HATRED AT HOME

AL-QAIDA ON TRIAL IN THE AMERICAN MIDWEST

Andrew Welsh-Huggins

Ohio University Press

Swallow Press

Athens

Swallow Press / Ohio University Press, Athens, Ohio 45701
www.ohioswallow.com

To obtain permission to quote, reprint, or otherwise reproduce or distribute
material from Swallow Press / Ohio University Press publications, please
contact our rights and permissions department at (740) 593-1154
or (740) 593-4536 (fax).

Printed in the United States of America
Swallow Press / Ohio University Press books are printed
on acid-free paper ⊗ ™

21 20 19 18 17 16 15 14 13 12 11   5 4 3 2 1

Library of Congress Cataloging-in-Publication Data
Welsh-Huggins, Andrew.
 Hatred at home : Al-Qaida on trial in the American Midwest / Andrew
Welsh-Huggins.
     p. cm.
 Includes bibliographical references and index.
 ISBN 978-0-8040-1134-1 (hc : alk. paper) — ISBN 978-0-8040-4046-4 (electronic)
 1. Terrorism—Prevention—Law and legislation—United States. 2. Civil
rights—United States. 3. Internal security—United States. 4. United
States—Politics and government—2001-2009. 5. Terrorism—Prevention—
Government policy—United States. 6. Qaida (Organization). 7. Terrorism
investigation—Middle West. I. Title.
 KF9430.W45 2011
 344.7305'32517—dc23

                        2011017688

For Pam

My companion in deadlines, life, and love

Contents

List of Illustrations   ix

Author's Note   xi

Introduction   1

Part 1: Morning

1	Call to Prayer	15
2	The Gymnast	19
3	Split Personality	23
4	Increasing Tensions	26
5	On the Move	28
6	Hardworking Truck Driver	32
7	Little Mujahideen	36
8	Diaspora	40
9	Ready at Any Time	42
10	Four Hundred Years	46
11	Busy Summer	50

Part 2: Night

12	We Need People Who Can Vanish	55
13	Collateral Damage	58
14	Winning the War on Terror	61
15	A Great Chapter	63
16	I'm Doing This as a Friend	67
17	Material Support	73

18	Guilty	79
19	A Secret, Double Life	82
20	Get This Done	90
21	Shopping Mall Plot	94
22	A Symphony of Unfairness	100
23	Life Goes On	104
24	Atypical Psychosis	106

Part 3: Evening

25	Radical Role-Playing	111
26	American Soil	117
27	Bureaucratic Sloth	120
28	Dirty Numbers	125
29	Disturbing Picture	132
30	The Ummah Is Angry	136
31	Changing of the Guard	141
	Conclusion	146
	Acknowledgments	153
	Notes	157
	Bibliography	187
	Index	189

Illustrations

Following page 108

Christopher Paul, born Paul Kenyatta Laws, in his 1984 high school yearbook photo

Christopher Paul, Franklin County Jail photo, 2007

Iyman Faris in Columbus, 1994

Iyman Faris's Freightliner truck

Iyman Faris and his wife, Geneva Bowling, c. 1999

Iyman Faris in Mecca, 2000

Nuradin Abdi, Franklin County Jail photo, 2004

Nuradin Abdi in prison

Author's Note

The term "al-Qaida" (or "the base," in Arabic) came into wide-spread use in 1998 after the group's simultaneous attacks on the U.S. embassies in Nairobi, Kenya, and Dar es Salaam, Tanzania. It is alternatively spelled as "al-Qaeda" or "al-Qaida"; the U.S. State Department's list of designated foreign terrorist operations transliterates it as "al-Qa'ida." As a reporter for the Associated Press, I elected to side with the *AP Stylebook* and its recommendation of "al-Qaida." Any exceptions involve usages in direct quotations from books or documents, such as court filings or government news releases.

Introduction

The terrorist attacks of September 11, 2001, serve as constant,
stark reminders that America has enemies in the world who
seek to kill American men, women, and children, any way
they can. Sometimes, the enemies are here at home.

—Attorney General John Ashcroft,
October 16, 2003, announcing plea agreements
in the Portland Cell conspiracy

I T WAS STILL dark when Nuradin Mahamoud Abdi stepped outside his apartment on the North Side of Columbus, Ohio, around
six o'clock on the morning of November 28, 2003. It was Friday, the
day after Thanksgiving, one of the busiest days of the Christmas
shopping season. Many others who were awake and leaving their
houses at the same predawn hour were headed toward the malls and
big-box stores like Target and Best Buy and Wal-Mart that were open
hours early to accommodate the traditional Black Friday shoppers.
Central Ohio's outsized retail centers, especially Polaris to the north
and Easton on the far east side, were sure to be jammed. By some
estimates, greater Columbus has too many malls for its million-plus
residents, a potential problem for some retailers but a boon, at least
temporarily, for bargain hunters.[1]

Abdi, however, was going in the other direction, both literally
and figuratively. As a Muslim, he had little reason to care about the
frenzy of gift giving leading up to Christmas. Keys in hand, the Somali native was still in his nightclothes, going out to warm up his
car before leaving for early morning prayers at Masjid Ibn Taymia, a
mosque catering to the city's large Somali population. After that, it
was off to work at his cell phone store in a small Somali mall about
a mile away. The thirty-one-year-old Abdi had a lot on his mind as
he opened the glass door of his apartment building, stepped under a
red awning, and walked into the chilly air of a dark, late-November

day. He and his wife, Safia Muse, had two young children and a third on the way. He was working long hours at the store he'd opened just two months earlier, hoping to get it off the ground. His goal was to save enough money to buy a house within the next two years. His mother, two brothers, and a sister also lived in Columbus, and the city, with its solid economy and Somali population second only to that of Minneapolis, was the place Abdi called home. Although he'd traveled out of the country in recent years, he told anyone who asked that he had no plans to leave Ohio. In any case, it wasn't as if his homeland, in its second decade without a functioning government, had much to offer a young entrepreneur.[2]

From the dark, someone called Abdi's name. He looked over, and a man approached him. The man said that his name was John Corbin and that he was an FBI agent. He showed Abdi his badge and asked him to wait a few minutes. While they stood there, Corbin made a call on his cell phone. "I have Abdi," he told the person on the other end. "He's standing with me here." The two waited for several minutes until at least five cars pulled up. Two men got out and began to search Abdi. They removed his wallet and the other contents of his pockets, then handcuffed him. Richard Wilkens, the Immigration and Customs Enforcement resident agent-in-charge for Columbus, told Abdi they had to check whether he had a bomb in his possession. He didn't. In his wallet, agents found a will, written in Arabic, that referred in part to his intent to travel to conflict zones in Afghanistan.[3]

A second ICE agent, Robert Medellin, told Abdi he was being arrested for violating federal immigration laws. When Abdi asked what type of violation, he got a curt reply: "You will know about it." Another FBI agent, Stephen Flowers, then asked Abdi for permission to search his apartment. He consented. One thing was clear: it looked like Abdi wasn't going to make it to morning prayers.[4]

Agents loaded him into an SUV and drove to FBI headquarters on the tenth floor of a building in the city's Brewery District just south of downtown. He was taken to a room for questioning, accompanied by Medellin and FBI agents. At 7:42 a.m., he signed a form waiving his *Miranda* rights. Medellin took the lead in the interview, telling Abdi he'd committed a lot of immigration violations and the only way to help himself was to cooperate with the FBI agents in the room. One of those agents, Flowers, then took over. The questions were numerous: Tell us about your background, your family here in Columbus, your travels abroad since you first came to the United States. Do you know of any threats or planned attacks against the United States or its allies? Do you remember a meeting FBI agents had with you last spring, when we discussed something a friend of yours—a man named Iyman Faris—had said about you? A statement he'd attributed to you?[5]

The questioning lasted for hours. Although the agents told Abdi he'd violated federal immigration laws, they didn't explain those violations or show him any documents detailing their allegations. Later that day, he was transferred to the Kenton County Detention Center in Covington, Kentucky, across the river from Cincinnati, where the headquarters for the FBI's southern Ohio division were located. Around noon, Medellin brought Abdi's lunch. He tried to reason with the prisoner. He'd been an immigration officer for twenty-seven years. He'd seen cases like this before. Medellin had observed Abdi's children at the apartment that morning, had seen his infant daughter; if he wanted to be with them, he told Abdi, he needed to cooperate. "What did I do?" Abdi asked. Medellin repeated he'd committed many violations.

"Can I see them?" Abdi asked.

"You are going to see them," Medellin said, before leaving him alone with his lunch.

Later that day, Abdi placed ten collect phone calls from jail, trying unsuccessfully to reach his family and a friend.[6]

The questioning continued Saturday, November 29, and lasted hours more, through the morning and afternoon, and well into the evening. Agents had a lot of information about Abdi, they reminded him, again and again, and he wasn't telling them what they needed to know.

At last Abdi said, "What are you looking for?"

Medellin glanced at Wilkens, then looked back at Abdi.

"We want to know information about Iyman Faris," he said.

Abdi countered by telling them he hadn't been brought in to talk about Faris, a friend of his from another mosque, and asked again what immigration violations he'd committed. He wanted to phone his wife to let her know he was all right, but the agents wouldn't let him place the call.[7]

The timing of Abdi's apprehension and the forceful way in which federal agents took him into custody were puzzling. But Abdi couldn't have been entirely surprised by this encounter. Of course he remembered their previous meeting. It had been April 2, when agents visited his cell phone store and asked him about conversations he'd had with Faris. Faris, Abdi well knew, was in a lot of trouble with the government. Big trouble. But what did that have to do with him? He'd already disavowed the things the agents said he and Faris had talked about. He was a Muslim, he told them. Our faith forbids us from harming anyone. Back in April, he'd even allowed the agents to search his apartment, and they'd found nothing. He'd produced a valid immigration document at the time and explained how he had come to the United States five years earlier after being smuggled through Mexico. The agents had dutifully noted all this and gone on their way.[8]

But that was then: nearly eight months later, something had changed. And the hours of questions were starting to wear Abdi down.

FOLLOWING THE 9/11 attacks, almost every American community experienced a moment of awakening from the illusory dream that such events happened only in faraway lands. For many, including people in Ohio, the new reality began with the calling up of active duty troops and reservists and National Guard members, first to help rout the Taliban in Afghanistan, then to take part in the invasion of Iraq. By the middle of 2003, Ohio in general and Columbus in particular had contributed their fair share of soldiers to fight the war on terror overseas. In tiny McConnellsville in southeast Ohio, more than four hundred members of a single Guard unit had been called up in one deployment. Eight Ohio soldiers had been killed in Iraq, including two—Private Brandon Sloan and Sergeant Robert Dowdy—on March 23, 2003, just three days after the invasion.[9]

Still, the idea that people in Columbus were in personal danger, that people living right next door meant harm, was not on people's minds. Of course Americans had seen such threats emerge elsewhere—in suburban Buffalo, for example, where several Yemeni Americans had been charged in October 2001 with providing material support to terrorists based on their visits to a training camp in Afghanistan. Or in Portland, Oregon, where almost exactly a year later, six defendants, including five U.S. citizens, had been charged with counts of material support, alleging they tried to go to Afghanistan to fight against American military forces. The televised perp walk of alleged homegrown terrorists across the cable news channels was familiar, but it was something that happened to someone else, some-place else.

All that changed on June 19, 2003, when Attorney General John Ashcroft stepped before the cameras in Washington to make a nationally televised announcement.

"On any given day, Iyman Faris appeared to be a hard working independent truck driver," the attorney general said. "Working out of Columbus, Ohio, he freely crisscrossed the country, making deliveries to airports and businesses without raising a suspicion."

"But Faris led a secret, double life," Ashcroft continued. "He traveled to Pakistan and Afghanistan, covertly met with Osama Bin Laden, and joined Al Qaeda's jihad against America."[10]

A secret double life? A meeting with bin Laden? Jihad against America? Above all, in Columbus, Ohio? This was as mild-mannered a place as a big American city can be. Overshadowed by Cleveland and Cincinnati, with their bigger metropolitan areas and more colorful histories, Columbus was a humble locale: the quiet state capital, a laboratory for the nation's fast food preferences, a white-collar town dominated by government and higher education. Generally speaking, the most consternation the city experienced involved the fortunes of Ohio State University's football team. It was a place where the threat of terrorism was something you heard about on the radio while inching along in rush hour traffic in the SUV President George W. Bush had told you to go out and buy as a sign of normality in a time of war.[11]

Now the city's time in the cable news sun had come. Over the next few days Columbus learned of and was amazed by the bizarre tale of Faris, a Pakistani American (and U.S. citizen) who had been married for a while to a preacher's daughter from Kentucky and who was alleged—when he wasn't playing cricket or driving his big rig or lying on the couch watching TV—to have cased the Brooklyn Bridge at the behest of none other than Khalid Sheikh Mohammed, the architect of the 9/11 attacks.

ONE WEEK AFTER the September 11 attacks, Congress passed Senate Joint Resolution 23, allowing the president to use "all necessary and appropriate force" against those who planned, committed, or aided in the attacks. The goal: to prevent future acts of terror against the United States "by such nations, organizations or persons." The resolution was the beginning of what would become a two-front war in Afghanistan and Iraq. Almost immediately, the government opened a third front on alleged terrorists operating within U.S. borders and presumably having the same goals as the 9/11 hijackers. This was a more complicated effort. It lacked any notion of a conclusion or what, exactly, would constitute victory, other than a lack of further attacks. One telling measure was the unprecedented growth of the FBI, the foot soldiers of this third front. When FBI director Robert Mueller assumed his job just one week before the 9/11 attacks, about a third of the agency's budget, or about $1 billion, and roughly 6,900 employees were assigned to counterterrorism and counterintelligence. By 2005, that spending had jumped to $2.2 billion, and 12,466 FBI personnel—an increase of nearly 80 percent—were devoted to terrorist-type threats.[12]

The targets of these beefed-up investigative efforts lived in ordinary American towns and cities. Alleged jihadists, homegrown or immigrant, had addresses in places like Lackawanna, N.Y.; the Virginia suburbs of the District of Columbia; Lodi, California; Liberty City, outside Miami; the Cherry Hill neighborhood of Philadelphia; Detroit; Cleveland; and Toledo. Because the government cast so wide a net, reports of the number of accused varied widely and were based in part on one's definition of terrorism—was fund-raising for Hezbollah, for example, equivalent to attending jihadist training camps in Pakistan or Afghanistan? One comprehensive 2010 study by researchers at Duke University and the University of North Carolina at Chapel Hill determined that 139 Muslim Americans had committed acts of terrorism-related violence or had been prosecuted for terrorism-related offenses in the eight years after 9/11. A 2009 study by Human Rights Watch analyzed 119 federal cases with 289 defendants, almost all of them from post-9/11 indictments. A 2006 study by New York University's Center on Law and Security cited a much higher figure of 510 individuals who had been classified at some point as terrorist cases.[13]

Many defendants were prosecuted under the "material support" provision of the federal terrorism laws (either 18 USC 2339A or 18 USC 2339B), facing allegations that they assisted terrorists by providing equipment, expertise, training, or, in some cases, themselves as participants. This charge of making available the basic fuel to feed the terrorist fire became the default accusation brought against most of the homegrown terrorism suspects after September 11. In cases in which deals were cut, the government often dropped other charges in exchange for a defendant's agreement to plead guilty to a single count of providing or conspiring to provide material support. Though the statute was challenged frequently, courts by and large upheld its constitutionality.[14]

The accusations were troubling, to say the least: plans to bring down the Sears Tower; blow up fuel lines at JFK Airport; shoot up Fort Dix; destroy synagogues in Brooklyn; detonate backpacks on mass transit throughout New York City; or in the case of Iyman Faris, cut the cables of the Brooklyn Bridge. And universally, charges were brought before violence was carried out. For better or for worse, the investigation of terror cases at home since 9/11 had consisted almost entirely of "what-if" scenarios.

OHIO IS A political bellwether—no Republican has been elected president without winning the state, and only two Democrats have done so in more than a century. As Ohio goes, so goes the nation. President Bush made the case for war in Iraq in a speech in Cincinnati in 2002. Senator John Kerry repudiated the war in a speech in the same Cincinnati hall in 2004. Bush returned to Ohio in 2005 to push for renewal of the Patriot Act. As the war on terror at home goes, so goes Ohio.

In January 2004, Fawaz Damra, the imam of one of Cleveland's largest mosques, was arrested on suspicion of hiding his ties to the group Palestinian Islamic Jihad when he applied for U.S. citizenship in 1994. Damra also had been criticized for hateful comments about Jews he had made in a 1991 speech, comments he later blamed on hostility from prejudice he picked up as a youth in the West Bank. His trial stirred up strong feelings about tolerance and the post-9/11 environment. Damra was convicted in June 2004 and deported to the Palestinian territories the following year.[15]

In 2005, police in the southeastern Ohio city of Marietta arrested two Arab American men from Detroit after they were discovered carrying hundreds of dollars in cash and several cell phones they'd purchased at area stores. The allegation: they were amassing tools of destruction that could be used as bomb detonators or hard-to-trace communication devices for terrorists. The men faced preliminary charges of terrorism until authorities discovered they were guilty of little more than the sin of American capitalism: the prepaid phones, it turns out, were a hot commodity overseas. All this unfolded and was resolved in a matter of days, but not before suburban Detroit's sizable Arab American population directed charges of prejudice and misunderstanding at police.[16]

In February 2006, federal authorities shut down an Islamic charity in Toledo and arrested three Arab Americans, accusing them of training and plotting for the purposes of waging jihad against U.S. forces in Iraq. The case against them was based on the work of an undercover FBI informant passing himself off as a former soldier disillusioned by the conduct of the war. The informant's early efforts at infiltrating Toledo's sizable Muslim community were so troubling that community members even contacted the FBI to report him.[17]

Early in 2009, the FBI began looking into the disappearance of as many as twenty young Somali men from Minneapolis. It was a case that resonated loudly in Columbus, which has the country's second-largest Somali population after that of the Twin Cities. Federal prosecutors said most of the men traveled to Somalia to join the terror group al-Shabab, linked to al-Qaida by the U.S. State Department. One of the men carried out a suicide bombing in Somalia in October 2008, the first American to participate in such an attack. People were not disappearing in Columbus, not yet, but Somali leaders and police had grown increasingly concerned about the alienation that many young men were experiencing, particularly after graduating from high school with few job prospects. In the fall of 2009, the Somali president, Sheik Sherif Sheik Ahmed, attended the United Nations General Assembly, then embarked on a tour of U.S. cities with large Somali populations. His trip included stops in Chicago, the Twin Cities, and finally Columbus, where in early October Ahmed addressed city and university leaders and later an overflow crowd of Somali residents at the Villa Milano hall on the north side of the city. Ahmed declared that solving his country's problems required both the help of the U.S. government, bound to Somalia by mutual threats from al-Qaida, and the help of Somalis who had immigrated to the United States.[18]

Stories of alleged terrorists in Ohio had faded by the summer of 2009, only to be resurrected by the case of a teenage girl named

Fathima Rifqa Bary. In July, the seventeen-year-old Muslim ran away from her family's suburban Columbus apartment to Florida, saying she feared death by honor killing for having converted to Christianity. Rifqa, a popular cheerleader, seemed an unlikely candidate to spark a national debate about religious tolerance. Then a lawyer in Florida known for taking up conservative causes stepped into the fray. He attempted to link a large suburban mosque the girl and her family occasionally attended with alleged terrorist conspiracies at another mosque earlier in the decade. The case ignited a storm of allegations and counterallegations in the blogosphere. Evangelical Christians warned of the evils of Islam and the dangers converts allegedly faced, while Muslims countered with accusations of kidnapping and brainwashing. As that debate raged, Rifqa went to live in a foster home in Columbus, estranged from her parents and even her younger brothers, all of whom she refused to speak to.

SOON AFTER THE U.S. invasion of Iraq in March 2003, a headline circled the wraparound digital news display on the *Columbus Dispatch* building on the east side of Capitol Square in downtown Columbus: "Another American Soldier Killed in Iraq." There had been a lot of those headlines recently, so many the words had become almost poetic in their dreary repetitiveness. On a smaller scale, the same was true of reports of the arrest of yet another Muslim American for plotting against the United States. The unconscionable had become commonplace. And despite years of investigations and prosecutions, such cases continued through the decade. On one troubling weekend in September 2009, the FBI announced the foiling of three separate plots: one to detonate backpacks in New York City subways and buses; another to destroy a Dallas skyscraper; a third to blow up the federal building in Springfield, Illinois.

One of the biggest concerns the FBI faced as the decade wore on was the lone wolf, the individual who expressed terrorist sympathies but was not connected to any organized cell. Take the case of Abdulhakim Muhammed, a young African American man who grew up in Memphis as Carlos Bledsoe. On June 1, 2009, in Little Rock, Arkansas, Muhammed allegedly opened fire on a military recruiting office, killing one soldier and injuring another. In two separate jailhouse calls to the Associated Press office in Little Rock, Muhammad said he didn't consider the killing a murder because U.S. conduct in the Middle East justified the shooting. The previous year, Muhammad had gone to Yemen as an English teacher. After overstaying his visa, he was jailed for a time: it was during this period behind bars, according to his father, Melvin Bledsoe, that he began to be radicalized. Here, too, was another Ohio connection. Muhammad had spent a very short time in Columbus sometime before 2007, living with a roommate in a low-rent apartment complex on the city's northeast side, his goal apparently to get an Ohio driver's license.[19]

IN 2003, THE government began pursuing three accused terrorists from Columbus. Though the three were considered co-conspirators, they were accused in separate indictments of vastly different crimes. Their alleged plots ranged from the Brooklyn Bridge plan to attacking civilians in Columbus to bombing U.S. military facilities and European tourist resorts. Like practically all defendants charged with material support since 2001, none of the three had carried out an actual crime of physical destruction. They never pulled a trigger; they never detonated a bomb; and the Brooklyn Bridge is still standing.

September 11 created unprecedented challenges for the federal agencies assigned to investigate and prosecute allegations of terrorism at home. Success was measured by the absence of new attacks; failure, by the unimaginable. By-the-book procedures were invisible; mistakes, a source of public outcry. Overzealous prosecutions were inevitable; less rigorous pursuits, out of the question. Relations between law enforcement and the country's growing Muslim population would ebb and flow—ebb, far more often than not—but would never be the same again. And most troubling, there did not appear to be an end in sight. The government investigated here; a new allegation emerged there. A cell was smashed one day; a lone wolf took up the cause the next. The specter of a perpetual struggle loomed large in November 2009, when U.S. Army major Nidal Malik Hasan allegedly opened fire at Fort Hood in Texas and killed thirteen fellow soldiers, and again the following month, when a Nigerian national allegedly attempted to bring down Northwest Airlines Flight 253 as it approached Detroit from Amsterdam on Christmas Day. As Abdulhakim Muhammad, the alleged Little Rock shooter and onetime Columbus resident put it, the attack he was accused of was "definitely not the end of it."[20]

ALMOST TWO DAYS had passed, and Nuradin Abdi still hadn't been able to contact his family. Finally, on Sunday, November 30, hoping cooperation would help, Abdi relented and told investigators things they appeared to want to hear. He confirmed information they'd learned from Faris. He told them additional details about his immigration status. The interrogation went on as agents moved him from his cell to an office for questioning and back again. Late that night, at 10:15 p.m., agents took an affidavit from Abdi, which he then signed. The following day, at 5:35 p.m., almost fifty-six hours after he'd first been taken into custody outside the Northland Arms apartment building on Tamarack Boulevard, Abdi was served with an arrest warrant by ICE agent Robert Medellin. At the same moment, Abdi was handed a notice that the government intended to terminate his asylum status in the United States.[21]

For the FBI, the need to take Abdi into custody the day after Thanksgiving of 2003 made absolute sense. They'd been keeping a close eye on the Somali immigrant for months, ever since Faris had told them of a chilling conversation he, Abdi, and another man had had a year earlier at a suburban coffee shop. The three were furious at civilian casualties in the ten-month-old U.S. campaign in Afghanistan and had discussed ways to vent their anger. Each had a different idea, a different plan. Faris threw out the possibility of blowing up the Hoover Dam, an idea the others agreed could cause widespread damage. But it was Abdi, Faris told the FBI, who suggested a terrorist attack as close to home as possible. He proposed shooting up a shopping mall with an AK-47.[22]

The FBI had learned of Abdi's threat months ago, but now, as Black Friday dawned and stores began to open to throngs of shoppers, agents believed the time had come to act. Investigators had found out too much since that April meeting. Apprehending Abdi on his way to morning prayers, even though agents lacked an arrest warrant, was the only way the FBI saw to thwart the possibility of a massacre in a packed shopping center on one of the busiest retail days of the year.

Two years and two months after the worst domestic terror attack in U.S. history, the government agents reasoned, what else were they supposed to do?[23]

PART.1
Morning

Against the widespread belief that jihad was a collective duty of the community and that only a legitimate political authority could lead such a fight, [Abdullah] Azzam declared the imperative of waging a defensive jihad: Muslim lands were threatened, and every Muslim man must join the fight, an obligation that had priority over everything else, including family and job.

—Daniel Benjamin and Steven Simon,
The Age of Sacred Terror

Call to Prayer

RIVERVIEW DRIVE on the northwest side of Columbus is a narrow street that travels west off Olentangy River Road, the main thoroughfare skirting the western side of the sprawling Ohio State University campus. The area is the typical American retail mishmash of gas stations, hotels, and fast food joints: here a Damon's, there a Bob Evans, a bit farther on a Kroger grocery store.

Riverview, a bumpy asphalt street with crumbling edges, is lined with several tired-looking brick apartment buildings. Bits of trash and paper collect by the edge of the buildings and next to bushes along the street. Some lawns are mowed more often than others. Illegible graffiti decorate a pair of Dumpsters. On the outside of one apartment building, someone has recently spray-painted "Free Leonard Peltier!" referring to the imprisoned American Indian Movement leader and convicted killer of two FBI agents.

There are no sidewalks along Riverview, and residents often walk in the street as they make their way to Olentangy to grab a bus or to shop—or in the case of many, to attend prayer services at the Omar Ibnelkhttab Mosque, one of the city's original Muslim houses of prayer. The beige mosque reflects the fatigue of the neighborhood. The small patch of grass at the front needs mowing, and leaves have collected along one side of the building. Its dusty parking lot is half brick, half gravel. The front entrance is unassuming. Few of today's Riverview residents have been around long enough to remember the aging building's original use as a Jehovah's Witness hall.

For years, the mosque was one of just a few Islamic worship centers in central Ohio. In the decades after World War II, the area's Muslim community was small, but diverse, and by the late 1960s included fifteen to twenty families from Pakistan, Turkey, Iran, Egypt, Lebanon, Morocco, and what was then Yugoslavia.

Most of the population could fit into a small enclosed shelter at the city's Park of Roses in the Clintonville neighborhood a few miles north of downtown, where they often held Eid prayers. Well into the 1970s, it was rare to see a Muslim woman in hijab in a public place like a shopping mall.[1]

A handful of Muslim families began to organize around 1965 and, in 1970, created the area's first formal body, the Islamic Foundation of Central Ohio. The foundation adopted a one-page constitution and started an Islamic weekend school for children, which met on the Ohio State campus. In 1976, the organization bought property for a mosque and offices on the east side of the city—property previously owned by the Boy Scouts of America—and hired an imam. Membership grew to between five hundred and a thousand.[2]

A growing number of Muslim graduate students arriving at Ohio State formed groups on and off campus beginning in the 1970s. In 1979, nine students began meeting for prayers in an apartment a couple of blocks south of Riverview. They discussed the possibility of a mosque, and on June 19, 1984, they bought the Jehovah's Witness hall and began converting it into the Omar mosque. It became a hub of activity for many Muslims in the Columbus area, but particularly for recent immigrants and among those, Arabic-speaking Muslims. Ohio State students and their families gathered there for prayers, study circles, and dinners. The mosque began offering marriage and funeral services and opened a weekend school for students.[3]

Muslims had a low profile in a community in which the dominant religions were Christianity and Judaism. If they showed up in the newspaper, it was usually at the beginning or end of Ramadan, the Muslim holy month of fasting and prayer, or because of an ecumenical event or announcement of a speaker at a mosque. Even in those years, Islam was still an exotic religion to most westerners, especially in cities like Columbus where people were just getting used to seeing robes and hijabs and prayer caps in public. In 1988, Muslims got an awkward chance to explain their faith when controversy erupted over the publication of Salman Rushdie's *The Satanic Verses,* which many Muslims believed was a blasphemous attack on their faith. Like their brethren around the country, Muslims in Columbus shared the burden of explaining Islam to people who were scratching their heads at televised images of angry religious rallies over a book few had ever heard of. "The Koran is full of fighting, but the question is why we fight," a prayer leader at the mosque on River-view tried to explain. "Islam respects the human life."[4]

Non-Arabic-speaking Muslims and those who didn't live near Ohio State or have a university connection tended to worship at the Islamic center on the city's east side. The Omar mosque, by contrast, served a heavily Arab and university-oriented community. For those immigrants, many of them poor and for a time transient, the mosque became an all-encompassing focal point. It was a resource that aided current residents and those moving to Columbus, providing financial assistance and help finding a place to live. In 1990, the mosque hosted two Afghan mujahideen injured in battle with occupying Soviet troops who were being treated at Ohio State's medical center through a medical program for such Afghan fighters. Over the years, the mosque helped refugees from Afghanistan and Bosnia and Iraq—particularly a wave of Iraqis who left the Middle East during the 1991 Gulf War.[5]

In 1991, the original Muslim Student Association that founded the Omar mosque transformed itself into the Islamic Society of Greater Columbus. The new group oversaw the mosque, the student group, and beginning in 1996, Ohio's first chartered full-time Islamic school, Sunrise Academy in Hilliard, a west-side Columbus suburb, which started with nine students. A decade or so after the school's founding, the mosque spun away from the Islamic Society and became an independent center. The society, in turn, devoted itself full-time to the school, which by now had grown to three buildings, fourteen employees, and an enrollment of four hundred students.[6]

As houses of worship, mosques differ somewhat from churches or synagogues. They are more like public libraries, open to all and visited at different times and on different holidays by Muslims who aren't necessarily members in the sense of, say, Christian parishioners. Muslims might affiliate themselves with one mosque but worship at another if it's closer to where they live or work. At the same time, just like churches, mosques acquire reputations for serving particular types of people and espousing particular types of theology. Some cater to a particular ethnic group: Somalis in Columbus, for example, tend to worship together with fellow Somalis.

When the Omar mosque first opened in the 1980s, men worshiped at the front of the building's main carpeted hall, women at the back. As immigrants with more traditional beliefs arrived in the

1990s, a room was created at the rear of the hall for women to ensure a starker separation of the sexes at prayer. Gradually, the Omar Ibnelkhttab mosque gained a reputation as the most conservative house of Islamic worship in Columbus.[7]

The Gymnast

THE PHOTO CATCHES high school gymnast Paul Laws in mid-swing as he pivots one-handed around the pommel horse at Ohio's state gymnastics championships in the late winter of 1983. He's making the move look easy, his left hand gripping one handle of the apparatus as he lifts his body up and around. His right arm is perfectly parallel with his right leg, the fingers of his free hand outstretched and relaxed. His wrists are taped, and he's wearing tight-fitting white gymnast pants and a dark sleeveless top. His face exudes concentration but not strain, the confidence of an athlete performing a task he knows he does well. It's another banner year for the gymnastics team at Worthington High School; each member competed at states, where the small squad scored 111.94 points, good enough for eighth place. In that year's team picture, Laws, a senior, towers above his fellow gymnasts. He looks handsome and strong and calm as he stares into the camera. He is the only black athlete on the squad. None of the boys' hair is exactly short, as the era demanded; but even so, Laws's Afro stands out, the longest hairstyle of any of his teammates. It's clear from Laws's confident expression that his hair length is of no concern to him.[1]

WORTHINGTON, OHIO, WHERE Laws grew up, is a community of about thirteen thousand, immediately adjacent to Columbus on the city's north side. Settled in 1803, the same year Ohio achieved statehood, it is older than Columbus by almost a decade, a fact that residents are wont to hold over the capital city. Today, Worthington is a comfortable inner-ring suburb spread across either side of High Street, a small city known for its quaint downtown, its good schools, and its genial quality of life. It has its share of new subdivisions with large, modern homes and street names like Loch Ness Avenue and

Bonnie Brae Lane, but the tree-lined streets and clapboard houses in the old part of town have a distinctly East Coast feel. "Worthington: New England in the Wilderness," was the title of a 1976 bicentennial history of the community. James Kilbourn, one of the city's founding fathers, was born in Farmington, Connecticut, in 1770, and later headed west as part of the Scioto Company, an organization of New Englanders determined to improve their lot in life. They named the city for Thomas Worthington, a federal land agent and later sixth governor of Ohio.

Blacks are a tiny minority in the mainly white city, accounting for less than 2 percent of the population. Of the more than five hundred seniors who graduated in 1983 from Worthington High School, only five or six, including Laws, were black. In years past, Worthington had been no more and no less prejudiced than other central Ohio communities; permissive—even liberal—but not quite color-blind. "Our blacks," an old-timer would say of the city's small African American population, implying that outsiders might not be so welcome.[2]

As early as 1821, a slave owner who brought a captured runaway slave named Isham into town on his journey south was met by Worthington citizens, including a local justice of the peace who determined the man lacked proof of ownership and set the slave free. Worthington abolitionists formed an antislavery society on March 28, 1836. A few blacks had long lived in the area, some of them associated with a brickyard east of Worthington. The city's African Methodist Episcopal Church was the fourth congregation in the city to build a church, and its black minister, James Birkhead, was a principal land owner in the decades after the Civil War. The city's earliest subdivision, known as the Morris Addition, was platted in 1855 and designed especially to attract Methodist ministers and free blacks.[3]

In 1935, Virdre C. Laws purchased two acres of land off East North Street, determined to find a better place to raise his daughters than the ghettoes of Columbus. Laws, who went by V. C., had moved north from South Carolina years earlier and gone to work at Columbus Malleable Iron on the city's east side. He bought the property at the height of the Great Depression with the help of a banker friend who bid on the foreclosed land on Laws's behalf. Laws and his wife, Esther, raised their children on what amounted to a small farm, growing numerous vegetables to sell to local markets and keeping cows, hogs, chickens, and ducks, which they slaughtered for food. In the 1930s, Ernest Laws,

Virdre's teenage nephew, migrated from the South and came to live with the family. After graduating from high school, he served overseas in World War II, then came home to make a career working for the city of Columbus. He and his wife, Arnetta, raised their six children in a house on the same land his uncle had farmed.[4]

Paul Kenyatta Laws was the youngest of six siblings born over nearly two decades; he graduated from high school in 1983, nineteen years after his oldest sister, Sandra. (Kenyatta was not an entirely uncommon name in the 1960s, perhaps reflecting black pride at Africa's changing fortunes: Kenya achieved independence in 1963, the year before Paul was born.) Paul had three brothers and another sister, who suffered from a mental disability following a childhood bout of encephalitis. Though a minority in their community, the Lawses' children grew up the way a lot of people did in the 1960s and 1970s. They played sports and worked part-time jobs and were in and out of the house constantly meeting friends and doing things. Theirs was an outdoors family and they loved to hunt and fish; Paul especially was a devoted angler. Their mother, a seamstress, made and repaired their clothes, so they always looked nice. But the children also kept a low profile at school, participating in almost no formal activities. Paul was the exception, competing in gymnastics three of his four years, including a trip to states his sophomore year, both individually and as part of the team competition, and again his senior year. Entering high school in 1979, Paul Laws was a typical skinny-looking kid of the era, his hair slightly outgrown, cool-looking in a T-shirt with "Camaro" spelled out in fat letters on the front. He volunteered in the high school office for a while and was friendly, cooperative, and polite. In his free time, he loved to go fishing. In his senior yearbook picture, Paul's smile is sincere and carefree as he poses in his best early 1980s wide-collar brown shirt and beige corduroy sports coat.[5]

After high school, Laws attended Ohio State University for a while, enrolling in the winter quarter of 1984 and taking classes most quarters through the fall of 1988. But he did not declare a major and did not graduate. Far more significant than his studies was the religious transformation he underwent at the time. After getting to know Muslim students on campus, Laws decided to convert to Islam. He grew a beard and began to wear long, earth-tone robes. Despite this change, Laws still visited his family often on East North Street and appeared to be the same sweet person the family always had known. A few years earlier, his conversion might have seemed more dramatic, but Muslims were becoming a more common sight in the United States, even in Ohio. Virginia Laws McCammon, one of V. C.'s daughters who lived next door to Laws's parents, said the family took it all in stride. "When we saw Paul, we understood because we were seeing others," McCammon would recall. "It wasn't that he stood out."[6]

In 1988, Laws moved to an apartment on Riverview Drive just up the street from the Omar mosque, and started taking computer and engineering classes at Columbus State Community College. As his passion for his new faith increased, so did his awareness of Islam around the world. And one of the things Laws became increasingly upset about was news of Soviet atrocities in Afghanistan.[7]

Split Personality

KASHMIR IS A mountainous land where the borders of India, Pakistan, and China meet, home to about seven million people and the site of two wars and numerous other territorial disputes between India and Pakistan. Its history embodies the postcolonial turmoil that gripped the region and set the stage for many of today's global conflicts. In the late 1940s, as the partition of India and Pakistan loomed, the rulers of Kashmir decided they wanted to join India. Pakistan had other ideas and thought the mostly Muslim region should be incorporated inside its borders. The two countries went to war over the region in 1947, and again in 1965. During those wars, Pakistan and China gained control of territory claimed by India, although India held on to the most populated areas. The dispute has cost fifty thousand lives over the years, and many experts fear Kashmir has the potential to trigger the use of nuclear weapons, now possessed by both India and Pakistan. It was here, in a land caught between two nations, that a boy named Mohammed Rauf was born on June 4, 1969.[1]

Rauf's father, Mohammed, separated from his mother around the time the boy was seven, and Rauf went to live with his father and his new family in Pakistan. He had several stepbrothers from his father's second marriage but was his father's only biological son. He was close to his father, who tended to pamper him, but was estranged from his mother, Gulzar. Even growing up he was known for his long, curly hair; his nickname in Urdu translated as "white man," perhaps because of his atypical look.[2]

In 1986, when Rauf was eighteen years old, he met a man named Maqsood Khan who would become a close acquaintance and companion over the next several years. Khan sparked Rauf's interest in the military conflicts of the region, first in Kashmir and then in

Afghanistan, where mujahideen were waging a guerilla war against the occupying Soviets. The Russians' 1979 invasion of Afghanistan had been a signal event for disenfranchised Muslims and a global rallying point for violent struggle. Thousands of young Muslim men flocked to the country, many from the Middle East but others from around the world, including the United States. Many returned home more radicalized than they left. The numbers of these foreign fighters grew from around four hundred in the early 1980s to, depending on estimates, as high as fifty thousand by decade's end. They were dubbed the Afghan Arabs.[3]

Rauf attended training camps in Kashmir and Afghanistan and took up arms for a short while, sustaining injuries serious enough to land him in the hospital for two weeks in 1989. During that time, he received a visit from Abdullah Azzam, the anti-American Palestinian cleric and disciple of the Egyptian Islamist Sayyid Qutb.[4]

Qutb was considered one of the founding fathers of the jihadi Salafi ideology, the idea that Islam needed to be reformed into something more closely resembling the pure state of the religion in the years after its founding by Mohammed. Qutb once had been an admirer of the United States but was shocked during a visit from 1948 to 1951 by what he considered the decadence of the country. After his return to Egypt, he joined the Muslim Brotherhood, a group that maintained among its goals the reestablishment of the Islamic caliphate. After a trial on charges of attempting to overthrow the government and assassinate public officials, the government of President Gamal Nasser hanged Qutb on August 29, 1966. A movement now had its modern martyr.[5]

In 1984, Azzam founded Maktab al-Khidamat (MAK) along with a Saudi acquaintance named Osama bin Laden. They used MAK to recruit and assist Arabs fighting the Soviet invasion of Afghanistan. One of the tasks the two jihadists took on was to create training camps and guesthouses, such as the one Rauf stayed in, including the Sidda camp, the Ma'sadat al-Ansar—or House of Lions—and the Beit al-Ansar, or House of the Companions, a reference to the companions of Mohammed. Over the next two decades, these camps trained some of the world's most wanted terrorists as well as scores of curious Muslims drawn more by the thrill of association than by true passion for jihad.[6]

After the defeat of the Soviets, Azzam and bin Laden decided to carry on their work in the form of a broader struggle, and created a new organization, dubbed al-Qaida, "the base" in Arabic. Rauf stayed with Azzam at a rehabilitation center the cleric had set up for injured soldiers. He claimed later to have respected Azzam and to have learned a lot from him, but said that the cleric didn't affect his own philosophy, whatever that was at the time. Azzam and his two sons were assassinated by bomb in 1989; the perpetrators were never identified.[7]

Around the same time, Rauf went to a camp in Afghanistan, where he received further training, including how to fire a Kalashnikov rifle, how to perform sentry duty, and how to throw live grenades. But not long after that, Rauf's father sent word for him to give up fighting and return home. Rauf obliged: for now, it seemed, family duty called.[8]

Increasing Tensions

LIFE WAS GOOD for Mohamoud Abdi Nur in the early 1970s. The
Somali businessman had been tapped to serve as an attaché in his
country's embassy in Germany, and he had a growing family that
eventually included eight children. But Nur's personal fortunes be-
lied growing problems in Somalia. The Somali Republic had been
formed in 1960 by the merger of the former Somaliland Protector-
ate, under British rule, and Italian Somaliland, which had been part
of a UN-administered trusteeship. Somalia adopted a constitution
and created a parliamentary form of government based on the
model of European countries. Like many other newly independent
African nations, however, the young country's experiment with democracy didn't last long. A bloodless coup brought Major General
Mohamed Siad Barre to power in 1969 and with his rule came the end
of democracy. Barre banned all elements of a representative government—suspending the constitution, abolishing the supreme court,
and closing the national assembly. The army renamed the country
the Somali Democratic Republic and replaced its former institutions
with a supreme revolutionary council composed of army officers
who had helped lead the coup. There were modernizing elements
of Barre's rule, which included the adoption of the Roman alphabet
for the Somali language, thus creating a nationwide standard for the
printed word. There was also an attempt, as part of a movement
dubbed the "Cultural Revolution," to undertake widespread liter-
acy campaigns. Barre allied the country with the Soviet Union and
proclaimed dedication to a political philosophy he called "Scientific
Socialism." But Barre also ruled with totalitarian force. He created
intelligence-gathering agencies to silence opposition; among them
was the National Security Service, whose brutal tactics earned it the
nickname "the Black Gestapo." Under the previous government, the

country had relinquished claims to portions of Kenya and Ethiopia with Somali populations; this had improved relations with both countries but angered many in the army, helping spur the 1969 coup. By 1972, tensions had begun to rise along the Somali-Ethiopian border. The same year, on May 22, Nur's third son, Nuradin, was born.[1]

One of Nuradin's uncles, the brother of his mother, was involved in politics, and sometime in the early 1970s, the family fell out of favor with the government. The rift was serious enough that Nur decided to leave the country, and in 1976, he and his wife, Nadifa, took their family to the United Arab Emirates. The move was timely. Somalia invaded Ethiopia the following year, sparking the 1977–78 Ogaden War. Though the country threw off ties to the Soviet Union and became a Cold War ally of the United States in the 1980s, Barre's suppression of opposition parties and ethnic groups sparked a civil war that eventually led to the demise of its government in 1991, the last time Somalia was a functioning state.[2]

Far from this conflict, the Nur family lived a middle-class life in their new country. Mohamoud and Nadifa ran a restaurant in Dubai, and the children attended UAE schools, where they became fluent in Arabic. Abdi, fourth-youngest of the eight children, was a good student who never got in trouble. But opportunities were limited in their adopted country, where citizenship was not an option, even for Abdi's younger siblings who were born there. At eighteen years old, Abdi left the UAE for Syria and the city of Aleppo. There he studied business and economics at the University of Aleppo for two years before leaving without completing his degree. Soon after, most of his family joined him there, but their plans to start a permanent life in Damascus were complicated by the death of Abdi's father in 1992. Abdi's mother eventually returned to Dubai, while Abdi went back to Africa for a time and stayed with uncles in Kenya and Tanzania. Along the way, he married for the first time. Abdi had formed a worldview by now, and despite his cosmopolitan upbringing, it did not permit many shades of gray. He was a fundamentalist, and to prove the point he returned to Somalia in 1993 to obtain training from Islamists who shared his outlook.[3]

On the *5* Move

BY 1989, PAUL Laws was immersed in his new life as a Muslim convert. On February 1, he filled out paperwork to change his name to Abdulmalek Kenyatta, taking his middle name as his last name, citing "religious reasons" as his motive. Abdulmalek, a common Muslim name, was appropriate for a convert: it means "servant of the king" or "servant of the master" in Arabic, with "king" or "master" usually a reference to Allah.[1]

A Franklin County probate judge approved the name change on March 16. Almost exactly one year later, on March 28, 1990, three days before his twenty-sixth birthday, Laws applied for a U.S. passport under his new name, seeking expedited processing for a trip he planned to take in April. He received his passport just two days later, on March 30, a turnaround time difficult to fathom in the post-9/11 era. As a high school student, Kenyatta had been surprised to learn of Christian assaults on Muslims in the Crusades. Now the passionate convert left the United States for Pakistan and his own crusade, one being waged in neighboring Afghanistan.[2]

KENYATTA STAYED FOR a time at the al-Qaida–affiliated Beit al-Ansar guesthouse in Peshawar, Pakistan, the resting spot for the faithful founded by Abdullah Azzam and bin Laden in 1984. There he met bin Laden's former personal pilot and got to know another member of al-Qaida whose responsibilities included logistics and transporting people to and from training camps in Afghanistan. It was likely Kenyatta was not the only African American in the camps in Pakistan or Afghanistan: subsequent reporting, trial testimony, and other research into the camps and events leading to 9/11 turned up several other black Americans who made a similar trip. Around that time, Kenyatta went to Afghanistan and learned how to use assault rifles and rocket-propelled grenades. He was also taught small-unit tactics and hand-to-hand combat techniques. Kenyatta was still abroad when Saddam Hussein invaded Kuwait on August 1, 1990, followed by the massing of U.S. and allied forces in Saudi Arabia in response, a gathering of nonbelievers on Islamic soil that was anathema to many Muslims.[3]

Around the middle of 1991, Kenyatta formally joined al-Qaida and stayed for a time at another Peshawar guesthouse, Beit ur Salam, reserved exclusively for members of the group. During this time, Kenyatta obtained further training, including map reading, climbing, rappelling, military history, and explosives. He made no bones about his purpose in being there: he told another guest he was there to "fight jihad." He was so passionate about his adopted cause that he told another member of al-Qaida he was furious the organization would even consider scaling back its military operations. Let me be clear, he said. Al-Qaida should continue those operations, and I'm committed to them even if they're not. Though Kenyatta traveled abroad too late to meet Azzam, he was linked to the cofounder of al-Qaida—and, inadvertently, to Rauf, who had met Azzam—through the places he stayed, the training he received, and the ideology he was exposed to.

Kenyatta's journeys at this time are difficult to track. But sometime in February 1992, he apparently went again to Afghanistan, where he met a man named Mohammedou Ould Salahi. Like Maqsood Khan, the close friend of Rauf, Salahi became a pivotal figure in Kenyatta's life.[4]

Salahi, sometimes referred to as Slahi, a native of the West African nation of Mauritania, had gone abroad in 1988, first to Germany, where he studied at the University of Duisburg. In 1990, he traveled to Afghanistan to fight against the communists still controlling the country following the Soviets' 1989 withdrawal. He spent six weeks at the al-Farooq training camp in Kandahar and swore allegiance to al-Qaida. In 1991, he returned to Germany to continue his studies, then came back to Afghanistan the following year with two friends, including Karim Mehdi, a Moroccan national. Salahi met Laws and fought as a member of an al-Qaida mortar battery in a battle in Gardez, Afghanistan.[5]

FOLLOWING THIS TRIP abroad, Kenyatta returned to the United States and to Columbus for a short time, teaching martial arts at the mosque on Riverview. By early 1993, he was overseas again, arriving at the U.S. consulate in Vienna to apply for a new passport in the name of Abdul Malek Kenyatta, stating his previous passport had been "lost/stolen." He received his new passport on February 23, 1993. It would have been telling to know Kenyatta's reaction to the events across the Atlantic just three days later, when a truck bomb exploded beneath the World Trade Center towers in New York, blasting a hole seven stories up, killing six people, and injuring more than a thousand.[6]

Ten days later, on March 23, Kenyatta entered Slovenia, staying just a day. He continued his travels throughout 1993 and early 1994, including an apparent three-week visit to Germany, where he may have met with both Mohammedou Salahi and Karim Mehdi. During that time, he began compiling a master list of terrorist contacts he would keep with him over the next decade. Kenyatta's visits also took him Croatia during the disintegration of Yugoslavia, where he was one of thousands of overseas Muslims seeking to support their Balkan brethren. One of those was Mohammed Rauf.[7]

Rauf and two childhood friends had obtained Turkish visas on Pakistani passports and traveled to Istanbul through Iran on an Iranian airline. It took a while, but eventually they obtained Croatian visas for the price of 1,000 deutsche marks, or about $700. They entered Bosnia from Croatia sometime in 1992. The world Rauf and his friends encountered was a heady mix of Muslims like themselves from around the world, drawn to the battles driving Yugoslavia's break-up. Although their exact numbers are in dispute, many of these outsiders were Arab veterans of the Afghan wars who based themselves around the Bosnian city of Zenica, where Rauf ultimately settled. The influx had begun in 1992, the same year Afghanistan's communist regime fell, and provided the next outlet for fighters who had learned their craft battling the Soviets. One report described a hundred Muslim volunteers arriving in early August 1992, who formed a unit based in Travnik and Zenica to fight alongside the Bosnian Defense Force. By one account, as many as four thousand foreign mujahideen ultimately fought against the Serbs. Part of the 1995 Dayton Peace Accord required all foreign forces, including freedom fighters, to leave Bosnia and Herzegovina. Although there is no evidence their paths crossed, Kenyatta and Rauf were in the same part of the world around the same time.[8]

In Bosnia, Rauf and his friends met up with Muslim fighters from Germany, Great Britain, the Netherlands, and Sweden. One of these fighters was a man named Iyman al-Ibraham al-Ali, a young man from Dubai who bore a striking resemblance to Rauf. According to Rauf, who told the tale to the FBI years later, al-Ali had an intriguing proposal. Al-Ali was returning to Austria to update an expired U.S. visa, and he was willing to give it to Rauf to allow him to leave Bosnia. Working with a Pakistani United Nations representative, Rauf managed to obtain UN "blue cards" allowing them to travel through the region. Rauf paid for this transaction with a surreal combination of money he claimed he received for fighting while in the Balkans and 3,000 deutsche marks he earned by selling two cows he had somehow come to possess.[9]

Blue card in hand, Rauf accompanied al-Ali to Sarajevo in a UN vehicle. From there they flew to Zagreb in Croatia. Rauf waited in Zagreb while al-Ali traveled to Austria to renew his visa. After al-Ali obtained the document, he gave it to Rauf, who took a train to Vienna and then flew to New York City. Rauf, now going by the name Iyman Faris, arrived in the United States in March 1994.[10]

Hardworking Truck Driver 6

IN JANUARY 1994, an immigrant from Turkey named Mehmet Aydinbelge began taking English classes through Ohio State University's continuing education program. Once his English improved, he intended to take graduate classes in agricultural engineering. Like many Muslim immigrants temporarily residing in Columbus, he was going to need a roommate to make ends meet. Just in time, Faris arrived in the city.[1]

Faris had flown from New York to Detroit and then driven to Columbus because friends had told him the cost of living was reasonable and there were a lot of Pakistanis living there. Having arrived with $1,500 in his pocket but little else, Faris checked in with leaders of the mosque on Riverview Drive, who, as they often did with new arrivals, found him a roommate and a nearby apartment. He found a school where he could improve his English, and using the visa he'd obtained overseas, got a driver's license and Social Security number.[2]

One of Faris's first jobs in Columbus was as a clerk at a Speedway gas station along a gritty stretch of Hudson Street on the city's north side, an area where many of the stores and gas stations were run by immigrants. Working at the station helped Faris improve his English, and it certainly led to his acclimation to American society. Women were drawn to Faris, a handsome man with a muscular physique, olive skin, and dark, wavy hair.[3]

It was at this gas station in 1994 that Faris met a woman named Geneva Bowling, who often stopped by for the station's cheap gas. Faris already had a girlfriend, but by the following year he and Bowling were dating and before long Faris had moved in with her and her ten-year-old son, Michael. The match was an unusual one from the beginning. Bowling, born in 1956, was thirteen years older than Faris. The daughter of a Pentecostal preacher from rural Kentucky, she had been raised by her grandmother and grandfather. She had been married four times before she met Faris, the first time at age thirteen when she lived in Pike County, Kentucky; her husband had been all of sixteen years old—her best relationship, she later recalled. Her most recent divorce had come in June 1994. Nevertheless, the two hit it off. "He was exciting," Bowling recalled. "Everything about him was different. He added that whole spice of life thing." Racism was a fact of life where Bowling had grown up in Kentucky. Yet her family immediately took to the dark-skinned Faris, in part because he was so friendly and respectful. The couple was married September 9, 1995, at the Omar mosque, with Bowling wearing a red Islamic-style dress that Faris's father had sent her from Pakistan. Just a few of Faris's friends and a handful of women from the mosque attended.[4]

After the wedding, Faris became a delivery driver for a local Pizza Hut and often worked nights. The family occasionally went out to eat at an American-style buffet up the street, the Taj Palace for Indian food in nearby suburban Hilliard, or a tiny Somali restaurant around the corner on Cleveland Avenue. They also liked watching movies: Faris leaned toward Jackie Chan films and comedies. Another favorite was *Air Force One,* in which Harrison Ford portrays a president battling terrorists aboard the presidential plane. Faris spent hours with Bowling's son, Mike, watching Steven Seagal's *Under Siege II,* examining martial arts moves frame by frame. When they played video and computer games together, Faris often picked Comanche II: Maximum Overkill, a helicopter combat simulation game. In fact, when Bowling first met Faris, he had told her he wanted to learn to fly. She took him to Don Scott Field, an airport operated by Ohio State University, to ask about lessons, but Faris didn't follow up. Throughout their marriage, he occasionally bought glider and airplane magazines. On one occasion in December 2000, Faris even traveled to South Bend, Indiana, where he paid forty dollars for a test flight on a gyrocopter, a small airplane-helicopter hybrid. Faris was also frequently at the Omar mosque, going on picnics with other "brothers" and playing club cricket on fields at Ohio State, where he was known for his bowling and batting skills.[5]

Early in their marriage, Faris announced to Bowling that a friend had talked him into becoming a truck driver. He left home and took a three-week truck driving course in South Carolina. He became one of several men at the Omar mosque who took to long-distance trucking. Faris worked for private companies for a few years, including Yowell Transportation in Dayton, then grew tired of the low pay and not being his own boss. The couple cosigned on a 1994 Freightliner, and Faris formed his own company. His jobs ranged from pickups and deliveries at airports to hauling processed tomatoes in Columbus. He took cross-country trips for a week at a time, occasionally calling Bowling from places like Florida, telling her she should be there to see the beach.[6]

Faris and Bowling lived in a small, white, one-story house on Grasmere Avenue in the Linden area of Columbus, a downtrodden racially mixed area that had seen far better days. Bowling worked in a Napa Auto Parts warehouse on the other side of town and was gone during the day. When he wasn't driving his truck, Faris was at home, where he spent hours outside working on the Freightliner and playing loud Arabic music to the annoyance of his closest neighbors. Some days he'd horse around in the small yard with Bowling's son. He had a carefree approach to life, once blowing past a parked police cruiser while driving with his stepson, then calmly pulling over and waiting for the officer to come and write him a ticket.[7] If he saw his seventy-something neighbor across the street, a woman still living in the house she'd been born in, he'd smile and wave almost like a big goofy kid. But he kept largely to himself; if anyone was neighborly and willing to talk to people on the street, it was Bowling.[8]

Faris was a study of contrasts in those years. For the most part, he eschewed traditional Pakistani clothes, preferring tight T-shirts and blue jeans, yet he spent hours at the Omar mosque, sometimes in robes. Yet he also stood out at the mosque for his long, wavy hair, which he occasionally wore in a ponytail, decidedly not a traditional Muslim look, and was teased for looking like one of the old French kings. At home, he ate mainly the ginger-and-garlic meals he had grown up with—which Bowling prepared for him, often late at night—yet satisfied a craving for burgers and fries by stopping by Burger King. "A pick-and-choose Muslim," Bowling recalled.[9]

Money was always an issue between Faris and Bowling. He'd been spoiled as a child, she felt, and was used to getting his own way. He refused to contribute to the household income or pay their bills. At the same time, he talked constantly about making money, a lot of money, how he was going to be a millionaire. "The money is on its way," he would say. Faris and a friend who also lived in Columbus had talked about creating an import-export business and on

February 11, 1997, paid $20 to formally incorporate Aymanes Imports with the state. Although he went by Faris in day-to-day life, he continued to use the name of Mohammed Rauf officially, listing that name on the business incorporation documents.[10]

By now Faris and Bowling were arguing frequently about bills, about the chores he wouldn't do, about how Bowling had to do all the cooking and cleaning. They were not wealthy people. Faris pulled down about $20,000 a year, after expenses, driving his truck, and Bowling's annual salary at Napa was only $24,000. While at home, Faris typically lay on the couch and watched TV, tossing his clothes on the floor and refusing to pick up. About the only household duty he participated in, Bowling recalled, was in the bedroom. They talked about having children together, but Faris wanted to take them back to Pakistan, and Bowling refused. "It has to be a partnership," Bowling recalled. "It has to be a give-and-take, and he didn't know how to give."[11]

Little Mujahideen

I T H A D T O be among the more unusual courtship letters written in Columbus in the 1990s. Wooing Frida Khanum Bashir, a British-born Pakistani woman, Abdulmalek Kenyatta wrote to her of his dream of raising "little mujahideen."[1]

In 1994, Kenyatta was back home in Columbus after his overseas travels and his official affiliation with al-Qaida, still a largely unknown entity in the United States outside of the intelligence community. Having previously converted to Islam and changed his name, Kenyatta now underwent another transformation. In March 1994, around the same time Faris came to Columbus, Kenyatta returned to Franklin County Probate Court to change his name yet again. As he had five years earlier, he cited "religious" reasons on his March 18 application to switch to the Anglo-Saxon–sounding Christopher Paul. Just as he had taken his middle name, Kenyatta, for his convert's name in 1989, now he took his former first name as his last. Kenyatta paid $85 in various fees and court costs, and on April 28 the former Worthington gymnast and current al-Qaida devotee became Christopher Paul.[2]

The newly christened Paul applied for another passport and, on September 8, 1994, received the new document, which along with his new name featured a new look: gone was the long beard grown in accordance with Muslim tradition. He wasn't alone in undertaking such a transformation during those years, and wasn't even the only American to do so. In 1996, Khalil Said Khalil Deek, a naturalized U.S. citizen born on the West Bank who allegedly helped facilitate the travel of individuals to terrorist training camps in Afghanistan, changed his name to Joseph Adams to obtain a new passport to travel to Jordan. Two years later, Mohamed Odeh, a Jordanian-born member of al-Qaida and a conspirator in the August 7, 1998, bombing of the U.S. embassy in Nairobi, shaved his beard to avoid looking Muslim before he fled Kenya the day before the attack. In February 2006, authorities say Daood Gilani, a U.S. citizen whose father was from Pakistan, changed his name to David Headley to travel to India and present himself as an American who was neither Muslim nor Pakistani. In October 2009, Headley was charged with planning terrorist attacks against a Danish newspaper and two of its employees. Two months later, he was charged with helping plan the November 2008 terrorist attacks on Mumbai that left almost 170 dead, including 6 Americans.[3]

During Paul's travels overseas, friends had introduced him to Bashir, and they married in England in late 1995 in an Islamic ceremony. She joined him in Columbus the following spring after he got a job working at Toledo/Mettler, a small factory that made scales. They moved into his apartment on Riverview near the mosque, where they lived frugally with few material goods. Frida didn't drive or work, and she relied on her husband or friends to get around. Soon afterward, Paul became close friends with Iyman Faris. He frequently visited Faris at his house on Grasmere, saying a few polite words to Bowling if she was present before the two men retired to a separate room to talk or pray. They were a striking contrast: Paul the African American from suburban Worthington in his traditional Muslim robe and prayer cap, Faris the Pakistani immigrant in his American jeans and T-shirt.[4]

THIS WAS THE period when al-Qaida coalesced into a terrorist organization powerful enough to ponder global operations. Osama bin Laden was not a religious cleric and was not educated in religious matters. But that didn't stop him from issuing fatwas, or interpretations of Islamic law by a respected Islamic authority. In August 1996, bin Laden condemned the Saudi monarchy for allowing American soldiers on Saudi soil and called on Muslims to drive the Americans out. (Two months earlier, a truck bomb had detonated in the Khobar Towers residential complex in Dhahran, Saudi Arabia, where U.S. Air Force personnel were housed, killing 19 Americans and wounding 372.) On February 22, 1998, bin Laden and his conspirator, the Egyptian physician Ayman al-Zawahiri, published a new fatwa in the London-based Arabic-language newspaper *Al Quds Al Arabi*. Along with other militant Islamic groups, they announced the creation of an organization called the "World Islamic Front for Jihad against the Jews and Crusaders." Bin Laden and Al Zawahiri declared that because America had declared war against God and his messenger, Americans anywhere should be murdered, as the "individual duty for every Muslim who can do it in any country in which it is possible to do it."[5]

THOUGH PAUL WAS settled in Columbus by now, he kept up his contacts with Mohammedou Ould Salahi, the Mauritanian he'd met years earlier in Afghanistan. Sometime in January 1997, Paul received a fax from Salahi, then living in Essen, Germany, asking him on behalf of a group of people they called "the brothers" to find them "a true group and place to make jihad." It was a busy time for Paul. On February 13, a month after getting the fax from Germany, Paul and Frida were married in an Ohio civil ceremony. Paul also had re-enrolled at Columbus State, where he was making enough progress that it appeared he'd soon have an associate's degree. Later that year, in September, Paul ordered a piece of equipment known as a "currency verifier," a device used for making fake documents. A vague manufacturer's note stated that it was for "export to Turkey." Court documents later alleged that he began accumulating videos of violent scenes in Muslim countries and watched them with others, hoping to exhort them to wage holy war. It was also around this time that Paul met Nuradin Abdi at the mosque on Riverview.[6]

The next year, 1998, held more milestones for Paul. He traveled abroad again, returning to Germany, where he visited Karim Mehdi for several weeks. (One of Paul's important possessions was a postcard from Mehdi addressing him as "Brother" Abdulmalek.) He and Frida had a daughter, Khadija, the name of the prophet Mohammad's first wife. In March, Paul graduated from Columbus State with an associate's degree in applied science in electrical engineering technology. The month after that, according to government documents filed years later, Paul and several others headed off to Burr Oak State Park, a popular camping and fishing area in the southeast part of the state. There, on a weekend trip that must have raised a few eyebrows among fellow campers, Paul led a group in hiking and camping techniques that allegedly replicated training he'd received in Afghanistan and Bosnia.[7]

Just over three and a half months later, on the morning of August 7, 1998, al-Qaida made its global debut. Operatives drove two bomb-laden trucks into the U.S. embassies in Nairobi, Kenya, and

Dar es Salaam, Tanzania, about five minutes apart. The Nairobi explosion killed 12 Americans and 201 others, almost all Kenyans, and injured nearly 5,000. The blast in Dar es Salaam killed 11 more people, though no Americans. Bin Laden later said it was permissible under Islam to kill Muslims—that is, the Africans who died in the blasts—to assault the Americans.[8]

Diaspora

WHEN ARCHITECT YUSUF Abucar arrived in Columbus in 1982, he was one of just a handful of Somali immigrants in the city. Abucar had left his home country in 1971 with a scholarship to study in Florence, Italy, where he earned a doctorate and met his future wife, an American artist. For almost a decade, he remained a minority within a minority of Muslim residents. All of that changed as waves of his fellow countrymen, displaced by the collapse of Somalia's last government in 1991, began to pour into the Midwest. By 2000, census figures showed more than three thousand Somalis in the greater Columbus area and another eleven thousand individuals describing themselves generically as "African." Among those coming to Columbus were Nuradin Abdi and his extended family.[1]

ABDI HAD BEEN back in the United Arab Emirates in 1995 when he paid someone to falsify a UAE passport by swapping photographs. With that faked document in hand, Abdi obtained a transit visa from the British consul and flew first to Heathrow in London and then to the United States, landing at Dulles International Airport outside Washington in September.[2]

Abdi, then twenty-three years old, had been in the country a little more than a month when he decided to take advantage of Canada's more liberal immigration laws and apply for asylum there. In November, he moved to London, Ontario, where he stayed with a cab-driving uncle and took classes at an English-language school. Everything about Canada was easier. In addition to the classes, he received papers allowing him to live there legally. He got medical care and rent money. The bar for obtaining refugee status also seemed lower.[3]

Abdi's parents eventually had left the United Arab Emirates and traveled to Syria, where they intended to settle. But after Abdi's father died in 1992, his mother decided to move on once more. The large family was scattered for a while, and two of Abdi's brothers spent time in the Ifo refugee camp in Kenya along with thousands of other displaced Somalis. Slowly, the family emigrated to the United States, first joining a cousin in Fairfax, Virginia, which has one of the country's larger populations of Somalis, then around 1998 moving permanently to Columbus, where rents were cheap and jobs plentiful. Finally settled, Abdi's mother entreated him to return to the United States.[4]

Abdi decided to leave Canada with his asylum application still in process. He reentered the United States at Detroit in August 1997. He still had the asylum issue to work out, however. In early October of the following year, he went to San Diego, where word was the application process was easier. He crossed into Mexico and then reentered the United States to apply. He obtained the proper paperwork and on October 19 filed for asylum, saying he feared for his life if he returned to Somalia, a country where he had spent relatively little time since childhood. After several weeks, the Immigration and Naturalization Service approved his request and on January 28, 1999, issued him a one-year work permit.[5]

Once Abdi joined his family in Columbus, he worked at Cell-U-Com, a cell phone store on Parsons Avenue on the city's east side. He also became involved in the welfare of the Somali community, many of whom had come of age in refugee camps, with little education or job training. Though he worshiped at the Omar mosque, Abdi was also interested in establishing a mosque that Somalis, with their shared heritage and tight community, could call their own. With his brothers and others, he helped found Masjid Ibn Taymia, named for the conservative thirteenth-century scholar Taqi al-Din ibn Taymiyya, who had urged a return to the purity of Islam as practiced in the first generations after Mohammed and often is cited by radical Islamists of the current generation. Abdi, fluent in English, Arabic, and Somali, cut a striking figure in the community, where he was respected for his willingness to help others and for his work with Ibn Taymia. Before coming to the United States, he had briefly given up his fundamentalist ways, but by 1997 Abdi had fully embraced the lifestyle of a radically committed believer and set about creating a group in Columbus with similar fundamentalist leanings.[6]

Ready at Any Time 9

EVEN AS THE shock of the Kenyan and Tanzanian embassy bombings sank in, the country also found itself occupied with another foreign policy crisis: growing concerns about a new conflict in the Balkans. Mindful of the 1995 disaster at Srebrenica, Bosnia, when Serbian forces overran Dutch peacekeepers and slaughtered thousands of Muslim boys and men—the largest mass killing in Europe since World War II—the United States now kept a close eye on events in Kosovo. In March 1999, U.S. and NATO forces launched a full-scale air war against Serbia aimed at protecting Muslim civilians.

FARIS AND PAUL had long been close friends, and by now Abdi and Paul had gotten to know each other better, in part by attending the same computer class in 1999 at a continuing education night school on the north side, not far from where Paul had grown up in Worthington. Abdi made friends easily, and he occasionally talked with Paul and Faris after prayers at the mosque. On one occasion, Paul, his wife, and their young daughter visited Abdi at his mother's house for dinner and conversation. Abdi put down Paul as a reference when applying for a job. As the Balkan conflict raged, the trio of Faris, Abdi, and Paul met one day at the Park of Roses in the Clintonville neighborhood, the same place where years before area Muslims held their first prayer services. There they discussed the possibility of going to Kosovo to protect fellow Muslims from ethnic cleansing by fighting the Serbs.[1]

The conversation settled it for Abdi: he was ready to attend a training camp to prepare for jihad. He figured he would need training in how to use radios, guns, bombs, and guerrilla warfare. Paul backed him up, telling him he would require such training to "be ready at any time." Paul did more than talk: he gave Abdi $3,000 for equipment and travel. Abdi contributed $1,500 of his own. On April

23, as NATO bombs rained down on Serbian targets, Abdi applied for a refugee travel document he would need to go overseas. He explained he'd be traveling to Germany and then Saudi Arabia to visit Mecca. He also applied for another document around the same time, for a Somali woman he was hoping to marry; he went ahead and referred to her as his spouse on a May 10 application for asylum. On June 1, the INS approved Abdi's refugee travel application and issued the document nine days later.[2]

In October, Abdi bought a black balaclava and a Gore-Tex watch cap from U.S. Cavalry, an online purveyor of military and law enforcement apparel and equipment. Abdi had to return his hood and cap when he and Paul learned just how difficult it was to get into Kosovo. Their attention turned to a possible training camp in Chechnya, but they scrapped that idea when Paul found out that the road on which Abdi had to be smuggled into the turbulent region was snow-covered and impassable. Abdi then recalled a place he'd learned of in 1995 when he was attending high school in the United Arab Emirates: a terrorist training camp in Ogaden, Ethiopia.[3]

WHILE ABDI WAS making overseas plans, Paul was on the move again himself. In mid-April 1999, he boarded a flight to Germany, where, during a short visit, he allegedly provided explosives training to fellow terrorist conspirators and helped them recruit new members. It's unclear whom he met with, though the evidence points to his Mauritanian acquaintance Mohammedou Salahi and the Moroccan Karim Mehdi. Back in the United States later that spring, Paul bought a device known as a laser range finder—he claimed it would be used in a training camp in Afghanistan—and came up with a novel way to demonstrate to Abdi how it worked. Standing near his apartment on Riverview one day that summer, Paul used the device to measure the distance to the local NBC station's transmission tower. In June, Paul shipped another unusual piece of equipment, a flat-bed scanner used to forge documents, to an address in Germany. In November, Paul wired $1,760 to an alleged conspirator in Germany. In December, Salahi, now living in Canada, called Paul twice.[4]

These were deep waters. In October 1999, Salahi provided a night's lodging in Germany for three men. One of them, Ramzi Binalshibh, was the primary contact for the 9/11 hijackers. The *9/11 Commission Report* concluded that the two others were Marwan al-Shehhi and

Ziad Jarrah, two of the hijackers, and that Salahi encouraged them to join al-Qaida and go to Afghanistan for training. Salahi denied that al-Shehhi and Jarrah were present and said the men who stayed with him were already on their way to Afghanistan. Years later, a judge weighing the government's right to hold Salahi as an enemy combatant downplayed the evidence, saying all prosecutors had proved was that three men, among them Binalshibh, had stayed with Salahi for a night in Germany. But the connection was enough to catch the attention of authorities after the attacks. Two years later, investigators linked members of the so-called Hamburg cell to the planning of the 9/11 attacks. There is no evidence that Paul was involved with the September 11 plot. But the visit to Germany, the ongoing contact with Salahi, and more than two score phone calls he made to Europe between March and the following January cemented his terrorist connections.[5]

JANUARY 1, 2000, dawned with a collective sigh of relief. Fears of an apocalypse triggered by the Y2K bug failed to materialize, thanks to billions of dollars in computer upgrades. But the celebration came with a somber footnote. Two weeks before the beginning of the second millennium, a man named Ahmed Ressam, a native of Algeria, was arrested at Port Angeles, Washington, as he tried to cross the border from Canada. An alert border guard found the trunk of his car filled with explosives. The so-called Millennium Bomber was foiled in what turned out to be a plan to blow up the Los Angeles International Airport.

A month later, on January 15, Abdi boarded a plane at Port Columbus International Airport on the city's east side, flew to Dulles International Airport in Washington, and then took an Ethiopian Airlines flight to Kampala, Uganda. Entering the country with a visa he'd obtained at the Ugandan embassy in Washington, Abdi paid a smuggler to get him to Nairobi. One of his tasks while in Kenya, he said later, was to serve divorce papers on his first wife. While there, he called Paul back in Columbus to tell him where he was. His next stop, he told him, was Ogaden, Ethiopia.[6]

Soon, though, the trip fell apart. Contacts in Nairobi told Abdi the camp in Ogaden no longer existed. He then attempted to attend a camp in Somalia known as al-Ittihad al-Islamiya. But once inside his native country, he couldn't find the facility. A government account of

Abdi's misadventures would be humorous were the context not so deadly: "Abdi admitted in his statements to the FBI that he was never able to find a training camp to actually attend." In Somalia, however, Abdi did encounter an Islamic warlord trying to create a Taliban-like government in Somalia who encouraged him to raise money in the United States. The warlord also asked Abdi to get in touch with operatives once he returned home. Abdi eventually asked Paul and Faris to contribute money, but he said later he didn't think they did. Faris did indicate that people in Afghanistan were at least interested in the plan.[7]

Abdi stayed in eastern Africa a few more weeks, but eventually it was time to return home. He flew back on an Ethiopian Airlines flight to Washington, then on to Columbus. Although Abdi hadn't found his training camp, he returned with at least one significant accomplishment under his belt: Christopher Paul, with his outspoken passion for jihad and his numerous contacts abroad, now believed Abdi was willing to do anything for the cause.[8]

Four Hundred Years

MOUHAMED TARAZI, THE imam who had married Faris and Bowling in 1995, could tell something was seriously wrong when he picked up the phone a couple of years later. Bowling was on the line and wanted him to hear something. In the background, Faris was screaming and ranting. "As if he's hearing something," Tarazi recalled. "Something talking to him."[1]

Bowling knew something was wrong with Faris. Her husband was prone to strange behavior from time to time, going on long walks during which he'd blank out and couldn't say where he'd been. One day, a few years into their marriage, she got a call from the police, saying Faris had tried to commit suicide by jumping off a bridge on the west side of town. He spent a week in a mental hospital. Even more disturbing, Faris told Bowling he was seeing things and referred to a "half-man" following him around like an imaginary friend. On one particularly bad day, Faris was at home, his face swelling as though he were being choked by some invisible hand. Christopher Paul, whom Bowling always referred to as Abdulmalek, came by and prayed with Faris until the attack, whatever it was, had passed.[2]

By 2000, despite Faris's difficulties, Bowling had had it with him. From the beginning, their marriage had been an odd match: a physical attraction with some shared interests that collided with their very different backgrounds. Five years in, the novelty was wearing off, and Bowling had grown tired of caring for her husband without much reciprocity, either around the house or financially. "I got tired of fighting for money all the time. I said, 'If you can't help me, we don't need to be together,'" she recalled.[3]

They separated in February 2000, the same month that Faris went to Mecca to perform Hajj. Photos he gave Bowling from the trip show a smiling, happy-go-lucky person who doesn't seem on the cusp of a major life change. Nevertheless, their amiable divorce went through two months later; the divorce papers show Faris still going by Mohammad Rauf. They split their meager assets and parted ways. These were dark times for Faris. His father fell seriously ill and died before Faris had time to return home to see him. This was a blow to Faris, who'd stayed close to his father even after he came to the United States. His father frequently had called and even sent gifts of clothing to Bowling; the two occasionally chatted over the phone with Faris translating. Faris eventually flew to Pakistan and spent several months in Karachi before returning home, where depression set in. He'd moved back to an apartment on Riverview near the mosque and did little but lie on his couch and drink Mountain Dew. Eventually, his stepbrother, with whom he'd stayed in touch, convinced him to return to Pakistan for a longer visit. On May 30, he arrived in Karachi for a trip that lasted nearly a year.[4]

IT WAS LATE summer when Faris and his old friend Maqsood Khan arrived at the camp, a collection of tents and buildings tucked between two mountains. They had traveled by bus from Karachi, first to Quetta, near the southeast border of Afghanistan, and then on to Kandahar. There they stayed at a safe house with several Arab men, then rode in a minivan to the camp about an hour away. Faris wasn't exactly sure where he was, but it wasn't hard to guess what the camp was with all the men wearing black scarves and bustling about, carrying guns. Earlier that summer, Khan acknowledged to Faris that he had joined al-Qaida and encouraged him to consider it as well. The confession came during a period of questions Khan put to Faris about his devotion to Islam and about how Americanized he seemed to have become. Faris assured him he still believed in Islam. The morning after their arrival at the camp, Faris, Khan, and others set out on a thirty-minute walk to another set of huts. There they had lunch, and a few minutes later, as a tall man arrived unexpectedly, surrounded by bodyguards, Faris's life changed forever.[5]

The visit with Osama bin Laden lasted about forty-five minutes and appears to have been about as sinister as a camp commandant welcoming the latest round of visitors touring the facilities. The al-Qaida leader greeted Khan with open arms and acknowledged Faris respectfully as a fellow Muslim. It was clear to Faris now: Khan was high up in the organization, bin Laden's "right foot," a top operative for finding materials and supplies. Bin Laden led the group in prayer, speaking in Arabic, a language Faris barely understood. Bin Laden reminded the visitors of their responsibilities to Islam, then departed with his security detail. Faris was both awestruck and fearful. He recalled later his concern that his Western-style ponytail, tucked beneath his turban, might have been discovered.[6]

As if meeting bin Laden weren't enough, Khan then introduced Faris to another important man wearing a turban, an individual who spoke in Urdu and kept his face covered. The man was called "Bocti," but in fact Faris was speaking with Khalid Sheikh Mohammed, a man who came to be known as the architect of 9/11. KSM, as he is frequently dubbed in court documents, peppered Faris with questions about ultralight planes, saying al-Qaida was looking to procure an "escape airplane."[7]

When the meeting with KSM and bin Laden ended, Faris and Khan got into a van that took them back to Kandahar. Faris was furious with Khan for bringing him to the camp and into bin Laden's presence. He wasn't stupid. Faris knew the kind of trouble he could face back home if anyone learned he'd met one of the world's most wanted terrorists. Khan told him not to worry, that they weren't being asked to do anything, and that the meeting was not an initiation or opportunity to swear allegiance to al-Qaida. Faris, shaken, wasn't convinced. "This is four hundred years right here," he told his friend.[8]

❖ ❖ ❖

HOW FARIS SPENT the remainder of his time during this year-long trip abroad is unclear, though a few details emerged over the years. Two months after his trip to the camp, Faris was back in Karachi, looking up information about ultralight planes on a computer at an Internet café and dutifully passing his findings to Khan. He bought a car for 174,000 rupees. At some point he and Khan went to a factory in Karachi and ordered two thousand lightweight sleeping bags which were later shipped to Afghanistan; Faris acknowledged he believed they were for use by bin Laden and al-Qaida.[9]

The day came when Khan asked him what he was doing with his life back home. Faris replied he was interested in investing in a business of some kind. I have just the person for you, Khan said. He's my brother-in-law, his name is Ali Khan, he lives in Baltimore and he owns his own gas stations. The day before Faris left, Khan told him that all he'd been doing during the past year was helping him out. But if he ever wanted to do something further—and Faris had a pretty good idea what that might be—just to let him know.[10]

After almost a year back home, Faris left Pakistan for the United States, arriving in his adopted country on May 25, 2001.

Busy Summer

I N THE SPRING of 2001, in the Buffalo suburb of Lackawanna, six Yemeni Americans made preparations for a trip similar to the one Faris had made a year earlier. Two members of the group traveled to an al-Qaida guesthouse in Kandahar, where they viewed videotapes of bin Laden speeches and the bombing of the USS *Cole* in the Yemeni port of Aden the previous October, an attack that killed seventeen crew members and wounded at least forty others. A third member met Osama bin Laden on his fourth day at the Kandahar guesthouse. From there, the trio traveled to al Farooq, the same camp attended by Christopher Paul's old friend Mohammedou Ould Salahi. Altogether, the six Lackawanna residents spent several weeks at the camp learning various techniques of the terrorist trade, such as using guns—including a Kalashnikov rifle—and being briefed on plastic explosives, TNT, detonators, landmines, and Molotov cocktails. Bin Laden made a guest appearance, speaking about the alliance of al-Qaida and the Egyptian Islamic Jihad, taking responsibility for the 1998 attacks on the U.S. embassies in Kenya and Tanzania, and declaring that fifty men were on a mission to attack America. The six eventually left the camps and were back in New York State by mid-August. They were some of the last U.S. Muslims attending alleged terrorist camps to have contact with bin Laden before 9/11.[1]

THE SUMMER OF 2001 was a busy one for Abdi, beginning with his June 14 marriage to Safia Hussein Muse, another Somali refugee settled in Columbus. Abdi also stayed in close contact with Christopher Paul. Abdi agreed to provide Paul with credit card numbers and corresponding verification numbers gathered from his job at Cell-U-Com. Abdi never figured out whether his friend used the numbers, but he knew what he wanted them for: buying laptops with satellite capabilities that freedom fighters in Afghanistan could use. Or so, Abdi said, Paul told him.[2]

Abdi was also in touch with Iyman Faris. In July, he e-mailed Faris links to websites that concerned items like night vision goggles and antisurveillance equipment and a Soviet monoscope. Faris was also occupied. After returning from his yearlong sojourn in Pakistan and Afghanistan, he took Maqsood Khan's advice and contacted the Khan family.[3]

ALI KHAN AND his family had moved to the United States from Pakistan in 1996, settling in Baltimore, where they ran their gas station. On Faris's first visit, he met with Khan to discuss the possibility of investing in the family business, then had dinner at the family's house, where he got to know Khan's son. Majid Khan had graduated from high school two years earlier and was fluent in English. The two talked about everything from Afghanistan and religion to Majid Khan's desire to work in construction instead of his father's business. Faris went back two or three more times to visit the family. On one of these trips, Majid Khan made an admission to Faris: he'd met KSM, whom he referred to as an uncle, in Pakistan. The teen told Faris something else. He wanted to conduct a mission to kill Pakistani president Pervez Musharraf by exploding a suicide vest. And there was something else, which Faris may or may not have known about: KSM had allegedly tasked Majid with orchestrating attacks on U.S. gas stations and water supplies. Majid's father worried that his son had come under the influence of some relatives with extremist views back home. As Faris got to know the family better, Ali Khan asked him to try to intervene with his son, to steer him off whatever path he was on. Faris was willing to help. But unbeknownst to him, that assistance would come at a high price. By now Majid Khan had attracted the government's interest, and soon authorities were tapping phones and listening in.[4]

PART 2

Night

The radical Islamist movement has never had a clear idea of governing, or even much interest in it, as the Taliban would conclusively demonstrate. Purification was the goal; and whenever purity is paramount, terror is close at hand.

—Lawrence Wright,
The Looming Tower: Al-Qaeda and the Road to 9/11

We Need People Who Can Vanish

SOMETIMES IN HINDSIGHT, it seems days of disaster always dawn brightly. But as anyone alive that day will recall, especially in the eastern United States, September 11, 2001, really did begin as a beautiful morning of blue skies and promise. Temperatures in Columbus were in the low fifties, and there were few if any clouds. The news wasn't all good—a massive fine against a megafarm egg producer, a narrowly avoided child abduction—but it was possible, on balance, to feel optimistic that day. The city was celebrating the first anniversary of its new arena in an up-and-coming development district just north of downtown. Residents of the crime-ridden east side were celebrating a massive police roundup of gang suspects. Advocates for people in nursing homes were celebrating a legislative victory requiring more contact between staff members and the people they cared for. And in news even people in football-crazed Columbus could appreciate, Michael Jordan was hinting at another return to professional basketball. A two-thirds-page Huntington Bank ad that ran in the *Columbus Dispatch* the morning of the attacks summed up the can-do mood, albeit in a layout that must have had bank executives banging their heads on the desk by midday: "Our Free Checking Is Such a Good Deal, It'll Make Your Ears Pop," read the script accompanying a striking photo of a jumbo jet taking off into the rising sun.

PAUL, AS A devout Muslim, could not condone the 9/11 attacks because of the likelihood that fellow Muslims were killed. Abdi long maintained he opposed the death of innocent civilians. Faris also questioned the motives of the hijackers. "How could anybody do that?" he said. "They're a bunch of idiots."[1]

A few days later, Faris had his first contact with the FBI. Agents visited him as part of a series of postattack interviews with Muslims and Middle Easterners around the country. Trip wires, the FBI calls them: people whose backgrounds and lives fit a pattern that helps agents paint a bigger picture. (Similarly, practically every crop duster pilot in America was interviewed after September 11 because of fears the next attack would come via small planes spreading poison.) An FBI agent also visited Faris's ex-wife at the auto parts warehouse and asked about her former husband and his friends. She didn't think much of it, assuming they were interested in anyone with connections to Muslims. That much was true, although officials acknowledged later they were also drawn to Faris because of several flags, including his Pakistani nationality, his commercial driver's license, and the possibility he could use his Freightliner to haul hazardous materials.[2]

About a month after 9/11, Faris was back overseas, traveling to Kashmir to care for his mother, who had had a stroke. Sometime during the same trip, he visited Karachi and met with Maqsood Khan. He pressed his old friend: did the people you're associating with have anything to do with the attacks? Khan claimed he didn't know. But he also enlisted Faris for another job. He asked Faris to visit a travel agency in Karachi to get extensions on several airline tickets, all for travel to Yemen. To do this, Faris dressed as a member of Tablighi Jamaat, an Islamic holy group. The movement, founded in rural India in the twentieth century, consists of itinerant Muslim preachers and is considered one of the most widespread and conservative Islamic movements in the world. Tablighi Jamaat describes itself as nonpolitical and nonviolent, interested only in religious recruiting and bringing back Muslims who have strayed from the faith. The trip piqued the interest of federal investigators because al-Qaida appeared to be using the group in its recruiting efforts: the Yemeni Americans from Lackawanna, for example, had traveled to Pakistan under the auspices of Tablighi Jamaat training.[3]

This stay was shorter, and Faris soon returned to the United States. But not long afterward, his mother became ill again, and he went back to Kashmir early in 2002. Once again, he visited family in Karachi, and once again, he met with Khan. During this trip, Faris had his second encounter with Khalid Sheikh Mohammed.

They met when Khan asked Faris to accompany his son on a trip to KSM to deliver a bag of money and cell phones. The trip made sense; Faris knew that Khan's son, according to a later federal complaint, was an "errand boy" for al-Qaida. During this Karachi meeting, Faris and KSM talked about Faris's job as a truck driver and the deliveries Faris made for cargo planes. The planes, KSM told Faris, hold "more weight and more fuel" than commercial jets. KSM was also interested in how people traveled around the United States, telling his American visitor, "We need people who can vanish into society." Faris later denied this and all such allegations regarding any meetings with KSM. But the federal government claimed there was a reason Khalid Sheikh Mohammed took such an interest in Faris: Majid Khan, the angry young man from Baltimore who referred to KSM as an uncle, had recommended Faris for a job.[4]

KSM told Faris that al-Qaida was planning simultaneous attacks in New York and Washington. Faris's help was needed to destroy the Brooklyn Bridge in New York by severing its suspension cables. Faris needed to buy equipment known as gas cutters, a type of blowtorch, to do the job, but should always refer to them in conversation as "gas stations." KSM also told Faris to start researching equipment, to be referred to as "mechanics shops," to derail trains. The secrecy around these alleged conversations was like something out of a spy novel: KSM told Faris never to access his e-mail immediately after logging onto a computer, but only after opening other Internet sites first.[5]

Thus tasked, Faris returned to the United States in mid-April 2002 and read up on gas cutters on the Internet. He also asked his Turkish roommate, Mehmet Aydinbelge, how such tools worked. They chatted about the idea as they worked on Faris's truck in a parking lot across the street from the Omar mosque. The reality was discouraging: it turned out that oxygen and gas had to be mixed together for them to work and that the tools were quite large. Over the next year, Faris communicated with Maqsood Khan through phone calls to Majid Khan, explaining that he was still trying to find those "gas stations" and "mechanics shops."[6]

Maqsood Khan was one of the central figures in Faris's life, his direct guide to meetings with bin Laden and Khalid Sheikh Mohammed, yet he remained a puzzle. Faris never saw Khan go to work, nor did he know anything about what he did for a living. Later, Faris reflected on ways that Khan perhaps had taken advantage of him. But Faris also hinted that his friend might be of benefit to him, that he might provide information that could make Faris money if he ever wrote a book. It was a consistent theme for Faris, who seemed at times a misguided entrepreneur or at worst an addled poseur, a carefree wannabe oblivious to the effects of the decisions he made and the people he associated with. Faris's stuttering attempts to acquire the gas cutters personified these traits: big ideas, flimsy execution.[7]

Collateral Damage

I N T H E E A R L Y hours of July 1, 2002, residents of the central Afghanistan village of Kakarak in Uruzgan province were celebrating an
upcoming wedding. Dozens attended a party at the home of Mohammed Sherif, brother of a close ally of Afghan president Hamid Karzai. The festivities honored Sherif's son, Abdul Malik, who was to be
married later in the week. Nearby, at the home of Muhammed Shah,
some partygoers were sitting on cushions in a courtyard, while others relaxed on the house's flat-topped roof. People were dancing and
singing and enjoying themselves in ways that had not been possible
under the authoritarian rule of the Taliban. Villagers could hear the
sound of planes overhead but didn't pay much attention. Such flights
had become common since coalition forces invaded the country the
previous fall after the Taliban's refusal to turn over Osama bin Laden.[1]

Suddenly, without warning, explosions and gunfire rocked the
village. An American AC-130 gunship roared overhead and opened
fire. As the plane's cannons and howitzers blasted away, terrified villagers, many of them women and children, ran into rice and corn
fields and nearby orchards to hide. Some survived by fleeing, others were killed or wounded as they ran. It was a scene repeated in
several nearby villages. At Sherif's home, 25 people were killed, all
members of an extended family. When the attack ended, at least 44
villagers were dead and 120 wounded. U.S. officials called the attack
a response to incidents of antiaircraft fire directed at the plane from
the compound. Villagers said they had been firing rifles as part of the
festivities, as was common at such events in Afghanistan, but had not
fired any shots for several hours before the attack.[2]

The incident further inflamed anger within Afghanistan over the
deaths of civilians during the invasion and later operations to hunt
down Taliban and al-Qaida fighters. The anger was as old as the war
itself. On October 27, 2001, two weeks after the United States began its

bombing campaign, a woman was sewing clothes for her brother-in-law's wedding in a village north of Kabul when a bomb went astray and landed on her house, killing her and seriously wounding her two young children. Earlier in the month, the Pentagon acknowledged that one of its missiles went off course and hit houses in Kabul, with reports that four people were killed. It also confirmed the deaths of four Afghans who had been working with a UN-supported demining program in Kabul. Near the end of October, Taliban rulers said that up to four hundred people, mostly civilians, had been killed in two weeks of air strikes around the country. The Pentagon called those figures exaggerated but also said civilian casualties were likely in a war.[3]

Collateral damage, the anticipated killing of nonmilitary combatants and destruction of civilian infrastructure, is as old as warfare itself. In Vietnam alone, an estimated 182,000 North Vietnamese civilians died during the United States' Operation Rolling Thunder bombing campaign from 1965 to 1968. The issue was especially problematic in Afghanistan, where hundreds if not thousands of civilians were killed in the decade following the U.S. invasion. As early as October 2001, UN secretary general Kofi Annan urged combatants to avoid such casualties whenever possible.[4]

In December 2002, Human Rights Watch reported the United States had dropped nearly a quarter-million cluster bomblets in Afghanistan that killed or injured scores of civilians, especially children. It cited data from the International Committee of the Red Cross that identified 127 civilian casualties from cluster bomb duds as of November 2002. As of March 2002, the provincial government of Kandahar had filed more than seventy compensation cases with the central government in Kabul involving U.S. air attacks.[5]

The Pentagon was defensive about its Afghanistan operations. It said military forces were doing all they could to avoid accidental killings. Defense Secretary Donald Rumsfeld blamed the death of every single Afghan and American on the Taliban and al-Qaida. "Their leaderships are the ones that are hiding in mosques and using Afghan civilians as 'human shields' by placing their armor and artillery in close proximity to civilians, schools, hospitals and the like. When the Taliban issue accusations of civilian casualties, they indict themselves," Rumsfeld said.[6]

ON AUGUST 6, 2002, one month after the Uruzgan killings, Abdi, Faris, and Paul met for coffee at a Caribou Café in suburban Upper

Arlington on the northwest side of Columbus. The three were furious at the way the United States had been waging war in Afghanistan. They talked about what to do in response, as they sipped $11.25 worth of gourmet drinks that August afternoon.

Faris tossed out the first big idea of the day, suggesting they destroy the Hoover Dam, perhaps using an airplane in a September 11–style attack. Abdi had another idea. They should use a bomb to blow up a shopping mall. Paul wasn't convinced by Abdi's suggestion. "It's not a good idea," he told the others. It seemed to Abdi that Paul felt the idea wasn't big enough, that it would not kill enough people.

But then Faris said, "Make the plan and you'll be financed." He added: "Do you know how to make explosives?"

"I don't know how to do it," Abdi replied.

Then Faris said, "I would have a better plan."

Abdi was angry as he drove the other two home. He dropped off Paul first, then Faris.

"I'll do whatever is necessary," he told Faris.

A few days later, Abdi went to see Paul, who gave him ten compact discs. "You will need this," he told Abdi.

"What is it?" Abdi asked.

"It's the good stuff," Paul replied. When Abdi asked him what he meant, Paul replied that it was information on how to make explosives. "Take a look at them and tell me what you think," he told Abdi.[7]

THE THREE CONTINUED to see each other that summer and into the fall. On the first anniversary of September 11, Abdi drove Paul, the world traveler with the sinister overseas connections, to Pittsburgh to meet someone and talk about attacking a U.S. military base in Qatar. Abdi took a similar trip in December, picking up this third individual and driving him back to Columbus for a meeting with Paul. The next day, Abdi took the man to the Columbus airport.[8]

Abdi stayed in touch with Faris through the fall by e-mail, periodically sending him messages about jihad, the status of Osama bin Laden, and related information. "A Message to the American People," read the subject line of one such e-mail about jihad. Paul also kept an eye on the Somali, at one point giving him a watch with global positioning satellite capabilities worth several hundred dollars. It was a gift, Abdi felt, to persuade him to stay involved with whatever the three were planning.[9]

Winning the War on Terror

BY NOW THE debate over whether to go to war in Iraq was at full boil. On October 7, 2002, President Bush came to Cincinnati and the city's old Union Terminal hall to give a landmark speech laying out the case against Saddam Hussein and in favor of invasion.

Ohio and George W. Bush went back a long way. The president's grandfather, U.S. senator Prescott Bush, had been born in Columbus, where his father, Samuel Bush, was a railroad executive and later president of a railway parts manufacturing company. The father of Barbara Bush, George W.'s mother, was from Dayton. George W. Bush drew on the connection often during his 2000 presidential campaign, as he and Dick Cheney crisscrossed the state. Ohio, with its eighteen electors and valued swing state status, was must-win territory. Bush underscored Ohio's importance when it became the first state he visited after his inauguration in 2001, traveling to a Columbus elementary school in a poor neighborhood west of downtown dubbed "the Bottoms." There he pitched the education plan that became known as the No Child Left Behind Act.[1]

Ohio made political sense for the speech Bush was about to deliver, as did Cincinnati, tucked into the most conservative corner of the state. Carl Lindner, majority owner of the Cincinnati Reds and former chief executive of Chiquita Brands International, was one of Bush's strongest supporters. A Super Ranger fundraiser for the president, Lindner was one of an elite few pledging to raise at least $300,000. Although hundreds of people protested the speech outside the terminal that night, Bush was guaranteed a supportive audience inside.[2]

Against this backdrop, Bush carefully and forcefully laid out the case against Hussein, from his alleged contacts with al-Qaida to his alleged pursuit of weapons of mass destruction to episodes of tyranny and brutality under his leadership. The president reminded his listeners that Iraq had promised as a condition of ending the Gulf

War in 1991 to eliminate any weapons of mass destruction. Instead, the country had gone back on its word; it now possessed biological and chemical weapons and was pursuing nuclear weapons, the president charged. "The entire world has witnessed Iraq's eleven-year history of defiance, deception and bad faith," Bush said.

Iraq was different from other despotic, dangerous regimes, Bush argued. The country had gathered in one place the most dangerous threats of the age, weapons of mass destruction, and placed them in the hands of a tyrant who already had used chemical weapons against minority Kurds within Iraq. Iraq also had ballistic missiles with a range of several hundred miles, powerful enough to strike Saudi Arabia, Israel, and Turkey. If that threat weren't serious enough, the president pointed out those missiles could strike in a region where tens of thousands of American service members and civilians lived and worked. Iraq had proven itself unique, Bush said, by its past and present actions, its technological capabilities, and the merciless nature of its regime.

The president zeroed in on the nuclear threat. Evidence was strong that the country was rebuilding its nuclear capabilities, though pointedly Bush said it was unclear how long it might be before Iraq had a usable nuclear weapon. But he offered a plausible-sounding possibility. If Hussein's regime acquired an amount of enriched uranium not much bigger than a softball, it could have a nuclear weapon within a year. The time frame, the president was quick to add, was not what mattered. The United States could not ignore the threat and wait for the ultimate proof in the form of "a mushroom cloud."

Along the way, the president acknowledged "legitimate questions" about the nature of the threat from Iraq and the urgency of the proposed action. He also tried to explain why it was necessary to deal with Iraq now, eleven years after the Gulf War. Bush also addressed a common concern of the time, that the United States had enough on its hands with Afghanistan and the attempt to find Osama bin Laden. He reiterated that America had already seen the consequences of the September 11 attacks. Inaction was no longer an option. It was a theme that became a hallmark of the Bush war on terror. "Some have argued that confronting the threat from Iraq could detract from the war against terror," the president told those gathered in Cincinnati that night. "To the contrary; confronting the threat posed by Iraq is crucial to winning the war on terror."[3]

A Great Chapter

IYMAN FARIS STAYED in touch with the Khan family in Baltimore that fall, even digging into his savings to send $17,500 to Ali Khan to invest in a gas station—a real one, this time. Late that year, Faris took a trip to New York City with two friends with one of two purposes: either as tourists checking out the city—Faris's story—or as a terrorist and operative of KSM—the government's version—scoping out the likelihood of destroying the Brooklyn Bridge with those aforementioned gas cutters. In December, back in Columbus, Abdi, Paul, and Faris were sitting in Abdi's car one day, parked outside a doughnut shop, when Faris made another typically bold pronouncement: he was now involved in a plot to launch simultaneous missile attacks against landmarks in Washington, D.C., such as the Capitol and the White House. On another day, in Faris's apartment on Riverview, he boasted to them about how he had met bin Laden.[1]

In February, Faris drove his Freightliner from Columbus to Brooklyn to deliver a load of candles for the Old Williamsburg Candle Company. For a second time, according to the government, he checked out the Brooklyn Bridge. This time, he concluded the plan was unlikely to succeed because of the security and the nature of the structure. After making this decision, Faris placed a two-minute phone call to Majid Khan in Baltimore during which he passed along the message that the job couldn't be done. He did so, according to the government, in his very best spy lingo: "The weather," Faris said, "is too hot."[2]

ON MARCH 1, 2003, Pakistani officials raided a two-story villa in the city of Rawalpindi around 3 a.m. local time. Inside they seized the sleeping Khalid Sheikh Mohammed and dragged him from his bed. The Pakistanis turned over KSM to American authorities, and both countries trumpeted what at the time was one of the most significant captures in the war on terror. White House officials said KSM had been trying to arrange an attack on the United States, adding that intelligence about this possibility had led them to raise the threat alert in February from yellow to orange. In reporting the arrest, *Newsweek* referred to an intelligence document it had obtained that indicated KSM was actively involved in planning attacks against the United States, including a directive to operatives "to target bridges, gas stations, and power plants in a number of locations, including New York City." Part of the plot, *Newsweek* reported, included slashing the suspension cables on bridges. Five days later, in Karachi, authorities apprehended another figure they believed was tied to KSM: Majid Khan, Faris's Pakistani acquaintance from Baltimore. He eventually became one of the so-called high-value Guantanamo Bay detainees.[3]

By now Faris was getting nervous. He had a feeling the government was after him. He'd stayed in touch with Geneva Bowling after their divorce, sometimes coming over and paying her $20 to do his laundry; sometimes they'd even make love again. She could tell he was upset. Late in February 2003 they'd had dinner together at a favorite Turkish restaurant. A few weeks later he called Bowling and sounded scared. The FBI had picked up his roommate, Mehmet Aydinbelge, he told her. The old opportunist, the guy who was going to be a millionaire, was suddenly not so sure of himself. Bowling tried to reassure him, but her pragmatic side also emerged. "Do what you have to do," she said.[4]

The world beyond Columbus was in turmoil. War with Iraq was imminent, sealed by President Bush's rhetoric, despite the national debate over the war on terror and the fundamental question of whether Saddam Hussein was connected, not in some way but any way at all, to bin Laden and al-Qaida. In the midst of all this, on March 19, 2003, Faris drove to Cincinnati to figure out what was happening to his old friend and onetime roommate Mehmet Aydinbelge, who'd been taken into custody by immigration officials pending deportation for overstaying his visa. As Faris walked into the lobby of the downtown Marriott where he was staying, FBI agents, including special agents Jack Vanderstoep and LaTisha Hartsough, approached and asked to speak to him. His fears realized, Faris agreed with little fanfare to meet them later that day in Columbus. I can help you, he added. I can give you information on people in al-Qaida. They rendezvoused at a Bob Evans restaurant just around the corner from the

Omar mosque. Faris reiterated his desire to cooperate. They could come to his apartment, look at his personal computer. He regaled them with descriptions of his overseas travel. It was all there, he said. Just check out my passports—U.S. *and* Pakistani.[5]

March 19 was also a big day for Nuradin Abdi and other members of Columbus's burgeoning Somali community. Masjid Ibn Taymia, a congregation that kept outgrowing its rented facilities, purchased a permanent site on the city's near east side, paying $425,000 for a former warehouse owned for the past thirteen years by something called the Church of Spiritual Unity. At last, one of the country's largest populations of Somali refugees had its own house of worship.[6]

The next day, March 20, the United States and a few coalition partners launched the "shock and awe" operation against Iraq. Eighteen months after 9/11, the United States had opened another front in its war on terror. That very afternoon, Faris arrived at FBI headquarters in Columbus and handed over his laptop to Hartsough. With him was his new girlfriend, Jennifer Keller, who told Faris not to say anything without an attorney present. A lawyer wasn't necessary, Faris recalled Vanderstoep saying to Keller. "He just joined the U.S. team." (Vanderstoep denies ever saying this.) Eventually, miffed, Keller left. The agents showed Faris pictures of several high-ranking al-Qaida leaders. Faris said he'd never seen them and pledged to take a lie detector test to prove it. OK, the agents said, and proceeded to set up the machine. Faris had second thoughts and approached Vanderstoep, asking if he could speak to him alone.

I've met with several terrorists, Faris told him, including Khalid Sheikh Mohammed. I have lots of information I can give you. But I need to keep it from getting out.[7]

Over the next two hours, Faris told the agents about his trips abroad and his contact with al-Qaida. The FBI persuaded him it was best, for his privacy and safety, to accompany them to a local hotel. He agreed and checked into a suite with room service at the Embassy Suites Hotel in the suburb of Dublin shortly after 7:30 p.m. on March 20. At his request, the FBI provided him with new clothes and toiletry items. It's difficult to say exactly what your status is when FBI agents eager to talk to you about your terrorist contacts move you into a hotel on their dime for more secure questioning. But legally, Faris was not under arrest or even in custody at this point.[8]

He spent the next five days at the Embassy Suites, a large hotel tucked into a development of office buildings. Each morning, Hartsough, the top agent on the case, led interviews with Faris in hotel boardrooms. They'd break for lunch, then plunge into another long stretch of questioning that in some cases lasted six or seven hours. At night, Faris hung out in his room and ordered dinner in. One day, Dana Peters, an assistant U.S. attorney from the Columbus office, came to the hotel and discussed with Faris whether members of his family should be moved from Pakistan for their safety or whether they might be eligible for an "S Visa," a special immigration card provided to people with information that could help the government prosecute a crime. Another day, when Faris complained of a rash, the FBI arranged to have a doctor come to the hotel and treat him.[9]

At the end of five days, agents suggested they take Faris to another, more secure location. He agreed, and they checked out of the Embassy Suites around 8:30 a.m. on March 26. Their first destination was Lane Aviation, a private chartered airplane company at the city airport, where they boarded an FBI plane. Over the years, Faris frequently had talked about the book he was going to write detailing his adventures. He said at one point he lied to KSM about his interest in al-Qaida to gain information for the book. Later, he claimed he didn't stop sending coded messages to KSM through the Khan family in Baltimore out of his desire to keep collecting book material. He made the same claim to his girlfriend, Jennifer Keller. He was going to earn a million dollars, he told her, writing a book about something very dangerous. On that morning, as he prepared to fly out of Columbus, Faris leaned back in his seat. "This," he said, "will make a great chapter in my book."[10]

I'm Doing This as a Friend

THEIR DESTINATION SHOULD not have surprised Faris: he was being transferred to the FBI Academy in Quantico in northern Virginia. The plane touched down at the airfield in Manassas about 10:30 a.m. Faris admired the view of nearby Lake Lunga during the short drive that followed. They arrived at the academy, tucked into the woods west of Interstate 95, about thirty minutes later, and Faris settled into his new accommodations.[1]

The setup was not luxurious, but not onerous either. The agents put Faris in a suite in the Jefferson dormitory, the most recently renovated residence at Quantico, an arrangement that included room service, his own bathroom, a kitchenette, a television, and a VCR. He was given new clothes and toiletries, had his laundry done, and got to keep his cell phone. Another doctor saw him and prescribed medicine for blood pressure, back spasms, and the rash he'd been treated for at the Embassy Suites in Columbus.[2]

But this was no vacation. Two guards always sat outside the door. He was allowed out for one hour a night for an escorted walk. Over the next few weeks, he submitted to interviews for hours at a time interspersed with lie detector tests. Though he still had his cell phone, he was warned he should expect electronic monitoring. He was not given any *Miranda* warnings about self-incrimination. A typical day began with interviews around 11 a.m., a break for lunch, then another round of interviews and lie detector tests that could run an hour or two in the afternoon. Since his girlfriend had first raised the issue of an attorney, Faris had wondered whether it might be a good idea. On March 28, Faris told the agents he wanted a lawyer. The agents conducting the interview that afternoon reminded him that he was a cooperating witness, that he was not in prison, and that he still had his phone. "Faris then stated that he wanted to continue to talk," according to an FBI log that provides a bare-bones summary of how he spent his days.[3]

Faris appeared to be intrigued with the position he was in. He talked often about what kind of deal he might get for helping the government. He proposed going abroad as a sort of FBI spy to root out al-Qaida members. (The government declined the offer.) The FBI played its cards close, reminding Faris that agents couldn't negotiate a deal because charging decisions weren't up to them. "We could only report to our superiors whether or not he had been fully cooperative during our interview sessions," Vanderstoep noted.[4]

Exactly what Faris told the FBI at Quantico is unclear, though a forty-four-page summary of nearly two weeks of interviews provides a comprehensive look at his travels abroad. But Faris also told them something of interest closer to home. As a result of that conversation, on April 2, FBI agents tracked down Nuradin Abdi at the Cell-U-Com store in Columbus. He agreed to answer questions. He told them how he had come into the United States via Mexico in 1998 and that he was married with two children and another on the way. He admitted he knew Faris and recalled the meeting at the Caribou Café. But he denied ever saying anything about weapons or shooting up a shopping mall. He was a Muslim, he explained politely, and his religion forbade him from harming anyone. He allowed them to search his apartment and produced a valid copy of an I-95 immigration form.[5]

Nothing further happened to Abdi that day, but the FBI wasn't taking any chances. Agents went immediately to shopping malls in the area, including Polaris on the north side, where rumors of a terrorist threat spread and security was tightened. Over the next few weeks, agents descended on malls throughout the Columbus area in the middle of the night with bomb-sniffing dogs and searched the facilities from top to bottom.[6]

On April 3, the day after agents interviewed Abdi, Faris agreed to let the FBI record a telephone call he placed to Baltimore to Majid Khan's father, Ali. The conversation lasted just two minutes, from 10:04 a.m. to 10:06 a.m. Afterward, Faris consented to another lie detector test, though he declined to sign the forms giving his consent. Instead, he scribbled at the bottom of the page, "I'm doing this as a friend." Faris was starting to get impatient. He repeated his desire to see an attorney. He wanted some resolution: what exactly was he going to get out of all this? He told the agents he wanted to talk to government "deal-makers." In response, shortly after 3 p.m. that day, Neil Hammerstrom, an assistant U.S. attorney from Alexandria, and

Joseph Kaster, a Department of Justice trial attorney, arrived at Quantico. They brought mixed news. They would grant Faris's request and provide him the best attorney possible. But any deal struck would have to include a guilty plea and prison time. If Faris was taken aback, he didn't show it. He said he understood and wanted to continue to cooperate. "I am here as a friend," Faris told the prosecutors, who in turn instructed the FBI it was time to suspend the interviews. Hammerstrom requested a lawyer for Faris the next day, and a federal judge appointed veteran Virginia defense counsel Frederick Sinclair.[7]

Faris had that Friday off; his only recorded activities were staying in his room and watching the movies *Clear and Present Danger* and *Donnie Brasco,* about an FBI undercover agent who infiltrates the mob. On Saturday, April 5, Faris stayed in his apartment most of the day, emerging only to take a forty-five-minute walk in the evening.[8]

The next day, April 6, Sinclair drove to Quantico to meet Faris. Hammerstrom rode along to brief him on the case. Sinclair, sixty years old at the time, knew his way around the courts after a long career first as a state and federal assistant prosecutor, then as a defense attorney representing hundreds of criminal defendants, including cases involving white-collar crime, drugs, guns, and national security. Hammerstrom, admitted to the bar in 1985, was a generation younger. As they drove, their conversation focused on how the government might deal with Faris. Considering the facts, Sinclair told Hammerstrom he assumed that if Faris didn't want to plead guilty, his options were to go to trial or be designated an enemy combatant. A fair assessment, Hammerstrom said.[9]

At Quantico, Sinclair got a complete briefing from the FBI on the evidence against his new client, including facts in their possession, Faris's admissions, and other evidence of his involvement with overseas members of al-Qaida. The agents also made it clear they thought Faris was holding back information. Sinclair asked several questions about the evidence. Finally, he met with Faris in the academy's administration building for two hours, beginning at 1 p.m. It was a tense meeting. Faris was reserved: not exactly hostile to Sinclair, but not friendly either. Faris confirmed Sinclair's worst fears, informing the attorney he'd already told the FBI a great deal about his involvement with al-Qaida. Sinclair advised Faris to stop making statements until they could work out some kind of immunity agreement that would cover any future statements. Faris was reluctant at first, saying he wanted to continue to help the FBI. He finally agreed it was time to stop talking. Faris wrapped up the day with two more movies in his apartment: *Analyze This,* and *The FBI Story.*[10]

The following day, April 8, Sinclair went back to Quantico. He had another FBI briefing about the evidence. The government, he learned, had corroborated Faris's involvement with al-Qaida through interviews with overseas sources. They had further corroboration from Faris's passport, telephone call records, and photographs from his laptop. Sinclair took the information and met again with his client. Sinclair was blunt, laying out the three options before Faris. He could plead not guilty and return to Columbus for a trial in federal court. If he did so, he could challenge the evidence against him, including the admissibility of statements he'd made to the FBI, and confront any government witnesses. The second option was military confinement in Guantanamo, though the likelihood of that was slim, since Faris would first have to be denaturalized—stripped of his citizenship—and declared an enemy combatant. Finally, he could plead guilty in federal court in Virginia and continue cooperating with the FBI. A fourth option, Sinclair emphasized, the outcome Faris really hoped for, to cooperate and then walk free, was not possible. Faris told his defense attorney, someone he had known at that point a total of three days, to pursue a plea deal and continued cooperation. "I want to help these people," he said.[11]

In hindsight, the idea of a U.S. citizen being sent to Guantanamo seems far-fetched. The prosecutions of the Lackawanna Six and the Portland Cell were well-known by then, and none of those defendants—including the Yemeni Americans who, like Faris, had attended al-Qaida training camps and met bin Laden—had suffered such a fate. But there were precedents. In December 2001, the government detained Yaser Hamdi, a U.S. citizen of Saudi descent, after the Northern Alliance captured him in Afghanistan. Hamdi was declared a military combatant and held in a military brig in South Carolina. Late that year federal authorities also arrested Ali al-Marri, a legal resident from Qatar, as he was studying at Bradley University in Peoria, Illinois. He, too, was declared a military combatant and held for years in South Carolina. In 2002, the government took U.S. citizen Jose Padilla into custody on allegations he was plotting to detonate a so-called dirty bomb, a low-level radioactive device. In June of that year, President Bush ordered Padilla held as an enemy combatant, and he, too, was transferred to South Carolina. Padilla and Hamdi ultimately were turned over to civilian courts, and al-Marri was released and sent to Saudi Arabia—but that was years in the future. As far as Faris knew in April 2003, he faced the same fate. The FBI was careful never to directly threaten Faris with the possibility of Guantanamo and military combatant status, but agents were just as careful to leave the door open if the subject came up. "We did not deny that this was a potential outcome," Vanderstoep would say.[12]

EVEN THOUGH FARIS now had an attorney, he was still not in custody. As if to drive this point home, after Faris begged to be allowed to see his girlfriend, the FBI arranged to have Keller flown from Columbus to Washington on April 9. The two spent about two hours together at a Days Inn off Interstate 95. It was hardly a romantic encounter; an agent outside their room knocked on the door every ten minutes to make sure they didn't make love, and eventually cut the visit short.[13]

Faris and Sinclair met twice more, on April 13 and April 16. Plea negotiations between Faris and the government had begun in earnest. One of the biggest advantages Faris had was the timeliness of any information he could offer about al-Qaida suspects. It was important to press forward now to seize the opportunity this information presented. The government's first offer wasn't promising: Faris could plead guilty to two counts of providing material support to al-Qaida in exchange for a thirty-year prison term. After researching the case law on material support charges, Sinclair decided it was a bad deal and advised his client to turn it down. Faris countered with a proposal to plead guilty to a single material support count. The government returned with a new offer: pleading guilty to two charges, providing material support to al-Qaida and conspiracy to provide material support, in exchange for twenty years in prison. The deal also included a broad grant of immunity from prosecution in other jurisdictions for the offenses and for any other information Faris provided. It would also give the government the option to file a Rule 35 motion for a sentence reduction if Faris's cooperation was valuable enough. Faris was reluctant, still wondering if there were other options. Finally, Sinclair laid it out in frank terms.[14]

"If you don't take the plea offer here in the Eastern District of Virginia with a twenty-year cap and ongoing cooperation," he told

Faris, "there's an agent, they're ready to take you back to at least Columbus tonight and then perhaps Guantanamo."[15]

On April 17, 2003, Faris consented to the deal and signed the agreement. Ironically, Sinclair had figured out by this time that Guantanamo was off the table. His clue: the arrival of Dana Peters, the assistant U.S. attorney from Columbus, to help with the negotiations. That was on a Thursday. Faris did further interviews Friday, then had the weekend off. He spent the next two weeks in legal limbo, his name on a document agreeing to plead guilty, but the deal not yet ratified by a judge. The FBI resumed questioning on Monday and Tuesday, April 21 and April 22, then took Wednesday off. Already there was a problem. FBI interrogators complained that Faris was not cooperating as promised. Hammerstrom relayed the concern to Sinclair, who met with his client that Thursday. He explained to Faris the prosecution was over and done with. The FBI couldn't take anything he told them at this point and use it against him for another set of charges. Conversely, Sinclair said, the deal couldn't change in Faris's favor, either. The government "was not going to agree to further modifications," Sinclair told Faris. The interviews resumed the next day from 10 a.m. to shortly after 5 p.m., with a break for lunch, and through the weekend. Faris agreed to lie detector tests both days.[16]

One of Faris's concerns had always been the effect of his cooperation on his family in Pakistan. Faris passed along a relative's name to the FBI, and agents talked with family members more than once, asking them to assess the danger they could face because of Faris. The government even offered to bring them to the United States, if needed. Faris's family assured the FBI it wouldn't be an issue. They took down the contact information but said they didn't feel at risk.[17]

On May 1, Faris left Quantico for good and was driven the thirty miles to the Albert V. Bryan U.S. Courthouse in Alexandria. He'd been up much of the night before, wondering if he was doing the right thing. Not that long ago, Faris had been a truck driver whose past jobs included delivering pizza and selling milk at a convenience store. Not that long ago, he'd done quintessentially American things: he ate out, he watched action movies, he played video games. Not that long ago, his biggest problem had been fending off complaints from his wife that he was a slob who didn't pick up after himself. Now here he was walking into a federal courtroom to formally acknowledge he'd consorted with two of the world's most wanted terrorists.[18]

Material Support

ONE OF THE stranger tales to emerge from the first few weeks of the U.S. war in Afghanistan was that of John Walker Lindh, the so-called American Taliban. Lindh, who grew up in California, was with a Taliban fighting group that surrendered to Northern Alliance troops in Kunduz in northeast Afghanistan in November 2001. A few weeks later, he was involved in a prison uprising in the nearby city of Mazar-e-Sharif that killed a CIA agent.

After Lindh was returned to the United States, he was charged in a ten-count indictment, including four counts of providing material support to two designated foreign terrorist groups, Harakat ul-Mujahideen, an Islamic militant group based in Pakistan but operating primarily in Kashmir, and al-Qaida. Material support, as defined by the statute at that time, included

> currency or monetary instruments or financial securities, financial services, lodging, training, expert advice or assistance, safehouses, false documentation or identification, communications equipment, facilities, weapons, lethal substances, explosives, personnel, transportation, and other physical assets, except medicine or religious materials.

Among other criminal acts, the indictment alleged that Lindh, as part of providing this support, attended the al-Farooq training camp, received weapons training, met Osama bin Laden, traveled with a fighting group opposing the Northern Alliance even after knowing U.S. forces had joined with the alliance, and participated in the prison uprising. The prosecution was one of the first to use the relatively new material support laws after September 11.[1]

THESE LAWS GREW out of statutes that originally focused on embargoes and other sanctions against U.S. enemies. The 1977 International

Emergency Economic Powers Act, for example, replaced earlier laws dealing with the president's ability to impose sanctions with more specific language allowing the seizure of assets and other actions during a formal declaration of a national emergency. Subsequent attempts to pass a law outlawing support for terrorist groups faltered because of concerns over free speech and definitions: one administration's terrorist group might be another administration's freedom fighters. The 1993 attack on the World Trade Center provided the impetus lawmakers needed, and in 1994 the original material support statute, 18 U.S.C. § 2339A, was enacted as part of the Violent Crime Control and Law Enforcement Act. The law targeted anyone who supported a group—regardless of who the recipient was—knowing the aid would be used to carry out specified violent crimes. But the law came with a big loophole: how to prove that someone was helping a group commit a specific crime. The National Commission on Terrorist Attacks upon the United States recognized this dilemma when it observed that "prosecuting a financial supporter of terrorism required tracing donor funds to a particular act of terrorism—a practical impossibility."[2]

President Clinton and Congress moved to address this problem, prodded again by outside events, including the April 1995 bombing of the Alfred P. Murrah building in Oklahoma City, at the time the worst terrorist attack in the nation's history. Despite concerns that the law was unconstitutionally vague and raised First Amendment questions, a new version of the material support statute, 18 U.S.C. § 2339B, became law as part of the far-reaching Antiterrorism and Effective Death Penalty Act (AEDPA) of 1996. The new statute banned support to any group explicitly designated a foreign terrorist organization by the State Department. The change was significant. Whereas 2339A targeted support of a group knowing the aid was going toward the commission of a particular crime, 2339B made any support illegal, regardless of the donor's understanding of how it might be used. On the surface, this seemed a textbook case of government intrusion that could unfairly—and perhaps unconstitutionally—limit well-intentioned and innocent charity work. The dilemma that the president and Congress faced was that donations, however harmless on their face, could also further the efforts of terrorist groups by freeing up funds they no longer had to spend on above-board causes like orphanages or food aid. In addition, those humanitarian gifts could give a dangerous entity a legitimacy it needed. That, in turn, could shield its ultimate and more insidious goals. Detaching support from intent, the government believed, was a crucial step toward battling terrorism.[3]

One of the earliest indictments using the newly enhanced statute targeted a North Carolina cigarette smuggling operation intended to fund Hezbollah. Otherwise, the law was used only infrequently until after the 9/11 attacks, when material support violations became a favorite choice of federal prosecutors. After Lindh, the statute's first major use came in the prosecution of the six Yemeni Americans from Lackawanna, New York, who had attended the same al-Farooq camp in Afghanistan. The case embodied the tensions at the heart of the law. Prosecutors promoted the ability to stop a homegrown terrorist operation by going after a group's activities based on the associations of its members. The defense said the government was overreaching to punish what was essentially the group's poor judgment. The backdrop of this debate: the smoking ruins of Ground Zero.

In the spring of 2002, the Department of Justice announced a significant change in the way the FBI would investigate crimes. The strategy, Attorney General John Ashcroft announced in a directive, would shift the investigation of crime from the prosecution of deeds to the prevention of further attacks. The goal: to free FBI agents from bureaucratic handcuffs and empower them to launch investigations more quickly and in a decentralized fashion, without an elaborate review by Washington. "Terrorism prevention is the key objective under the revised guidelines," Ashcroft announced on May 30. "Our philosophy today is not to wait and sift through the rubble following a terrorist attack." The approach fit perfectly with the intent of the material support laws.[4]

Critics said the government was using the law to punish people when it had only sketchy evidence of criminal intent. Georgetown University law professor David Cole, who has led challenges against the law in the Ninth Circuit Court of Appeals and the U.S. Supreme Court, has said that under the law, someone who sent a designated terrorist group a book about Gandhi for the purpose of persuading them to adopt nonviolence could then be considered a terrorist. In a series of federal lawsuits, the Center for Constitutional Rights argued the law violates the First Amendment by prohibiting activities with no malicious intent, such as the distribution of literature, participating in peace conferences, or providing pure humanitarian assistance. The law "imposes guilt by association by punishing moral innocents not for their own culpable acts, but for the culpable acts of the groups they have supported," CCR has said.[5]

Nevertheless, courts upheld the law, and material support prosecutions piled up through the decade: Jose Padilla, once held as an enemy combatant for allegedly plotting overseas jihad; Yemeni cleric Mohammed Ali al-Moayad, sentenced to seventy-five years in prison for attempting to raise money for terrorist organizations; Syed Haris Ahmed, convicted of conspiring to provide material support by sending video clips of potential targets in Washington, D.C., to overseas jihadists; Hamid Hayat, convicted of a material support charge for attending a jihadist training camp in Pakistan; the Liberty City Seven, charged with plotting to blow up the Sears Tower; and on and on. A 2009 analysis by two former New York City federal prosecutors concluded that the material support provisions were the laws used most frequently in charging domestic terrorists after 9/11. "Although these cases can potentially result in overreaching, and although not all material support cases have resulted in convictions, the government's overall record of success in this area is impressive, and most if not all of the convictions seem sound," the report said.[6]

The 1996 material support law was challenged almost as soon as the United States began designating foreign terrorist organizations. A 1998 federal lawsuit in California, *Humanitarian Law Project v. Reno,* argued the statute violated First Amendment rights of freedom of association by criminalizing donations to groups regardless of whether the intent was purely humanitarian. The suit argued on behalf of groups and individuals who had supported two organizations in the past and wanted to continue supporting them—namely, the Kurdistan Workers' Party (PKK), a Kurdish political group in Turkey, and the Liberation Tigers of Tamil Eelam (LTTE), a group in Sri Lanka advocating the rights of Tamils to engage in self-determination. Both district and appeals courts acknowledged the law's impact on the First Amendment but upheld the statute's constitutionality. In a related case challenging the charges against Lindh, U.S. District Court judge T. S. Ellis, ruling in the Eastern District of Virginia, said there was a difference between associating with a "disfavored or subversive group," and, as Lindh was accusing of doing, joining groups intent on carrying out the terror and violence they advocated. "There is, in other words, a clear line between First Amendment protected activity and criminal conduct for which there is no constitutional protection," Ellis wrote in July 2002.[7]

Congress amended the law over the years, adding "expert advice or assistance" to the list of banned activities in the 2001 Patriot Act. In response to federal court decisions that criticized the law for vagueness, Congress in 2004 again revised 2339B in the Intelligence Reform and Terrorism Prevention Act (IRTPA), adding definitions for "service," "training," "personnel," and "expert advice or assistance." In 2005, a federal judge in California found the terms "service" and "training" remained unconstitutionally vague but also ruled that the new definition for "personnel"—involving one or more individuals working under a terrorist organization's direction or control who organize or otherwise direct the organization's operation—eliminated vagueness concerns. The Ninth Circuit Court of Appeals agreed with the finding in December 2007.

The case was appealed, and the U.S. Supreme Court heard oral arguments in 2009. David Cole argued that the ban on "training," "expert advice or assistance," "service," and "personnel" were unconstitutional because they are vague, punish protected speech and the right of association and discriminate on the basis of content. "The right to engage in peaceable political speech is at the very core of the First Amendment, and government attempts to criminalize such speech warrant the Court's most skeptical scrutiny," Cole wrote in his brief to the Supreme Court. The government disagreed. Solicitor General Elena Kagan said the law does not prohibit independent advocacy or expression, but rather a separate act of giving aid to terrorists, regardless of the form that help takes, whether money, training, or advice. "The material-support statute provides persons of ordinary intelligence with reasonably clear, and therefore constitutionally sufficient, notice of the types of direct aid that it prohibits," said Kagan, who a few months after making her argument in December 2009 was nominated to the Supreme Court by President Obama.[8] On June 21, 2010, the Supreme Court upheld the law's constitutionality when applied to the four remaining terms under challenge: "training," "expert advice or assistance," "service," and "personnel." The decision did, however, leave the door open for future litigation. "We conclude that the material-support statute is constitutional as applied to the particular activities plaintiffs have told us they wish to pursue," concluded Chief Justice John Roberts. "We do not, however, address the resolution of more difficult cases that may arise under the statute in the future."

❖ ❖ ❖

JUDGE T. S. ELLIS upheld the use of the material support statute in Lindh's prosecution on July 11, 2002. Four days later, both sides were gathered in Ellis's Alexandria courtroom for a hearing in which Lindh was challenging the admissibility of statements he'd made to the FBI, military officials, and the media after his capture. Suddenly, Lindh's attorney stood up and made a surprising announcement. His client had reached an agreement with prosecutors to plead guilty. The judge turned to Lindh and asked him to explain what he was doing. "I provided services as a soldier to the Taliban last year," Lindh said. "I carried a rifle and two grenades." He added that he knew his actions were illegal. "I plead guilty," he said.[9]

As part of the deal, prosecutors dropped all but one charge of supplying services to the Taliban. Lindh also agreed to plead guilty to what is called a criminal information that charged him with illegally carrying explosives. Prosecutors dropped the remaining charges, including all the material support counts. Lindh went from suspected terrorist to a man violating the older federal prohibition against helping a wartime enemy.[10]

The use of material support charges against Lindh was the beginning of the statute's prominence in the war on terror, not its end. The goal, after all, was no longer just to prosecute those who meant harm. The objective was to stop the harm from happening in the first place. Speech, action, and association had new significance in the post-9/11 era. As Attorney General John Ashcroft put it, the time for sifting for clues in the rubble of an attack was over. But the trade-off was a precarious balancing act that inevitably tipped against the defendant: at what point do angry words and misguided deeds rise not just to the level of criminal acts, but to the realm of terrorism?

Guilty

THE FEDERAL DISTRICT Court for the Eastern District of Virginia in Alexandria has seen its share of big national security cases over the years, starting more than a century ago with the 1866 indictment of Jefferson Davis on a charge of treason. Spies Arthur Walker, Aldrich Ames, and Robert Hanssen are among those who have been prosecuted in Eastern District courtrooms. The judge overseeing Faris's plea and sentencing, Leonie Brinkema, was also no stranger to the national security spotlight. Three months before Faris appeared before her, she had ordered the government to allow Zacarias Moussaoui, the so-called twentieth September 11 hijacker, to question Ramzi Binalshibh, the attacks coordinator, by videotape. Brinkema started her legal career in 1976 as an attorney with the bulldog public corruption unit in the Justice Department known as the Public Integrity Unit, then served as a federal prosecutor and later as a trial attorney in the criminal division of the Office of International Affairs. President Clinton appointed her to the bench in 1993.[1]

Brinkema opened the May 1 plea hearing by asking Faris about his command of English, and then slowly walked him through the questions typical of such appearances. Was he on any medication? Was he under the influence of any drugs or alcohol? Was he feeling all right? Faris, behaving calmly, indicated he was fine, though his brief responses left the impression of someone less than happy about his circumstances. Brinkema then sought assurances that he understood he was giving up his right to a grand jury and that he wasn't being unduly pressured to make this court appearance and enter this plea. Again Faris—with the help of Sinclair—indicated he understood the circumstances and acknowledged his choice in being present. Brinkema phrased her questions carefully: as a judge she regularly posed inquiries that sometimes required a "yes" and sometimes a "no" to ensure defendants were truly aware of what they were saying and not just uttering rote responses.[2]

Brinkema moved on to the punishment Faris might face when he was sentenced later that year. She went over the terms of the deal and the options before her.

"That would mean that the Court could—doesn't mean that I will—but it could add the sentences together so that, in fact, your exposure on Count 1 is up to five years, your exposure on Count 2 is up to 15 years, so at least theoretically, the Court could sentence you to 20 years of imprisonment. Do you understand that?" Brinkema said.

"I do," Faris said.[3]

Brinkema pressed the point by raising the issue of where Faris might end up once he was sentenced.

"I think Mr. Faris needs to be aware of, you know, the worst things that can happen to him with a guilty plea," Brinkema said.

Sinclair explained that he'd had several previous clients go to Ashland Federal Correctional Institution in Ashland, Kentucky, a medium-security facility. (On its website, however, the Bureau of Prisons classifies Ashland as low security.)

"All right," Brinkema said. "Mr. Faris, do you understand that?"

"I do," Faris said.[4]

Brinkema reviewed what Faris's obligations to the government would be once he pleaded guilty. Did he understand he had to cooperate with all state and federal authorities if they needed information about criminal or terrorist activities? He did. Did he understand he had to testify truthfully at any grand juries, trials, or military commissions? He did. Did he understand that he was assigning the government any profits he might make from publishing a book about his experiences?

"I do," Faris said, with no mention of his get-rich dreams from writing such a book.[5]

Brinkema moved on to the business of the day, reviewing the elements of the offenses Faris had been charged with: the trips abroad, the orders of the sleeping bags, the meetings with bin Laden, the introduction to bin Laden's "right foot," the extension of the tickets to Yemen, the research into ultralight planes, the plan to destroy the Brooklyn Bridge, the sending of coded messages. Faris acknowledged them all.

"Do you make any claim whatsoever that you're innocent of the conspiracy charge in Count 1 of the information?" Brinkema asked him.

"No," Faris said.

"How then do you plead to that charge?"

"Guilty."

"Do you make any claim whatsoever that you're innocent of the charge in Count 2 of providing material support and resources to al Qaeda?"

"Say that again?" Faris said.

"Yes. Do you make any claim that you're innocent of the charge in Count 2 of providing material support and resources to al Qaeda?" Brinkema said.

"No, I'm not."

"How then do you plead to that charge?"

"Guilty," Faris said.[6]

The hearing over, Faris, now a convicted terrorist, was placed in handcuffs and taken to jail to await sentencing. It was the first time he had been formally detained since FBI agents approached him in Cincinnati six weeks earlier. A strange journey that stretched back to the day he met his old friend Maqsood Khan decades earlier was coming to an end.

A Secret, Double Life

THE DAYS THAT Turkish graduate student Mehmet Aydinbelge had left in the United States were running out. It had been almost a decade since he arrived in Columbus, and his student status had long since expired. A week after Faris pleaded guilty, an immigration judge ordered Aydinbelge deported to Turkey. Before that happened, the government wanted one last word with him. In early June 2003, as the FBI sifted through the reams of information Faris had provided, Aydinbelge told agents that Faris, Nuradin Abdi, and Christopher Paul were close associates affiliated with a radical branch of Islam.

That the three were friends was true, as was the fact both Abdi and Paul were religious conservatives. (It's hard to know what Faris believed in.) Whether friendship and heated conversation rose to the level of "associates" was another question. But shortly afterward, on June 5, agents opened an official investigation into Abdi. On June 6, Aydinbelge, the onetime Ohio State graduate student and Faris roommate, left the United States permanently, flying home out of New York's JFK Airport on Delta Flight No. 72.[1]

Prosecutors could hardly be faulted for congratulating themselves on a job well done with Faris. His was a textbook example of how such cases were meant to proceed. Acting on information gained from sources including Khalid Sheikh Mohammed, one of the world's most wanted fugitives, the government had interrupted a potentially deadly attack on U.S. soil involving another New York landmark, the iconic Brooklyn Bridge. Furthermore, Faris represented a valuable source of continuing information. Thanks to him, the government was now aware of at least two other conspirators in Columbus. Faris's interrogation had gone smoothly, relatively speaking, and the final plea negotiations, while bumpy, had been concluded without undue complications. And then, as sometimes happens, everything went to hell.

Up until now, Faris's arrest and conviction had been well-kept secrets. Brinkema, the federal judge, had made it clear she wanted it to stay that way. "I don't expect to see anything about this in the press," she warned Hammerstrom during the plea hearing on May 1.

"It certainly won't come from our office, your honor," Hammerstrom replied.

"I hope not," Brinkema said. "We've had too many of these problems, all right?"[2]

On June 13, however, someone in the government leaked word of the investigation into Faris and his subsequent disappearance. This leak was still unknown to Faris and in all likelihood, to the FBI and government prosecutors—who were not likely the source of the information—when agents and Sinclair visited Faris in the Alexandria jail for a follow-up interview on June 14. Suddenly, an hour into the questioning, Faris announced that he had been wrongly accused and that everything he'd told the government was a lie. Among other things, he said, he was frustrated by agents' inability to tell him how much of a break he might get on his sentence under the Rule 35 provisions. This was a big headache, but nothing compared to what came next. *Newsweek* broke the news about the investigation with an online story, followed by a June 19 report by MSNBC Online that Faris had disappeared without being publicly charged with a crime.[3]

The government scrambled to repair the damage and assess its options. Faris had always feared that his cooperation might endanger his family back home. Shortly after midnight on June 19, Vanderstoep got one of Faris's close relatives in Pakistan on the line to explain the situation. The relative, who spoke excellent English, was taken aback at the news, but after discussion said he didn't feel as though word of Faris's arrest was going to put anyone in Pakistan in danger. One reason may have been that Faris had few direct relatives left: his father had died, he didn't have any full siblings, and the rest of his relations were stepbrothers and stepsisters.[4]

Still, in light of the leaks and unwelcome publicity—some of it inaccurate—the government decided it was time to unseal the record and make the case against Faris public. "The whole story really hasn't been told, and I think the Department would like to try to get ahead of the story and avoid any erroneous reporting," Hammerstrom told Brinkema and Sinclair during a teleconference on June 19, the day the MSNBC story appeared. Sinclair wasn't so sure. He acknowledged the source was likely not the FBI or the Justice Department, but perhaps someone in the Defense Department. "There's a lot of people in this loop," Sinclair said. Nevertheless, he wasn't happy with the government's backtracking on going public.[5]

"My problem is it's the same agency, the same government, the same entity that apparently leaks it in the first place and now wants to unseal it, and I just find that somewhat distressing," Sinclair said. Brinkema said she was inclined to go along with the government's request, particularly since there didn't appear to be any danger to Faris's overseas family. But she also noted the unusual nature of the proceeding. "This is the first time I've had the government pushing for things to be made open and the defendant arguing he wanted them kept closed," she said, before unsealing the plea agreement the same day.[6]

LOSS OF INNOCENCE is probably too strong a phrase for the effect that word of Faris's guilty plea had on Columbus. Twenty-two months after 9/11, after all, the country had grown used to arrests of locals for plotting alleged terrorist attacks. In May alone two members of the Lackawanna Six had pleaded guilty to material support charges. Still, the June 19 news conference in Washington held by Attorney General John Ashcroft, when he told the world of Faris's "secret, double life," was startling.

"In apprehending Faris and reaching this plea agreement, we have taken another American-based Al Qaeda operative off the streets, who appeared to be a hard-working American trucker, but secretly scouted terrorist strikes that could have killed many of his fellow citizens," Ashcroft said.[7]

By now Columbus and Ohio were more than accustomed to members of the National Guard, reservists, and active-duty personnel shipping overseas to fight our enemies. But this was different: this was that same enemy at home. Right next door. The streets and highways Faris traveled, the restaurants and the mosque he frequented, even the air field where he considered ultralight lessons, were familiar to many in the community.

As news spread, FBI agent James Turgal assured people there was never a threat to anyone in Columbus. He added, somewhat curiously, "There is no cell in Columbus, not at all." Tarazi, the former imam at the Omar mosque who now ran a charter school, recounted the story of Faris's mental troubles. Negla Ross, who lived next door to Bowling and Faris on Grasmere, recalled him as "a nasty man, a mean man." Geneva Bowling was at work when friends told her about the arrest of her ex-husband. She professed shock and a feeling akin to physical illness at the news. She said it just didn't seem like the person she knew—although she must have had some inkling given Faris's panicked phone calls to her in the weeks before he disappeared. Bowling and her son, Michael, had the requisite morning TV appearance, on *Good Morning America,* a week after the announcement. "He liked America. Never said anything negative. He liked the freedom here," Bowling said on the program. "That's why I was so shocked. I couldn't see that happening."[8]

Back in Virginia, things went from bad to worse. The day after Ashcroft's news conference, Faris saw a doctor in the Alexandria city jail who prescribed antidepressant and antipsychotic medications. Five days later, when FBI agents—with Sinclair present—again tried to interview him, Faris threw a fit, demanded an 80 percent reduction in his sentence based on his cooperation, then began banging his head against his cell door.[9]

It's clear Faris was not in his right mind at this point; to what degree he was mentally ill or unstable would be argued later. But it's not hard to understand what he was feeling. The leak and subsequent publicity had done considerable damage to his value as an informant, and hence to the possibility he could receive a reduced sentence. The existence of a possible al-Qaida conspirator known in court documents as C-1—Maqsood Khan, in fact—was now common knowledge worldwide. It wouldn't have taken much to figure out C-1's identity and then to connect the dots to Baltimore and Majid Khan. That likely ended any hope the government had of pursuing Maqsood Khan, and in truth, there wasn't a whole lot more Faris had to offer. The FBI was already investigating Abdi's coffee shop comment, and the agency had never taken seriously Faris's offer to go to Pakistan as an ad hoc spy.[10]

By July 24, Faris was on suicide watch at the Alexandria City Jail and taking Prozac. Sinclair filed a motion asking that his client's mental competency be evaluated, noting he was having a hard time communicating with Faris and needed to know if he was even capable of helping Sinclair represent him. Brinkema granted the request, which was unopposed by the government, and appointed Richard Ratner, a veteran Washington-area psychiatrist, to do the evaluation.[11]

Sinclair also asked for the first time for a transcript summarizing the interviews the FBI had conducted with Faris from March 19 until he came aboard as Faris's attorney. Known as 302s, these are not verbatim transcripts but narratives that sum up the gist of such interviews. Sinclair received a copy of the forty-four-page document on September 4. After reviewing its contents, he started to have doubts about the validity of what Faris had told agents. In particular, Sinclair was bothered by discrepancies between the government's official version of Faris's reconnaissance of the Brooklyn Bridge and what the 302s contained.[12]

This is how the statement of facts, released June 19, described what Faris did:

> In late 2002, the defendant traveled to New York City. After examining the particular bridge, he concluded that the plot to destroy the bridge by severing the cables was very unlikely to succeed because of the bridge's security and structure. In early 2003, after scouting the bridge, the defendant sent a message to C-1 which stated "the weather is too hot." This message was coded and meant to convey the defendant's assessment that the bridge plot was unlikely to succeed.[13]

THE PROBLEM, SINCLAIR realized, was that the 302s contained no specific account of Faris examining the bridge in late 2002. At best, they describe a trip Faris took to the city with two friends in December 2002 during which, on a day trip to New York City, his friends took pictures "of the bridges, tunnels and landmarks." There was another problem. Faris told the FBI he had driven his truck over the Brooklyn Bridge on that February 2003 trip, but in fact the bridge had been blocked to truck traffic. For that, Faris had a simple explanation: he'd lied, he said, because he was afraid of being sent to Guantanamo.[14]

Withdrawing Faris's guilty plea seemed a logical response to such questions. But that option raised considerable complications. By acknowledging he had lied, for example, Faris now faced the possibility he could be charged with perjury. But he persisted, and Sinclair, as his attorney, felt he had to comply. On September 24 Sinclair filed a notice of Faris's intent to withdraw his plea. Once again, Faris's mug shot was repeatedly broadcast on cable news channels nationwide.[15]

On October 28, the day previously scheduled for Faris's sentencing, Ratner's mental evaluation of Faris was filed in federal court. The defendant, Ratner concluded, likely suffered from a significant mood disorder and personality disorder. Faris told Ratner that when he emerged from the depression and despondency he was suffering at Quantico, he finally had enough strength to read the reports of what he'd testified to. He decided he'd made the wrong decision. Ratner concluded none of this affected Faris's ability to stand trial. Although Faris did not always tell the same story about his activities, those inconsistencies didn't rise to the level of mental illness. Faris, Ratner said, was "currently competent for whatever legal procedure" he faced. Brinkema opened a hearing on the findings and Faris's request.[16]

She began by addressing the central issue before her: Faris's desire to take it all back and start over. Sinclair must have known what he was up against from the beginning, she told the defense attorney. "Some discrepancy between detailed FBI briefings and the statement of facts," Brinkema warned, "in and of itself does not in my view establish either legal innocence or that the plea was not knowingly and voluntarily made."

Sinclair, his client sitting nearby, soldiered forward. "I make this motion on his behalf with a heavy heart," he began. "If the court were to allow him to withdraw his plea, his options are somewhat grim." Faris knew that, and had heard Sinclair say it before in open court. It was his choice, Sinclair emphasized, and he'll have to live with it.[17]

That said, Sinclair went on, there were troubling questions about the May 1 plea agreement. He had become aware of Faris's past mental problems, including the Columbus suicide attempt and hospitalization years earlier, only when he sat down with Faris and a probation officer weeks after the plea had been signed. Given that history, Faris's brusque behavior during their attorney-client sessions in April, and then the noticeable difference in Faris after he began taking antidepressant and antipsychotic medications, led Sinclair to wonder whether Faris was really in his right mind when he was talking to the FBI. Moreover, the comparison of the statement of facts with the FBI 302 had revealed discrepancies at the heart of the government's case, which after all had been built around the idea that Faris was trying to destroy the Brooklyn Bridge. Compounding those discrepancies was the fact that much of the government's case was based on Faris's own admissions. And Sinclair was starting to doubt the validity of those statements. Without the bridge corroboration, Sinclair said, "some of the elements of material cooperation or providing material resources and a very important element may no longer be there."[18]

The government responded by attacking Sinclair's position point by point. The records of Faris's hospitalization alluded to severe depression, not psychotic episodes, Hammerstrom said. There were no major differences between the statement of facts and the FBI 302. Moreover, such an allegation was rendered moot by the hearing Brinkema had conducted May 1 when Faris agreed with the judge's detailed outline of the allegations against him. Brinkema interrupted Hammerstrom to read a portion of the May 1 transcript as a way of agreeing with his position. "There's nothing in that statement that indicates he drove his tractor trailer across the bridge or how he did that surveilling of the bridge," Brinkema said. "That's not critical, how he did it."[19]

Furthermore, Sinclair had it wrong on the corroboration, Hammerstrom said. Faris's statements weren't the only source of the government's case. Agents backed up the information he gave with other sources, including his contact in the United States—presumably Majid Khan in Baltimore—as well as telephone and toll records that confirmed his presence in New York City. Not only was Faris guilty of the charges he had pleaded to, he knew exactly what he was doing, irrespective of any allegations that he wasn't in his right mind. "You have a calculating, devious individual and not a person suffering from a mental disease or defect," Hammerstrom said. Joseph Kaster, the Justice Department attorney attending the hearing, pressed the point. Faris made a decision to align himself with al-Qaida, Kaster said, a decision exacerbated by the fact that he was a U.S. citizen and that his outreach happened after the events of 9/11. In the fight against terrorism, Kaster said, Faris "chose sides by casting his lot with al Qaeda."[20]

Prosecutors Hammerstrom and Kaster weren't guaranteed Brinkema would be friendly to their argument. This was the jurist, after all, who the previous January had given Zacarias Moussaoui permission to depose a top government witness, a move strongly protested by prosecutors. But today, she had little patience for Faris's backtracking.[21]

"Any defendant who has no significant mental problems, which this defendant does not have . . . who has no problem with the English language, who has an education, who stands up in court, takes an oath to tell the truth, and consistently answers questions the way this defendant did, can walk back into the same court and say it was all a bunch of lies," Brinkema said. "I will not accept that." Given the sensitive nature of some of the witnesses who might testify, it would be a problem for the case to go to trial, she continued. Moreover, the government had already expended scarce resources on the mental evaluation. Allowing Faris to withdraw his plea, Brinkema said, would be a waste of money.[22]

After denying the motion, Brinkema then called Faris forward for sentencing, and asked if he had anything to tell the court. As Faris spoke, a bailiff kept reminding him to face the judge.

"I don't have any connection to al Qaeda except my best friend has worked for al Qaeda. Yes, on that extent, I have," Faris said. "I wanted to fool them in order to I can gain something to write a book. That's the only thing I wanted to do, to get an opportunity out of this."

Brinkema asked him why he shouldn't be sentenced.

"Because I'm innocent."

"That certainly is different from what you told the court several months ago, Mr. Faris."

"Your Honor, you have every right to—I mean, I don't have a word for you, but every right to petition me because of my stupidity." He went on, saying it was ridiculous for the government to argue he wasn't in custody during his closely supervised time at Quantico.[23]

"Am I a free man? How do you qualify a free man? You put one person for a day in a room, man go crazy. I'm thirty days sitting with these people, same thing over and over and over and over," Faris said.

Brinkema had had enough. "All right," she said.

"I'm innocent," Faris said again.

He tried to go on, but Brinkema cut him off. The only other word Faris said the rest of the day was "yes" responding to various questions about the twenty-year term she was handing down. She agreed to Sinclair's request that a prison close to Columbus be considered. She reminded Faris that under his plea agreement his conviction could not be appealed. But he could appeal her decision today to deny his motion to withdraw that plea. The day's business done, she ordered Faris taken back into custody and concluded the session.[24]

Three weeks later, on November 17, Faris filed notice he would appeal Brinkema's decision. Two weeks after that, on the morning of the post-Thanksgiving shopping frenzy known as Black Friday, FBI and ICE agents took Nuradin Abdi into custody outside his north-side apartment.

Get This Done

AFTER THE FBI formally opened its investigation into Abdi, agents began following him and tracking his phone conversations. By November, they had confirmed calls to as many as forty different people the government associated with terrorism suspects. To the agents assigned to Abdi, he seemed to behave like someone with something to hide; his erratic driving including U-turns and random stops suggested someone taking countersurveillance measures. Abdi treated it more like a joke, priding himself on the day agents lost him because he had to drive his sister's car. He kept on with his life. On September 17, he and a cousin cosigned papers to incorporate Abdi's own cell phone store, Cell Station, in the Global Mall, an indoor conglomeration of clothing stores, a restaurant, a money transfer business, and other outlets, tucked between an Old Pottery store on one side and a Waterbeds 'n Stuff on the other. His brother had a small book and tapes shop across the street, and Abdi would often wander over, buy a cappuccino at a neighboring coffee shop, and visit with his brother and mother, who also worked there.[1]

It was a surreal standoff. Abdi, knowing full well he was in the government's crosshairs—especially since Faris's conviction—tried to proceed as if nothing were wrong. On November 22, a Saturday, Abdi went to the Ibn Taymia mosque where he sneaked a look at his cell phone to see how Ohio State was doing in the annual football showdown against Michigan. Meanwhile, FBI case agent Stephen Flowers, convinced Abdi was on the cusp of a horrifying attack, worked feverishly behind the scenes to find a way to arrest the Somali. Eventually, the FBI and Immigration and Customs Enforcement concluded Abdi was a threat to national security and should be arrested. The agencies agreed the best approach was to make the arrest based on violations of federal immigration laws. But making that arrest happen wasn't going to be easy.[2]

Normally, the heads of local ICE offices can issue administrative arrest warrants by themselves. Headquarters gets involved when the arrest is based on national security concerns. In that case, agents typically submit an affidavit or some other document explaining their evidence. Early in October, Flowers starting giving information about his investigation to Turgal, the chief general counsel for the Cincinnati division—an FBI position that serves as a sort of in-house attorney for agents on the ground. The information included Abdi's forty-plus phone calls along with a July e-mail Abdi sent Faris showing him websites where he could purchase spyware: night vision goggles, small cameras, listening devices, and the like. Turgal drafted a five-page declaration over the next few weeks. He finished on October 28 and submitted the document to Washington.[3]

Flowers and Turgal both believed the information they provided was unclassified. ICE lawyers in Washington weren't so sure; they were reluctant to issue the arrest warrant if that information was in the affidavit. The portion causing the most problems was Paragraph 8, which detailed the heart of the case: the analysis of Abdi's cell phone calls and e-mail between June 3, when the investigation opened, and October, when Flowers submitted his evidence to Turgal. FBI and ICE lawyers in Washington spent nearly a month debating the document and trying to decide what information was, as one jurist later quipped, "classified, unclassified, declassified or about to be declassified." Flowers and the ICE agents in Columbus were starting to get antsy. They still believed Abdi might carry out an attack on Black Friday, and then, assuming he survived, try to disappear.[4]

The debate reached a fever pitch in the days before Thanksgiving. Agents and government lawyers all the way to the highest echelons of FBI and ICE headquarters in Washington hashed out whether they had the authority to arrest the Somali, and if so, how? The last thing anyone wanted was a high-profile arrest in a crowded mall parking lot as Christmas shoppers streamed into stores. Complicating matters, the allegations against Abdi involved a falsified application for political asylum. That was one of the most coveted immigrant statuses available. Arresting a political refugee was rare and ran contrary to America's reputation as a welcoming harbor for the persecuted. More practically, what would happen if Abdi refused to talk? They could deport him, but where? Back to Somalia, a lawless land with no government, where he might face torture or worse? For Abdi's part, if he was concerned about minimizing guilt by association, he wasn't showing it. On Wednesday, the day before Thanksgiving, he loaned Paul $250 to buy something for Frida.[5]

On Thanksgiving Day, Kevin Cornelius, supervisor of the Columbus joint terrorism task force, spent much of the afternoon in a back room at his in-laws', glued to a cell phone plugged into a charger. Flowers, John Corbin, and LaTisha Hartsough were among the many agents and other law enforcement officers who came into the FBI Columbus office to work the phones on the holiday. Finally, late in the afternoon, the call came: ICE was granting authority to take Abdi into custody based on the Turgal declaration, even though authorities still didn't have an administrative arrest warrant.[6]

After the weeklong production of deciding whether to pick up Abdi, the operation nearly fell through the next morning. The team of arresting agents, basing their movements on Abdi's normal routine, was still driving to the apartment complex on the city's north side when Abdi left his apartment and headed for his car. Only Special Agent John Corbin was present, and it was he who stopped Abdi, told him to wait, then got on his cell phone and let the startled team know he had their man.[7]

On the day he was arrested, Abdi signed a form at 7:42 a.m. waiving his *Miranda* rights and giving agents consent to search his apartment, his car, and his business, Cell Station ("Your source of wireless connection," according to the business's stationery). The agents seized four computers, five CD-ROMs, and numerous documents from Cell Station, along with VHS tapes, CD-ROMs, audio cassettes, floppy disks, a GPS watch, and several documents from the rooms in Abdi's apartment, including the bedroom of one of his children. An analysis of one of the Cell Station computers—the one that used Abdi's log-on name, "alnasrojay" and had pictures of Abdi's wife and brother—found numerous photographs on the hard drive with such captions as, "Bin Laden is in our hearts," "Our war is with America," and "Do not consult anyone in the killing of Americans." On one of the floppy disks investigators found an Arabic text titled "Pillar of the preparing of the Jihad."[8]

As Abdi sat in government custody, first at the FBI's Columbus office, then later in the detention cell in Kentucky, one thing became clear: both his immigration status and his ability to see his family hinged on his willingness to cooperate. Within twelve hours of his apprehension, according to Abdi, both Stephen Flowers, of the FBI, and Robert Medellin, the veteran ICE agent, told Abdi that the process was going to take a while but that he could shorten things considerably—and return home—by helping them. They repeatedly mentioned his children. Abdi believed them, thinking if he would get this "done faster," it would get him home. "As each day passed by," Abdi recalled, "the concern of seeing my family was heightened, and thus the pressure was heightened." The pressure increased when agents revealed they really wanted information about Iyman Faris. They knew they had a limited window of opportunity to question Abdi and so focused their questions on the most crucial details.[9]

Abdi told the agents most of what they wanted to hear almost immediately. The key confession came on November 30, two days after he was taken into custody. ICE agents had moved him from the Kenton County Jail to the Cincinnati FBI office for further questioning late that morning. He signed a *Miranda* waiver, his second since his arrest. Feeling isolated and worried about his family, Abdi confessed that he had falsified his asylum application. The FBI agents, Flowers and Corbin, listened in but didn't participate. They left the building around 1:30 p.m. for lunch. When they returned, they learned Abdi had acknowledged the discussion Faris had first tipped them to, but with a correction: the talk was of opening fire in a mall, he said, not blowing it up. ICE agents immediately instructed a clerical assistant to type up the notes of Abdi's confession and between about 5 p.m. and 10 p.m. Abdi, the assistant, and the ICE agents reviewed the transcript. At 10:15 p.m. the assistant, Richard Wilkens—the top ICE agent in Columbus—Medellin, and Abdi signed the sixteen-page statement, which Abdi acknowledged was "a true and correct transcript." Abdi then agreed to be interviewed by the FBI agents about the mall threat. He signed his third *Miranda* waiver at 10:40 p.m. and was questioned for almost two hours, the interview ending around 12:45 a.m. the morning of December 1, 2003. Abdi's ordeal was far from over, as he returned to jail in Kentucky. But the bulk of the government's case against him was now complete.[10]

Shopping Mall Plot

Late in the spring of 2004, Abdi found himself incarcerated at the Seneca County Jail in Tiffin, Ohio, a city of seventeen thousand about two hours north of Columbus. His then attorney, Doug Weigle, had visited him regularly when he was in the Pickaway County Jail in Circleville, just south of Columbus. On May 28, however, on a day that government agents were meeting with Abdi, Weigle couldn't make the trip. Instead, he dispatched his colleague, Matt Benson, in his stead. But when Benson arrived at the jail, Abdi refused to speak to him. When Benson handed him his business card, Abdi took it and ate it.[1]

Abdi had a special status in the Somali community in Columbus. Many looked up to the quiet, religiously devout man, the entrepreneur who spoke excellent English and Arabic, the husband and father of a growing family who was always respectful and never used inappropriate language. His arrest had sent shock waves through the community; most people were angry and in disbelief at the news. Defense lawyers knocked on the government's door almost immediately. On November 30, a lawyer contacted ICE claiming to represent Abdi on behalf of his family. Abdi refused to speak with him. On December 5, another attorney faxed Medellin, saying Abdi's wife had retained him; the same day, a third attorney left a voicemail for Medellin, saying she now represented Abdi. Abdi denied any of them was his lawyer and continued to consent to interviews without representation. On December 6, he told investigators, apparently for the first time, about a conspirator who was then unknown to them. On December 7, Abdi agreed to a polygraph test. In the middle of the procedure, Weigle, a Cincinnati lawyer with experience in immigration cases, arrived to say he now represented Abdi. The Somali accepted Weigle but decided to finish the test before meeting with him.

Almost ten days after his arrest, with considerable water over the dam, Abdi finally had a lawyer.[2]

The pace of interrogations slowed. Abdi would undergo only four more interviews after December 7, during which he repeated much of what he'd already said. He still believed his cooperation would lead to his release. On December 15, 2003, after almost three weeks in his Kentucky detention cell, Abdi was moved back to Ohio, to Seneca County. Once there, in the ICE-approved jail on the outskirts of Tiffin, Abdi entered an anonymous solitude. Guards knew him only as "John Doe." He was not allowed to know where he was, was not allowed to be around other prisoners, and for reading material was given only the Quran and *USA Today*. On December 26, in part to make it easier for Weigle to visit his client, Abdi was transferred again, this time to Pickaway County Jail in the small Ohio city of Circleville. He was now allowed a television.[3]

The winter passed with a series of interviews with the FBI and hearings over Abdi's immigration status: that was, after all, the purported reason for his arrest in November. Abdi appeared before U.S. immigration judge Elizabeth Hacker in Detroit in late January, where she ordered his detention to continue on national security grounds. FBI agents interviewed him for the last time on February 17. On March 9, Abdi appeared again before Hacker. The small immigration court is tucked into a corner of the fourth floor of the Crain's Brewery Park building, part of the redevelopment of the site where the Stroh Brewery Company once sat. Abdi's wife, mother, sister, and brothers drove up from Columbus. A cousin flew from Virginia to testify on his behalf. Abdi's family, barred from entering, waited outside the courtroom for six hours. They got a brief glimpse of Abdi as he was led into court, the first time they'd seen him in six months.[4]

During the hearing, Abdi gave a full accounting of his past, in hopes of avoiding deportation to Somalia. He paid people in San Diego, he said, to draw up an application for asylum because he needed the document to stay in the United States.

"Other than your name and maybe some biographical details, is anything in this document true?" Hacker asked Abdi.

"No, unfortunately," he replied.

Abdi also explained he told the FBI where al-Qaida operatives were training in Somalia and where those camps were. He acknowledged identifying and discussing al-Qaida conspirators with the FBI. He admitted he had met with Mohamed Haji Yusuf in 2000 in Somalia and was later visited by an operative in Columbus whom Yusuf had identified for him. He acknowledged meeting with Faris and the discussion about an attack on a shopping mall. If word of his cooperation with the FBI got back to Somalia, Abdi testified, his life could be in danger. People he knew in Mogadishu and Kismayu, a port city, would not be happy. "Islamists in Mogadishu and Kismayu . . . have strong ties with Al-Qaeda, and my help or cooperation with the government will put me at risk," he told the judge. In Somalia, he said, "news flies right away."[5]

At the end of the hearing, Hacker ordered Abdi deported as a security risk. She said he constituted a danger to the United States based on the shopping mall plot. "Your interruption in this continued activity appears to be as a result of your arrest," the judge said. "After your arrest, you appear to have cooperated with authorities, certainly in an attempt to ameliorate the effects of your earlier actions. There's very little doubt in my mind with respect to that."[6]

On Weigle's advice, Abdi decided to waive his right to appeal. It was a calculated risk: doing so triggered a ninety-day window for the government to deport him. Because Somalia did not have a central government and didn't issue passports, however, it was a challenge to officials in Detroit to carry out the actual deportation.[7]

As Abdi left, he glanced at his family and spoke quickly and cryptically. "They refused, I refused," Abdi said in Somali. They puzzled over the comment at first, then figured out later he was explaining that, while the judge had refused to let him stay, he had refused to appeal and thus forced the government to figure out what to do with him. From there, Abdi was returned to the Pickaway County Jail in Circleville.[8]

Two months later, on May 7, the government offered Abdi a plea deal to settle the charges against him. Under the arrangement, Abdi would serve five years or less in prison and be allowed to stay in the United States. In return, the government wanted his cooperation in its ongoing terrorism investigation in Columbus, which could mean testimony against people like Christopher Paul.[9] It was a generous offer by any stretch of the imagination. Although Abdi might not have followed every case of alleged terrorism prosecuted in the United States since 9/11, he must have been aware that some heavy sentences had been handed out—members of the Lackawanna Six, for example, had received sentences of seven to ten years for little more than attending terrorist training camps in Afghanistan. The last of those defendants to be sentenced, Sahim Alwan, received his nine-and-a-half-year term on December 17, two days after Abdi was taken to the Seneca County Jail. Abdi also had to know about Faris's twenty-year sentence. But Abdi was adamant: he had no reason to accept a plea deal to charges he was innocent of, and he was never going to testify against a fellow Muslim.[10] He rejected the offer.[11]

Abdi may have been influenced by unfolding international news. On April 28, *60 Minutes II* aired a segment on alleged prisoner abuse in the Abu Ghraib prison complex in Iraq by soldiers assigned to the 372nd Military Police Company. On April 30, investigative journalist Seymour Hersh posted an article in the online edition of the *New Yorker* detailing the abuse and including photos of prisoners, followed by publication in the magazine's May 10 print edition. The shocking photos, including images of guards posing naked inmates in humiliating positions, became instant fodder for the twenty-four-hour news cycle. The news reached everywhere, including Pickaway County Jail. For Abdi, whose anger at the death of civilians in Afghanistan first caught investigators' attention, the prisoner abuse was too much to bear. On May 16, he returned his television set, saying he no longer wanted to watch coverage of the scandal.[12]

Returning the TV marked the beginning of a change in Abdi and his behavior. He started to chant and pray and refused to talk to guards. The sheriff's office called Immigration and Customs Enforcement to report what was going on. Abdi's mother and wife were shocked when they visited on May 21, finding Abdi slouched in a chair, chin on his chest, hands handcuffed behind his back. His wife called his name but got no response. He responded to his mother with grunts. When Abdi stood up suddenly, pushing his chair back, ten guards pounced on him and hauled him from the room. The next day, at the jail's request, ICE officials transferred Abdi back to Seneca County. Things deteriorated further. A social worker tried talking to Abdi the same day but gave up because of his odd behavior. Abdi started drinking water from the toilet, refusing to eat, and growling.[13]

On May 26, Attorney General John Ashcroft and FBI director Robert Mueller held a news conference warning of credible intelligence of an al-Qaida attack in the next few weeks or months. The potential targets were significant: the upcoming G-8 Summit in Georgia, the Democratic National Convention in Boston, or the Republican National Convention in New York City. Ashcroft and Mueller also released the names of seven wanted al-Qaida individuals and warned that the group was evolving, seeking newer converts, even recruiting people who could pass for Europeans.[14]

Two days later, federal prosecutors and Special Agent John Corbin visited Abdi to ask him to sign a waiver of the statute of limitations for his forthcoming indictment. Matt Benson, the Cincinnati lawyer substituting for Weigle, tried unsuccessfully to talk to Abdi. When offered Benson's business card, Abdi put it in his mouth and proceeded to chew.[15]

Just over two weeks later, on June 10, a grand jury indicted Abdi on four criminal counts. The first, conspiracy to provide material support to terrorists, targeted the travel document he'd applied for in 1999 purportedly for a trip to Germany and then Mecca, when in fact the government alleged he planned to seek out terrorist training in Africa—the bungled trip to Ethiopia to find a terrorist training camp. Count two was a second material support conspiracy charge, alleging collusion with others—presumably Faris and Paul—between 1997 and 2003 to help al-Qaida. The third and fourth counts related to his alleged possession and use of refugee documents he had obtained by lying about his refugee status. Significantly, he was not charged with plotting an attack on a shopping mall. Whatever the allegations against him, Abdi was now a long way from an emotional conversation about the war in Afghanistan over coffee in a suburban café.

On June 14, U.S. magistrate judge Mark Abel ordered the indictment against Abdi unsealed, almost exactly one year after the announcement of Faris's conviction. "America offers freedom and the protection of human dignity to oppressed people who come to our shores," John Ashcroft said as he announced the charges. "Unfortunately, some American citizens, as well as others given haven here, have chosen to betray these values and to support the terrorists' goals and plots." By coincidence—or not—the news of Abdi's indictment competed with the other big news in Columbus that week: the appearance of Democratic presidential candidate John Kerry at a park on the city's west side. The 2004 presidential campaign was under way, and Ohio was once again the epicenter of a battle with a single, overriding issue at its core: the efficacy of the Bush war on terror.[16]

Abdi's abnormal behavior continued during his initial hearing before Abel. He stared left and right, at times grinning at the courtroom artists sketching his picture. He gazed at the tabletop in front of him, once striking his head on it gently. It was a painful moment for his family, who were seeing a far different, far more troubled person than the son and brother they'd briefly glimpsed in Detroit three months earlier. The next day, Abdi refused to take a shower, urinated on the floor of his cell and smeared feces around the walls, then turned on the sink to flood his cell and chanted at the walls. Two days later, Abel granted Weigle's motion for a competency hearing. Abdi slammed his face onto the table where he sat during the hearing, keeping it there for several minutes. Near the end of the proceeding, he began muttering. Dozens of Somalis were crammed into the courtroom, while outside hundreds more protested Abdi's arrest. "Nuradin is 100 percent innocent," said a sign held by one. "What we know about him is unlike how he is portrayed," Ahmad Al-Akhras, then president of the Ohio office of the Council on American-Islamic Relations, said. Abdi had a new attorney now, a fellow Muslim named Mahir Sherif, a private defense lawyer from San Diego hired by Abdi's family with the help of community fund-raising. Sherif declared the government had taken a healthy person and turned him into a broken man. (Assistant U.S. attorney Dana Peters, representing the government, said there was no evidence Abdi had been abused.) One thing was clear: Abdi's family knew they were in this for the long haul. On June 28, Abdi's cousin signed papers dissolving Cell Station.[17]

The next day, authorities transferred Abdi from Seneca County Jail to the Bureau of Prisons Federal Medical Center in Rochester, Minnesota, for evaluation. For the next month, nurses and doctors visited and interviewed Abdi every day. The staff also talked with people who had interacted with Abdi since his arrest and incarceration and reviewed documents related to his case. Abdi remained in Minnesota until August 4, when the government returned him to Ohio and placed him in the Franklin County Correction Center just south of Columbus's downtown. For a time, Abdi seemed no better and continued to show signs of instability. Jailers placed him on suicide watch. Family members tried in vain to visit him each Thursday and Sunday; because he refused to acknowledge anyone who came to his cell, jailers wouldn't bring him to the visiting area. Nevertheless, on August 13, the medical center issued a report, signed by psychologist Andrew Simcox and medical doctor Daniel Shine, which found that Abdi understood the seriousness of the charges against him. The report concluded that Abdi was malingering and was competent to stand trial: that is, he was faking his illness.[18]

A Symphony of Unfairness

A GUILTY PLEA eliminates one foundational safeguard of the American justice system: the ability to appeal one's conviction. The tradeoff is basic. In exchange for acknowledging participation in a crime, and oftentimes fingering others, a defendant receives some benefit from the government, typically a reduction in sentence. He also avoids the risk of a trial, where acquittal is rare and sentencing a gamble.

Iyman Faris's guilty plea won him ten fewer years in federal prison, based on the government's first offer back in April 2003. That didn't matter to Faris, who was determined to restart his criminal proceedings. Several things burned inside him: his experience with the FBI, his long days at Quantico, his after-the-fact dissatisfaction with his first attorney, Fred Sinclair, and his belief that the government had manipulated and conned him into a prosecutorial corner that ended with a twenty-year sentence. His new government-appointed lawyer, Washington, D.C., attorney David Smith, believed Faris had grounds for a successful do-over. The appeal that Smith filed early in February 2004 raised several legal issues, but came down to two essential allegations: Sinclair had done a lousy job representing Faris, and the information in that forty-four-page FBI interview summary was so significant that the failure to provide it to Faris before his plea was a violation of his rights to items possessed by the government, information referred to in legal parlance as *Brady* material.

Smith contended Brinkema should have held a full evidentiary hearing to allow Faris to explain why he wanted to withdraw his plea. At the heart of that hearing should have been the threat of being sent to Guantanamo as a military combatant. It was a false threat, Smith argued, since it was not government policy to send U.S. citizens to Guantanamo, and furthermore, there was no basis for holding a defendant there who had been apprehended in the United States. "The court was not aware Faris was laboring under this terrible Hobson's choice at the time he entered his plea," Smith wrote. "Thus, Faris did not have an accurate understanding of what his true choices were."[1]

Smith argued that Brinkema should have explored whether the government reneged on promises for a further reduction in sentence based on information provided by Faris. (Ironically, some of that information, unbeknownst to Smith at the time, led to Abdi's apprehension.) The judge should also have researched the discrepancies in the FBI interview summary, which seemed to cast doubt on whether Faris really intended to bring down the Brooklyn Bridge. The delay in providing that report to Sinclair was inexcusable and hobbled the attorney's ability to represent Faris. Brinkema also should have studied Faris's mental history, which included that attempt to jump off a bridge on the west side of Columbus in 1995. Finally, Smith took issue with the notion that withdrawing the plea was a waste of judicial resources. Faris, Smith declared, had undergone "a veritable symphony of unfairness" leading up to the day he was sentenced.[2]

The government summed up these arguments as a case of cold feet. "At its heart, Faris's position distills down to this farfetched syllogism," Hammerstrom, the assistant U.S. attorney, wrote in a court filing. "'Believe me now when I say am [*sic*] innocent because I previously lied to the FBI and the district court.'"[3]

The May 1 hearing, when Brinkema questioned Faris about the conspiracy point by point, had been fair and exhaustive; not once had Faris suggested he was an innocent man, Hammerstrom argued. Furthermore, Faris never requested the evidentiary hearing he was now asking for, which meant, among other things, it was not eligible to be raised on appeal. The fact that Faris's plea had been unsealed after the media began reporting on the case was not sufficient evidence that an implied promise of secrecy had been broken. Faris also waited too long between his guilty plea on the first day of May and his decision to withdraw that plea in July, Hammerstrom said. The government had done nothing to violate the defendant's rights by not producing for Faris a copy of his own statements to the FBI.

"During the interviews Faris may have rationalized his conduct, contradicted himself, or minimized his assistance to al Qaeda. But such self-serving efforts to deceive the investigators are legally irrelevant," Hammerstrom argued. "When Faris pleaded guilty, he swore the statement of facts were 'true and accurate'—nothing he said during his interviews with the FBI altered that reality." There was another reason not to allow Faris to withdraw his plea: doing so could affect the status of ongoing terrorist investigations. As a defendant who had pleaded guilty, Hammerstrom said, Faris was a useful witness in other cases, presumably starting with the one against Abdi. In essence, the argument went, to withdraw his conviction would create a domino effect on other open cases.[4]

Smith went back to how much pressure Faris felt over the possibility of being sent to Guantanamo. The night before Faris pleaded guilty, after all, Sinclair had told him there were FBI agents ready to take him to the base in Cuba if he didn't accept the deal. "One could understand how, in these unusual circumstances, with the threat of being sent to Guantanamo hanging over him, an uncounseled, unsophisticated, depressed, foreign born defendant with suspicious al Qaeda connections could be pressured into admitting facts that were not true in the false hope of propitiating the FBI and getting himself off the hook," Smith said.[5]

The fact that Faris might have been depressed years ago or the fact that he might have been despondent at the thought of going to prison, were not by themselves sufficient reason to allow him to withdraw his plea, the government said. Hammerstrom also took issue with the idea that Guantanamo ever had been raised by the government in its plea negotiations. "To reiterate, the United States did not in this case—nor does it ever—threaten criminal defendants with the designation of enemy combatant status to obtain a guilty plea."[6]

Smith and Justice Department trial attorney Joseph Kaster argued before a panel of Fourth Circuit Court of Appeals judges on June 4, 2004, which happened to be Faris's thirty-fifth birthday. Just six weeks later, the panel returned its unanimous decision siding with the government. The court's fourteen-page opinion made short work of most of Faris's arguments. "This conclusion is amply supported by the transcript," wrote Chief Judge William Wilkins, "which reflects that the court thoroughly explained to Faris the facts he would admit by pleading guilty, the rights he would waive, and the sentence he would face. Faris's statements in response to these explanations demonstrate that he understood the information he was being given." The government's delay in turning over the FBI summary of Faris's interviews didn't impress the court, nor did the panel give much weight to discrepancies between the summary and what Faris said. Faris's assertion that it was impossible for him to have driven a truck over the Brooklyn Bridge also mattered little to the judges.[7]

"No evidence specifically indicates that Faris drove across the Brooklyn Bridge in his truck," they concluded. As a result, Brinkema properly discounted Faris's denials of his guilt after the May 1 hearing, "In light of the possibility that he used another vehicle, as well as his multiple attestations that he had in fact examined the bridge." Faris's fight wasn't over, but a significant door had been closed.[8]

Life Goes On

MARK ELLWOOD WAS a regular at World's Gym on the north side of Worthington. He and his wife went there often to use the treadmill. Ellwood, a high school teacher, was working out in the winter of 2005 when recognized a former student, though he couldn't recall his name right away. The man had set the treadmill to a steep incline and was running hard. He was a striking person, an African American with a full beard and closely cropped hair. He did not look like others at the gym his age, probably early forties, who did their best, not always successfully, to fight off middle-aged paunch. This guy was fit. Seriously fit. Ellwood went through his own jog on the treadmill, which seemed pedestrian by comparison, then headed for the locker room. There the man came right up to him and introduced himself as Paul. Of course, Ellwood now recalled, Paul Laws. He'd had him in a sophomore social studies class at Worthington. They chatted for a few minutes. Paul said he'd been traveling and was about to take a class at Columbus State Community College, but he was vague about what else he was up to and didn't offer any specifics.[1]

Paul was living a life of contrasts in those days. He worked at Toledo/Mettler. He was devoted to Frida and their daughter, Khadija. He maintained a simple existence; they'd stayed in his one-bedroom, $350-a-month apartment on Riverview all these years. They had a TV and a computer and pots and pans, but not much else. Paul was well known in the neighborhood and always friendly. He was on good terms with the landlord, though he insisted on being present for any repairs to the apartment; Frida was not to be alone with another man. Paul was taking computer courses at the community college and in his free time, apparently, pushing himself physically. Whenever he could spare a few extra minutes he would go fishing, possibly the one thing he was most passionate about after his faith.[2]

But Paul had begun organizing things he'd acquired over the years that spoke of a different, less simple existence. Beginning in 2004, he stored several pieces of equipment in his apartment and at his parents' house in Worthington: night vision scopes, a laser range finder, a GPS watch, a military survival knife, and his passports, one with his current name, one when he was known as Abdulmalek Kenyatta. And other things: a fax allegedly listing names, phone numbers, and contact information for al-Qaida leaders and associates; books on how to make explosives; lists of book ISBNs, including *Guerilla's Arsenal: Advanced Techniques for Making Explosives and Time-Delay Bombs* and *Home Made C-4: A Recipe for Survival;* a note on the al-Farooq training camp in Afghanistan; currency from Middle Eastern countries; and listings for range finders, high-powered binoculars, and sniper guns. Paul also kept letters he'd written over the years. One was the love note he'd sent Frida years earlier, talking about raising "little mujahideen." The other was a letter to his now aging parents.

It explained that he would be "on the front lines" and told them how to find information on jihad.[3]

Atypical Psychosis

BY THE FALL of 2004, the presidential campaign had hit full throttle in Ohio. Kerry, Bush, Cheney, and Kerry's running mate, John Edwards, made multiple stops across the state. On September 8, Kerry traveled to the Cincinnati Museum Center at Union Terminal, the same place that Bush had made his case for the invasion of Iraq in 2002. In a sharp rebuke to the president, Kerry called the war a catastrophic choice that had cost $200 billion to date along with hundreds of American soldiers' lives. "George W. Bush's wrong choices have led America in the wrong direction on Iraq and left America without the resources we need here at home," Kerry said. Two weeks later, Cheney and Edwards campaigned for two days in the state; Edwards concluded with visits to Cleveland and Cincinnati, while Cheney made stops near Columbus and Toledo. On September 23, Kerry spoke at a Columbus firehouse, while on Friday, September 24, Republicans announced Bush events the following Monday in southwest Ohio they predicted would draw tens of thousands of supporters.[1]

That same day, in Columbus, jailhouse guards moved Nuradin Abdi out of the mental health wing and into a regular housing unit. He was slowly starting to resemble his old self. He began to visit with his family again. "I thought you were all dead," he told one of his brothers on a visit. His case had been transferred to the docket of U.S. District Court judge Algenon Marbley, and one of Marbley's first acts was to order a second psychiatric evaluation for Abdi for mid-November.[2]

The presidential campaign wound down, but not without a last Ohio-related drama: at Kenyon College in tiny Gambier, about an hour northeast of Columbus, students waited in line for up to twelve hours to vote for Kerry after one of the precinct's two machines malfunctioned. The lines were the longest in the nation and bolstered later allegations that Ohio ballots for Kerry were somehow sabotaged. Early the next morning, Ohio was finally called for Bush and the election was over. Back in Columbus, one week later, on November 11, 2004, Abdi was taken permanently off suicide watch.[3]

The doctor conducting Abdi's second evaluation, psychiatrist Robert T. M. Phillips, started by reviewing the previous analysis of Abdi's mental health. He went over the materials Marbley provided him and then evaluated Abdi on November 16, 17, and 18. He concluded on December 23, 2004, that Abdi was competent to stand trial. Phillips added a proviso: it was possible, he said, that rather than malingering, the legal phrase for making up an illness, Abdi had been suffering from some type of "atypical psychosis" in May and June, possibly a condition known as Ashanti psychosis. The symptoms of this condition, observed in people in Ghana and West Africa, bear some resemblance to Abdi's behavior in Circleville and Tiffin. Subjects who fear they are being punished become frightened, then frenzied, then suffer hallucinations and are sometimes seen tearing off their clothes and eating their feces.[4]

Phillips's finding was a victory for the government. But it was also moot in a way: with Abdi on the mend, it was a foregone conclusion he would have to face the charges against him. And that's what his attorney was now preparing for, starting with the event at the heart of the case: Abdi's warrantless arrest on the day after Thanksgiving. It was an act, Abdi's attorney was ready to argue, that was illegal and without provocation.

Born Paul Kenyatta Laws, Christopher Paul grew up in the old Columbus suburb of Worthington, the youngest of six children in one of the community's few African American families. Paul, pictured here in his 1984 high school yearbook, was regarded in high school as pleasant and polite, and was chiefly known as an excellent gymnast who went to state championships with his team.

The FBI spent several years building a case against Christopher Paul before he was arrested on April 11, 2007, as he walked back to his apartment after prayers at a nearby mosque. Once indicted, he put up almost no defense and quickly agreed to plead guilty to conspiring to use a weapon of mass destruction in terrorist attacks. *Franklin County Jail photo*

Iyman Faris arrived in Columbus in 1994 and found housing with the help of the Omar Ibnelkhttab Mosque, a place where he would spend much of his free time over the years. Yet Faris, who often wore Western clothes and loved video games, never quite fit the image of a devout Muslim. Members of the mosque teased him about his long, dark hair, saying it was reminiscent of a French king. *Photo courtesy of Geneva Bowling*

Iyman Faris spent three weeks at a South Carolina driving school to get his trucker's license, then purchased his own Freightliner. His cross-country trips involved mundane shipments like processed tomatoes, but his hazardous materials license worried authorities after they learned that Khalid Sheikh Mohammed, the architect of the September 11 attacks, had enlisted Faris to look into opportunities for additional terrorist attacks. *Photo courtesy of Geneva Bowling*

Iyman Faris met his American wife, Geneva Bowling, when he was working as a clerk at a gas station where she would stop for the cheap gas. Theirs seemed an unusual match: a native of rural Kentucky and the daughter of a preacher, Bowling had been married multiple times already and had a stepson. But her family immediately took to Faris, in part because he was so friendly and respectful. The couple was happy for a time, but clashed over what Bowling considered Faris's lazy habits around the house. *Photo courtesy of Geneva Bowling*

Iyman Faris and Geneva Bowling finally separated in February 2000, the same month that Faris went to Mecca to perform Hajj, the pilgrimage required of all Muslims who can afford it. Photos from the trip show a smiling, happy-go-lucky person who doesn't seem on the cusp of a major life change. In a few months he would be divorced and would embark on a trip to Pakistan and then Afghanistan, where he would ultimately meet Osama bin Laden. *Photos courtesy of Geneva Bowling*

Nuradin Abdi's first court appearance following his June 2004 indictment shocked his family and friends. The confident family man and community leader had been replaced by a wild-looking individual prone to abnormal behavior. During a competency hearing two days after his indictment, Abdi slammed his face onto the table at which he sat during the hearing, keeping it there for several minutes. *Franklin County Jail photo*

Nuradin Abdi is serving out his prison time at a federal penitentiary in Marion, Illinois, where he contemplates the possibility of deportation to Somalia in 2012, an action complicated by his homeland's continued lack of a functioning government. His wife explains to their young children that Abdi is away working and will rejoin them eventually. One photo he sent his family from prison shows him standing by a wall without revealing his location. "I don't think he's happy here," his six-year-old son said when he saw the picture. *Photo courtesy of the family of Nuradin Abdi*

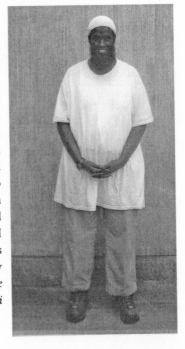

PART 3
Evening

The idea that al-Qaeda is a coherent hierarchical terrorist group with a single leader, a broadly uniform ideology and an ability to conceive and execute projects globally through well-disciplined cadres, sleepers and activists spread around the world is misplaced. Saying what "al-Qaeda" was during the period, and thus to a large extent, is now, is far more difficult.

—Jason Burke,
Al-Qaeda: Casting a Shadow of Terror

Radical Role-Playing

To be a Muslim in Ohio or anywhere else in the years after 9/11 meant a periodic walk across eggshells. Each time the government announced a new set of charges against alleged Islamic terrorists in the United States—be it Atlanta, Buffalo, Miami, Portland, or suburban Washington, D.C.—a wave of suspicion followed. Muslims experienced firsthand the fear of the broad brush, the burden of having to explain that such actions weren't tolerated and weren't representative. Muslims, many of them born in the United States, sometimes second- and third-generation Americans, once again had to defend both their faith and their loyalty as citizens. Making this delicate dance all the more difficult were the questions many in the Muslim community were asking about the government's approach to domestic investigations.

Skepticism at new allegations was understandable, especially in light of such disasters as the discredited prosecution of four North African defendants in Detroit in 2002. Often such skepticism melted away as the gravity of the charges and evidence became clear: the courtroom jammed with supportive Somalis at the initial appearance of Nuradin Abdi, for example, was getting emptier as the case continued. But suspicion lingered over indictments in which it seemed the government did more instigating than investigating.

Shortly after the 9/11 attacks, an angry man showed up in Toledo, Ohio, looking for people who shared his outrage at U.S. conduct abroad. A stocky African American in his thirties with close-cropped hair and a beard, he said he was a former soldier now intent on violence against America. Known as Bilal, he was shunned by many Muslims, some of whom contacted the FBI. Those concerns fell on deaf ears: Bilal was an FBI informant assigned to monitor extremist activity. Dubbed "the trainer" in government documents, his real name was Darren Griffin, a fourteen-year U.S. Army veteran with a history of using cocaine and marijuana who had gone to work briefly for the Drug Enforcement Administration before the FBI recruited him in October 2001.[1]

The community that Griffin infiltrated was large and well-established, the first sizable group of Muslims anywhere in the state. Arab immigrants to Toledo, mostly from Syria and Lebanon, began arriving after World War I. By 1939, their numbers multiplied to the point that they organized the state's first Muslim society. The community built a mosque in 1954, spurring further immigration. In 1959, Mike Damas, whose parents had emigrated from Lebanon decades earlier, became the first Arab American elected mayor of a major American city. In 1982, as Toledo's Muslim community outgrew its old religious center, construction began on the Islamic Center of Greater Toledo. The finished building, with a large dome and two soaring minarets, sits prominently at the intersection of interstates 75 and 475, the first mosque in North America built in the classical Islamic architectural style.[2]

Griffin had a part-time job at KindHearts, a Muslim charity in Toledo, doing data entry and loading and unloading trucks. As his assignment proceeded, he visited a couple of local mosques, where he got to know three men: Mohammad Amawi, a citizen born in the United States who also had Jordanian citizenship; Marwan Othman el-Hindi, born in Jordan but also a U.S. citizen; and Zand Wassim Mazloum, a permanent resident who had come to the country legally from Lebanon in 2000 and, with a brother, operated a Toledo car lot. Sometime in 2002, Griffin said, el-Hindi began making threatening statements about kidnapping Israeli soldiers and asked Griffin to help him with bodyguard training.[3]

Over the next three years, Griffin insinuated himself into the lives of Amawi, el-Hindi, and Mazloum. He supplied them with terrorist training books and manuals. He paid for trips to an indoor shooting range where they rented a Beretta 9-mm pistol and a Glock 40-caliber pistol and practiced in two shooting lanes. He secretly recorded their conversations for hours on end. For his efforts, he received an annual salary of $56,000 from the government, part of an estimated $350,000 he earned from the FBI since first going to work for them as an informant in 2001. Throughout the time Griffin associated with the three friends, he later testified, they frequently accessed jihadist websites. They registered for a basic training course in weapons instruction and physical fitness and copied instructions off the Internet on how to make and use explosives, including improvised explosive devices, or IEDs. One video that Amawi allegedly downloaded, "Martyrdom Operation Vest Program," explained how to make a suicide bomb vest. "Blow them up! Blow them up! Blow them up!" Amawi sang along while watching an IED video, according to Griffin.[4]

Amawi traveled to Jordan in October 2003 and, according to the government, tried unsuccessfully to enter Iraq to wage jihad against U.S. forces. The goal of the conspiracy, according to an indictment issued against the three, was to find ways to provide support—material support, possibly including themselves as freedom fighters—to groups attacking U.S. troops in Iraq. Amawi returned to Jordan in August 2005, this time with Griffin, ostensibly to deliver laptops to a contact in Syria to be used by mujahideen brothers. But that delivery never happened, and they spent the entire trip visiting Amawi's family. The relationship with the "trainer" and the alleged plotting came crashing to a halt on February 21, 2006, when federal authorities arrested the three and announced a material support indictment alleging a plan to attack and kill U.S. soldiers.[5]

Defense attorneys attacked Griffin almost immediately and alleged he all but entrapped their clients. El-Hindi, in an early court filing, argued that the recordings proved Griffin had pushed, encouraged, and incited the defendants for more than three years and that "the conversations with his handlers indicate that the government told him how to do it." On March 9, 2005, el-Hindi said, Griffin went so far as to tell his government handler that he encouraged the three to get together to go shooting but left it to them to pick a date so it "wouldn't be like I [Griffin] pushed them." Amawi said he was targeted only because he spoke out against the war in Iraq. Griffin lied, he said, when he testified that Amawi considered traveling to Iraq to become a martyr. "I'm against suicide bombing," he said. "I made this very clear."[6]

Similar arguments alleging government entrapment of alleged terror suspects arose time and again around the country. In October 2002, Attorney General John Ashcroft announced indictments against members of the so-called Portland Cell. The government said six defendants—five of them U.S. citizens—trained to fight violent jihad in Afghanistan. According to prosecutors, five of the members tried to travel to Afghanistan in October 2001 to join forces with Taliban and al-Qaida troops battling American and allied military personnel. Defense lawyers zeroed in on the role that government informant Khalid Ibrahim Mostafa played in the investigation and whether he went beyond observing the group's activities and statements and crossed the line to encourage them to express hatred for the United States. During the investigation, the FBI outfitted Mostafa—like Darrell Griffin a former informant for the DEA—with a body wire, which he then used to record numerous conversations, including some held during religious services inside a Portland mosque. Despite these concerns, all six were convicted on charges including conspiracy to levy war against the United States, conspiracy to provide material support to foreign terrorist organizations, and conspiracy to contribute services to al-Qaida and the Taliban.[7]

In 2006, the Justice Department charged seven men, arrested in Miami and Atlanta, for an alleged plot to blow up the Sears Tower in Chicago, as well as FBI offices in Miami and other federal buildings in Miami-Dade County. Most of the defendants worked small construction jobs and met over religious study in the Miami neighborhood of Liberty City. According to prosecutors, Narsearl Batiste, a former FedEx deliveryman from Chicago who believed he was a divine messenger sent to overthrow the U.S. government, persuaded the men to join in the attacks. Ultimately, all seven allegedly swore *bayat,* or an oath of loyalty to al-Qaida. Defense lawyers argued the plot was a ruse and the men only feigned support for al-Qaida to get money from an informant. They argued the informant prodded their clients to make radical remarks and vows of terrorist allegiance. They pointed out an FBI search of the group's Liberty City headquarters found no evidence of weapons or preparation for an attack on the scale that prosecutors alleged. The arguments had temporary traction: in December 2007, a federal jury acquitted one man and deadlocked on charges against the other six. A new jury deadlocked again in April 2008. On May 12, 2009, a jury finally convicted five of the defendants and acquitted a sixth.[8]

In June 2007, the government announced the end of a sixteen-month investigation with charges against six men accused of plotting to attack Fort Dix, a U.S. Army base in New Jersey, by attacking and killing soldiers using assault rifles and grenades. The FBI arrested the men as two of the defendants, according to the government, were meeting a confidential government witness to purchase three AK-47 automatic machine guns and four semiautomatic M-16s. Five of the alleged conspirators had conducted training missions in the nearby Pocono Mountains and distributed training videos among themselves that included depictions of American soldiers being killed and Islamic radicals urging jihad against the United States. The plot unraveled when a Circuit City clerk grew alarmed at what he saw on a videotape he was asked to convert to a DVD: men firing automatic weapons and shouting angrily about holy war. Defense attorneys said the case was classic entrapment. Troy Archie, representing defendant Eljvir Duka, argued that two informants, known in government documents as CW1 and CW2, egged on his client and other defendants, who had recently become practicing Muslims, to take advantage of their new faith. "Throughout the entire Governmental investigation involved herein," Archie argued, in language that recalled the same allegation in the Toledo case, "the defendants were induced or persuaded by agents, CW1 and CW2 to prepare to commit a crime that they had no previous intent to commit under the banner of their newly acquired Islamic beliefs and practices." There was no conspiracy, Archie said, before the informants' "fanatical Islamic discussions and exchanges of religious extremist ideology." The jury didn't buy it, and the five defendants were convicted in December 2008. The families of the men remained adamant that the whole case was a setup.[9]

IN TOLEDO, ENTRAPMENT allegations were raised and just as quickly shot down. If the defendants were innocent, prosecutors argued, why did they continue meeting with Griffin in the first place? Gregg Sofer, a Justice Department trial attorney prosecuting the case, hammered this point home in his closing arguments in June 2008. Amawi, el-Hindi, and Mazloum weren't passive bystanders: they were enthusiastic participants. "Why didn't the defendants simply walk away?" Sofer asked. "Nothing forced them to talk with him." Jurors had little patience with the defense argument and convicted all three on June 13, 2008. The case left behind a troubling legacy of tension between Toledo's large Muslim community and law enforcement. For many, it wasn't the prosecution of the individuals that bothered them so much as the use of an outsider like Griffin and the hype that surrounded the arrests and the trials, which left the impression of, as one Muslim leader put it, a "heartland conspiracy."[10]

Controversy over informants has had little impact on the government's prosecutorial successes so far. The three trials of the Liberty City defendants were the exception, not the rule. But the debate continues. (One 2008 analysis of Attorney General John Ashcroft's post-9/11 mandate stated that FBI agents and U.S. attorneys interrupt terrorist groups by prosecuting them as soon as charges can be brought, found the approach actually reduced the number of informants the government could use and almost eliminated its ability to infiltrate groups with undercover agents.[11]) On April 21, 2009, a federal judge in California ordered the FBI to turn over more than one hundred pages of documents related to agency inquiries into several Muslim groups and activists who claimed they were unfairly spied on and questioned. Later the same month, Terrence Berg, the U.S. attorney in Michigan, encouraged Muslims to report suspicions that the FBI had hired informants to infiltrate mosques and spy on leaders and worshippers. "If there's misconduct going on," Berg told a community meeting of Arab and Muslim leaders, "we'd like to know what it is."[12]

American Soil

IT WAS KNOWN as the "1 Percent Doctrine," a hallmark of the Bush administration's war on terror, a way of emphasizing the magnitude of the threat facing the United States.

"To protect our country, we have to be right 100 percent of the time," President Bush said in the summer of 2005. "To hurt us, the terrorists have to be right only once. So we're working to answer that challenge every day, and we're making good progress toward securing the homeland."[1]

It was June 9, and Bush was back in Ohio. He had come to the highway patrol academy at the state fairgrounds complex on the city's north side. He was there to talk about a cornerstone of the war on terror, the 2001 Patriot Act, now up for renewal. What better place to campaign for the nation's premier antiterrorism law than the Midwest, which recent events had shown was as allegedly vulnerable to enemy infiltration as New York or Washington?

"As we wage the war on terror overseas, we'll remember where the war began—right here on American soil," Bush began. "In our free and open society, there is no such thing as perfect security."

The president continued by bringing the nature of the challenge home more directly. "Federal, state, and local law enforcement have used the Patriot Act to break up terror cells in New York and Oregon and Virginia and in Florida," Bush said. "We've prosecuted terrorist operatives and supporters in California, in Texas, in New Jersey, in Illinois, and North Carolina and Ohio."

Tellingly, the president said, these efforts have not always made headlines—referring, presumably, to attacks thwarted without publicity. The Patriot Act had done what it was supposed to do: made average American communities safer, protected American liberty, saved American lives. To do that, the president said, it was important to share information across bureaucratic lines in a way that was not possible before the Patriot Act, thus enabling law enforcement to communicate with intelligence officials. And there was no better example of the benefits of information sharing than right here in Columbus.

"For several years," Bush told the audience, a friendly gathering of law enforcement officials, "Iyman Faris posed as a law-abiding resident of Columbus. But in 2000, he traveled to Afghanistan and met Osama bin Laden at an al Qaeda training camp."

The value of the Patriot Act kicked in after Faris returned to the United States, Bush explained, as federal investigators used the law to piece together details about his time in Afghanistan and his plan to launch an attack on the United States. The case against Faris was so strong, the president said, that after investigators confronted him with their evidence in 2003, he chose to cooperate and spent weeks explaining his al-Qaida connections. And then the high note: "And today, instead of planning terror attacks against the American people, Iyman Faris is sitting in an American prison."

Bush pressed ahead, hammering home the value of the Patriot Act in apprehending Faris. "The agents and prosecutors who used the Patriot Act to put Faris behind bars did superb work, and they know what a difference information-sharing made," the president said. "Here is what one FBI agent said—he said, 'The Faris case would not have happened without sharing information.'" According to Bush, another investigator said, "We never would have had the lead to begin with." The gist was clear: teamwork was critical to protecting the United States. For the sake of national security, the president said, Congress must not rebuild a wall between law enforcement and intelligence.

Bush used the rest of the speech to tick off elements of the Patriot Act that needed to be renewed. One key provision was roving wiretaps, which allow investigators to seek a warrant covering multiple cell phones used by an individual who switches phones frequently to thwart tracking. Another controversial provision granted Internet providers immunity from lawsuits over divulging information to investigators about threatening e-mails. (The anecdote that Bush chose to illustrate this aspect of the law cleverly shifted the perspective of the war on terror: the FBI had used information from an Internet provider to arrest a man in El Paso, Texas, who had e-mailed a mosque threatening to burn it down.) Finally, Bush said, with a nod to his critics, aspects of the Patriot Act that protected civil liberties must also be renewed.

The Patriot Act, Bush concluded, had strengthened Americans' freedom, not diminished it. "My message to Congress is clear," he said. "The terrorist threats against us will not expire at the end of the year, and neither should the protections of the Patriot Act."[2]

ONE THING BUSH was right about: Faris was definitely sitting in prison. In fact, on the very same day, hundreds of miles away in the government's supermaximum facility in Florence, Colorado, the subject of Bush's speech was lying on the floor with several guards piled on him. According to Faris, he was being escorted back to his cell after a phone call from his attorney, David Smith, when he passed the cells of fellow Muslim inmates reciting their prayers in Arabic. The inmates greeted Faris through the bars and he shouted back, in Arabic, that they should say the prayers louder so he could hear them in his cell. The next thing Faris knew, six guards tackled him and threw him to the ground. He was taken to a cell for punishment and chained to the floor for a day. After an internal prison hearing, he was punished with the loss of seven months of good time and denial of television and commissary privileges. "Sometimes I wonder whether I would have been better off in Guantanamo," Faris pondered dramatically in a court document recounting the incident.[3]

ONE MONTH LATER, the world got a cold reminder of the 1 percent doctrine. On July 7, four suicide bombers struck central London, setting off bombs on three underground trains and a double-decker bus, killing fifty-two people and injuring more than seventy. A month after that, Ohio received its own reminder. On August 3, a roadside bombing in Iraq killed eight members of Lima Company, a Columbus-based Marine Reserve unit, in an attack that took the lives of fourteen Marines overall. The news came two days after the same battalion—the suburban Cleveland-based 3rd Battalion, 25th Marines—lost five members in fighting. One of the survivors of the attack was J. D. Coleman, the oldest son of Columbus mayor Michael Coleman.

Bureaucratic Sloth

FROM THE BEGINNING, attorney Mahir Sherif had argued that FBI and federal immigration officers, in essence, had taken a backward approach in charging Nuradin Abdi. First, they arrested the Somali without probable cause. Then they gathered information during three days of questioning. Finally, using what Abdi told them, they obtained an arrest warrant that they served on November 30, alleging an immigration violation. From a legal perspective, they had reached back in time to justify taking Abdi into custody. When the government agents arrested Abdi, Sherif maintained, they had no evidence that he had committed an immigration violation or that he was likely to abscond before they got a warrant. When Abdi was formally detained, "the only basis for the arrest was from defendant's own statements he made after his arrest," Sherif argued. Thus, nothing Abdi said during his initial interrogations should be used as evidence.[1]

The agents, Sherif's argument went on, were guilty of official misconduct and had violated both Abdi's Fourth Amendment rights against unlawful search and seizure and his Fifth Amendment rights against self-incrimination. They had kept Abdi in isolation, then cajoled and tricked him into talking by convincing him his only hope of seeing his family was to cooperate. Through Sherif, Abdi also argued that he was poorly represented by Doug Weigle because the Cincinnati attorney previously had represented Mehmet Aydinbelge—Iyman Faris's roommate and onetime FBI informant— who had given an interview alleging Abdi's terrorist ties. Sherif was a passionate advocate for Abdi from the beginning and used strong language to make his case. (At one point he suggested that the U.S. invasion of Iraq itself was a form of jihad.[2]) In Abdi's case, he said, "it is fundamentally unfair to the defendant to allow the Government to make an unlawful warrantless civil arrest and then 'torture' the defendant with interrogations and isolations until he provides something the officers can use to make an immigration charge."[3]

Prosecutors turned the timing argument upside down. Dana Peters, the assistant U.S. attorney who also had worked on the Faris case, maintained that even if the arrest were problematic, it didn't justify the kind of sweeping suppression of evidence Sherif was demanding. As Peters put it, "even if the arrest, in hindsight, is found to be technically flawed, the defendant's statements should not be suppressed." Immigration officials made a good-faith arrest on national security grounds, and any taint of an illegal arrest was quickly overcome by statements Abdi made after signing numerous *Miranda* waivers. In essence, the government added, the only thing backward about the arrest came as a result of Abdi's actions, not those of the interrogating agents. ICE and the FBI were just doing what they were supposed to when they came across a situation that potentially affected national security. The argument boiled down to this: ICE had sufficient reason to arrest Abdi and deport him on national security grounds. Once Abdi was arrested, he informed them that he'd falsified his asylum papers. The admission, unknown to ICE at the time, allowed new charges. Abdi then acknowledged statements that affected national security, which gave the FBI another approach to follow. It was Abdi, in other words, who triggered the sequence of events that led to his postcustody arrest, not the government. "Defendant Abdi's confession," Peters said, "was simply an unintended consequence of what ICE and FBI believed was a national security immigration arrest."[4]

Peters laid out the facts of the case known to the government the morning of November 28, 2003. There were the phone calls Abdi had placed to more than forty numbers associated with ongoing terrorism investigations. Abdi also behaved like a man up to no good as he drove suspiciously to avoid being followed. Abdi had had contact with Iyman Faris, who had been receiving instructions for a possible attack from none other than Khalid Sheikh Mohammed. Abdi had sent Faris an e-mail containing a list of websites for acquiring spyware. Faris had detailed the substance of a coffee shop conversation in which Abdi expressed a desire to carry out a deadly act of vengeance. You could not ignore the context either of the times or of the people Abdi had consorted with, Peters said.

"Abdi's threat was made during a volatile political situation when our troops were hunting Al Qaeda in Afghanistan and war was imminent with Iraq," Peters argued. "His threat was made in the presence of a now-admitted Al Qaeda operative, who, at the very time Abdi made the threat, was conducting ongoing Al Qaeda target selection in the U.S. for Khalid Sheik Mohammed (KSM), supposed mastermind of the 9/11 terror attacks."[5]

Marbley, the federal judge hearing the case, was a Clinton appointee who'd been on the bench eight years by the time he received the Abdi prosecution. He accepted written arguments on the motion to suppress evidence over the summer of 2005 and held a hearing on August 25 and 26 during which he grilled the FBI about the warrantless arrest and the delay in apprehending Abdi. It was a long two days for agents at the federal courthouse, which sits on the edge of the Scioto River in downtown Columbus. Why wait so long to deal with a terrorism threat? Marbley asked James Turgal, the FBI special agent who'd drafted the declaration seeking the warrant. Marbley added, somewhat dryly, "This is a priority in light of 9/11 isn't it?" Turgal, who acknowledged they had probable cause to arrest Abdi in September, emphasized the need to arrest Abdi by November 28, 2003, because of Black Friday. That didn't hold much water for Marbley. "If you knew at least as early as September, and you know the court's preference for an arrest with a warrant, why didn't the FBI get a warrant?" Marbley demanded. Richard Wilkens, the ICE special agent in charge, did his best to explain the debate in Washington over the classified material. But it was clear Marbley was skeptical.[6]

One week later, the judge received a letter from a Franklin County Jail inmate who had some new allegations about Abdi, housed in the next cell over. The Somali, the inmate said, had talked about how Americans were evil and should be killed. Abdi also explained that he knew how to make bombs from cell phones. It was a development that hardly helped Abdi's case, though it didn't show up in the court record for another year and there is no indication that Marbley considered it as part of the official record before him. Three weeks after that, on September 25, Marbley issued his decision on Abdi's request to suppress his initial interviews.[7]

As his questioning during the August hearing had foreshadowed, Marbley was far from persuaded by a number of the government's arguments. The notion that Abdi posed a flight risk, for example, seemed absurd. After all, he'd been aware of investigators' interest in him at least since the previous April when the FBI first had talked to him about Iyman Faris. He hadn't moved out of Columbus or made travel plans since then. He owned a cell phone business, leased a storefront, rented an apartment, and had a wife, two children, and a third on the way. His mother and some of his siblings lived in Columbus. The fact he had car keys in his hand when he was arrested was meaningless, and proved nothing other than the fact he was on the way to the mosque when agents arrived.[8]

Marbley also wasn't convinced by the Black Friday argument. The government offered no proof that Abdi planned any sort of attack that day, nor was the arrival of the post-Thanksgiving shopping blitz much of a surprise. "It is beyond peradventure that the agents were aware of the day's status as a high volume shopping day," Marbley wrote. He was unmoved by the delay obtaining the warrant while ICE and FBI lawyers wrangled over the wording of the Turgal declaration. The judge was not going to overlook what the law required "because of bureaucratic sloth."[9]

Marbley believed the FBI arrested and interrogated Abdi as part of a criminal investigation, not because of immigration violations. Because Abdi did not meet with a lawyer until December 7, more than a week after his arrest, Marbley ruled on September 12, 2005, that all statements Abdi had made up until that point were inadmissible. "The governmental misconduct in this case may have been more subtle than flagrant, but the Court finds that it was calculated to ensure that the government's investigation continued unimpeded by the requirements of criminal procedure," Marbley said. The decision, robbing the government of crucial evidence, was good news indeed for Abdi.[10]

Yet it was not a complete triumph. Marbley wasn't convinced by Abdi's Fifth Amendment argument, that his confinement in Kentucky was so severe and the psychological coercion so harsh he was forced to incriminate himself. When it came to the bigger picture—whether to dismiss the case altogether because of government misconduct—Marbley sided with federal investigators. Abdi had argued that the lengthy interrogations he endured, the government's refusal to let him see or talk to his family for months, his isolation from other prisoners, and the government's alleged collusion with Abdi's first lawyer were egregious enough to throw the case out. The government countered that Abdi never had asked to see his family and pointed out that Abdi, thirty-one years of age, fluent in English, and well-versed in immigration law, was hardly a defenseless innocent. Marbley agreed, finding that the government's behavior, though troubling, did not meet the threshold known as the "shock the conscience" standard, named for a California case in which police pumped a suspect's stomach in search of evidence.[11]

Prosecutors had a lengthy appeals process ahead of them to try to overturn the suppression order. But Marbley had backed them where it counted. As Dana Peters, the assistant U.S. attorney, had argued, "Whatever Mr. Abdi's motivation ultimately to confess his deeds to agents, it was prompted by something other than government coercion."[12]

Dirty Numbers

A S BOMBSHELLS GO, this one was right up there. On Friday, December 15, 2005, the *New York Times* broke one of the biggest stories of the Bush administration. "Months after the Sept. 11 attacks," the article began, "President Bush secretly authorized the National Security Agency to eavesdrop on Americans and others inside the United States to search for evidence of terrorist activity without the court-approved warrants ordinarily required for domestic spying, according to government officials."[1]

Under a presidential order signed in 2002, the article continued, the NSA had monitored the international telephone calls and e-mails of hundreds or even thousands of people inside the United States without warrants. The goal was to track so-called dirty numbers linked to al-Qaida. The effort meant a significant new role for the NSA and a departure from the traditional method of obtaining warrants from the Foreign Intelligence Surveillance Court. "This is really a sea change," a former senior administration official specializing in national security law told the *Times*. "It's almost a mainstay of this country that the N.S.A only does foreign searches."[2]

Officials said the program monitored up to five hundred people in the United States at any one time and between five thousand and seven thousand people overseas suspected of terrorist ties. One of the individuals monitored in the United States, the *Times* reported, was Iyman Faris. Several officials said the program had helped uncover the plot to destroy the Brooklyn Bridge.

As soon as the story appeared, attorneys for several defendants convicted of terrorism-related crimes, including Faris, announced their intentions to ask whether the program had been directed at their clients. They included lawyers for Jose Padilla; Ali al-Timimi and Seifullah Chapman, sentenced to long prison terms as part of the so-called Virginia Jihad case; the Lackawanna Six; and the Portland Cell.[3]

For David Smith, the report was an unexpected boost for a motion he planned to file to vacate Faris's conviction on the basis of the poor legal help Smith believed Fred Sinclair had provided his client. "I want to know in what way NSA's surveillance program impinged on his case," Smith said December 27, two days after the program's existence was revealed. "Did they actually listen to conversations of Mr. Faris, or was it merely that his phone number came up in a surveillance of another target?"[4]

The report's timing was good news for Faris for another reason. After the Fourth Circuit had rejected Faris's attempt to withdraw his guilty plea in 2004, Smith had had a brief patch of good luck when the U.S. Supreme Court, in March 2005, ordered the appeals court to consider whether Faris should be resentenced. It was a glimmer of hope for Faris, who was grinding out his sentence in the federal supermax without much hope of reducing his time behind bars. Jack Vanderstoep and another FBI agent had visited him in early January of 2005, hoping to get his help in identifying suspected terrorists from photos. In typical fashion, Faris proposed a deal: arrange a lie detector test for him, and if he passed, propose a reduction in sentence based on his cooperation. The deal fell through after Faris insisted on taking the test before looking at the photos, an arrangement Vanderstoep rejected.[5]

Smith based his argument on a Supreme Court decision earlier in the year that had called into question federal sentencing procedures. On December 29, however, as the repercussions of the warrantless wiretap news still reverberated, the Fourth Circuit reaffirmed Faris's conviction and sentence, determining that he was not affected by the ruling on sentencing. As Faris's legal options dwindled, the wiretap allegations were prime fodder for an additional challenge. On February 3, 2006, Smith asked Brinkema in a thirty-eight-page filing to overturn Faris's conviction on the basis of ineffective assistance of counsel.

Smith laid out two basic arguments. Had Sinclair properly investigated the facts of the case and talked to Faris about them, there was a good chance Faris never would have pleaded guilty to begin with. Once the deal was cut, had Sinclair done a better job investigating the law regarding withdrawal of a plea, there was a good chance Brinkema would have granted Faris's decision to start over. Many of the arguments were similar to previous allegations Smith had made about Sinclair: he pressured Faris to accept the plea, he failed to properly investigate the facts of the case—including the legal basis for Faris's being declared an enemy combatant—he didn't mesh the FBI's summary of its interviews with Faris with the statement of facts that Faris had agreed to. Smith added another allegation in the new filing, that Sinclair was so cozy with federal prosecutors in the Eastern District of Virginia that it compromised his ability to represent Faris. But front and center in Smith's new argument was Sinclair's failure to ask the government whether Faris had been subject to any sort of electronic surveillance. "Had he done so," Smith argued, "the government would have been in a real bind and this would have enabled Faris to, at a minimum, negotiate a much more favorable plea bargain." It was a mistake Smith said he was not going to make.[6]

On March 1, Smith requested copies of all documents and tapes related to any electronic monitoring of Faris, with or without a warrant. Sinclair, meanwhile, refuted the allegations about his conduct. He never pressured Faris to plead guilty, he said in a sworn statement. He never told Faris he was facing at most a seven-and-a-half-year sentence because of his cooperation. He never failed to explain Faris's legal rights to him or to remind him he could go to trial instead. And he never offered his advice simply to help the U.S. attorney's office.[7]

The government dismissed the filing as a new twist on an old argument. Two strikes down, having failed to convince Brinkema or the appeals court he should withdraw his guilty plea, Faris was looking for the same result by arguing he had had a bad lawyer. Such allegations, the government prosecutors said, were baseless. Sinclair had advised Faris on the legal options in front of him. He had bargained the government down from the original offer of a thirty-year prison sentence. Once Faris insisted on withdrawing his plea, Sinclair did the best he could to advocate for his client. Don't forget, the prosecutors added, that the backdrop for all of maneuvering was the fact that Faris had cooperated with the government almost from the moment FBI agents approached him in Cincinnati in March 2003.[8]

The government also downplayed the significance of electronic surveillance to the case, particularly the NSA program. When explaining why agents first reached out to Faris, the government referred to information gleaned from a "court-ordered" wire interception in another investigation. They made sure Brinkema was aware that Smith had told *Newsweek* in January he was skeptical of the impact the warrantless monitoring had had on the Faris investigation. They pointed out Smith's concession that the statement of facts Faris pleaded to was based entirely on the incriminating statements he gave the FBI. "Indeed, the factual basis for Faris's guilty plea came from his own lips, with corroboration from other stated sources," prosecutors argued. Faris had no one to blame for his guilty plea and conviction but himself.[9]

AS FARIS TRIED to turn the clock back on his conviction, Nuradin Abdi was trying to go back in time himself: to the early morning of November 28, 2003.

Prosecutors immediately appealed Marbley's decision putting off-limits the statements Abdi had made before he got a lawyer. Their argument went like this: Federal agents had ample reason to suspect that Abdi was likely to attack a shopping mall. That suspicion was based in part on statements made to Faris—damning evidence by itself, given the allegations against Faris. But agents also conducted additional investigations of Abdi over several months. It was obvious, the government contended, that Abdi would try to escape following such an attack. That consideration alone permitted a warrantless arrest under U.S. immigration law. Once Abdi was in custody, he made several statements to agents after signing *Miranda* waivers. Those statements shouldn't be suppressed because they came as a result of his detention, not his arrest. At the very least, the government argued, even assuming Abdi's arrest had been unlawful, the fact that immigration authorities issued a warrant for his arrest on December 1—along with all those *Miranda* waivers he signed—should have been enough to allow any statements he made from that day on. The government bolstered its case with a new argument it hadn't raised earlier: when arresting someone in public, the only thing required is probable cause of an alleged crime. An arrest warrant itself is not needed. Hence, Abdi's arrest did not violate the Fourth Amendment.[10]

Abdi filed a relatively brief response several weeks later, on March 6, 2006. Sherif revisited the arguments he'd made earlier to Marbley, though the cursory summaries in his eleven-page document hint that his heart may not entirely have been in the debate at this point and he was ready to move on and prepare a trial defense. Sherif reiterated that an allegedly illegal arrest and nine days of custody in isolation outweighed any suggestion that Abdi's statements had been made freely.[11]

Attorneys argued the case before the Sixth Circuit on July 19, 2006. Two months later, on September 22, a panel of three judges returned a new verdict: by a 2–1 vote, they sided with the government and declared all of Abdi's statements, from the morning of November 28 on, admissible as evidence. Judge Thomas Wiseman Jr., a federal district court judge in Tennessee sitting temporarily on the Sixth Circuit, delivered the opinion on behalf of himself and Judge Danny Boggs.

> Thus, despite Abdi's argument to the contrary, it is constitutionally irrelevant that the ICE officers' reason for arresting him was their belief that he was in violation of immigration laws, and not that he was a felon. There is no question that, at the time of Abdi's arrest, the arresting officers possessed all of the information contained in the Turgal Declaration, and that the information was sufficient to establish probable cause to believe that Abdi was a national security risk.[12]

Judge Guy Cole dissented, saying that since the government hadn't raised the probable cause argument earlier, it was a moot issue; appeals courts generally aren't allowed to consider arguments brought up for the first time on appeal.[13]

The court's decision was an obvious blow to Abdi's case, though perhaps by this time not an unexpected one. With no further appeal pending, both sides could now concentrate on trial preparations. That work would proceed without a great deal of scrutiny over the next few months, since recent events had given the country something else to focus on. On August 9, 2006, British authorities announced they'd thwarted a terrorist plot to blow up several transatlantic flights by smuggling aboard chemicals that could then be mixed to deadly effect. Travelers had long grown accustomed to post-September 11 lines getting through airport security. Thanks to shoe bomber Richard Reid, removing footwear in the presence of strangers was also commonplace. Now, the era of liquid-free bags had begun.

A MONTH AFTER the Sixth Circuit cleared the way for Abdi to go to trial, Judge Brinkema began to shut down Faris's second extended round of appeals. On October 26, in a sealed order, she denied Faris's request for information collected about him under electronic surveillance as well as for information about the NSA program. Two weeks later, on November 6, in a second sealed order—she would unseal it two weeks later—she again upheld his conviction.

Brinkema skewered Faris's arguments point by point. There was no merit, she said, to the notion that Sinclair should have delayed his plea bargaining efforts for months until he reviewed the FBI's forty-four-page interview summary. The reason was obvious: Sinclair was basing his knowledge of the case on what Faris himself had told him. Faris, under oath at his May 1, 2003, plea hearing, had acknowledged the accuracy of what he told investigators. Inconsistencies between the summary and Faris's statements were not the same thing as innocence.[14]

Nor, Brinkema said, should Sinclair be faulted for not having demanded extensive information from the government about its case against Faris. Instead, the defense attorney had gambled correctly that Faris's usefulness as a witness outweighed the benefit of collecting that evidence. There was nothing wrong with recalling the context of the case: the tensions of post-9/11 America combined with the threat that Faris could be declared an enemy combatant if he didn't cooperate. Brinkema also shot down Faris's argument that Sinclair should have collected more information about electronic surveillance. The case against Faris, Brinkema said, had always relied on his statements to the FBI, not information gleaned from wiretaps. Moreover, even if Sinclair had requested such information, he would have come up empty. The warrantless wiretap program was completely secret in 2003, so clandestine that not even prosecutors were aware of it. Though the government agents acknowledged that Faris had come to their attention because of electronic surveillance in another case, Faris himself did not have the standing to challenge the surveillance of a third party.[15]

Brinkema was also unconvinced that Sinclair should have investigated the enemy combatant issue more fully. Even though the government was unsuccessful in holding Jose Padilla, she said, that case was far from settled in the spring of 2003.

In summary, Brinkema said, Faris hadn't met the burden of refuting the sworn statements he'd given May 1. He had participated actively in negotiating his plea bargain. He had bargained a prison term from thirty down to twenty years, received a broad grant of immunity from further prosecution, and left open a window for further sentence reduction. Case closed, the judge ruled.

"On this record, there is no evidence of involuntariness and Faris's contention that he was pressured into pleading guilty is unfounded," Brinkema wrote.[16]

Disturbing Picture

BY 2006, CHRISTOPHER PAUL was getting accustomed to unwanted visitors. FBI agents were dropping by to talk to him. They were interviewing family members. They were following him and his wife and coming by the factory to interview people he worked with. They'd searched his apartment the previous year, and in November 2006, they'd searched his parents' house on North Street in Worthington. Paul politely, but steadfastly, declined to talk to the agents. Privately he complained he was being unfairly harassed, that he hadn't done anything wrong with Faris or Abdi or anyone else, that at worst he'd been in the wrong place at the wrong time, that anyone who attended the Omar mosque automatically became a terrorism suspect. He went to the Ohio offices of the Council of American-Islamic Relations and asked the legal director, Jennifer Nimer, for her assistance. When Toledo/Mettler suddenly fired him in 2006, they gave him a generous severance package. Paul was convinced they'd been spooked by the FBI's visits and just wanted him gone. He showed Nimer the severance agreement and asked if it checked out. The document appeared normal, but Nimer had her doubts about Paul. He didn't seem the type of person capable of getting involved in the things he said he was being pursued for. In any case, there wasn't much she could do. He hadn't been arrested or indicted. And frankly, his wasn't the first such story she'd heard. The office had had visits from a lot of people with similar concerns.[1]

IN THE SPRING of 2007, Iyman Faris was serving his twenty-year sentence in the federal supermax in Florence, Colorado. Nuradin Abdi was still in Franklin County Jail, preparing for his upcoming trial. In April, a military tribunal in Guantanamo Bay was about to hold a hearing on whether to declare Majid Khan, Faris's friend from Baltimore, an enemy combatant. Officials at the highest levels of the

FBI were seething over an editorial in the *Seattle Post-Intelligencer* on March 29 that accused the agency of "flying high on the wings of the Patriot Act," using it to collect private information, "telephone and financial records, e-mails, whatever—almost on a whim." In Columbus, terrorism had faded from people's minds. More pressing concerns included the fate of the general manager of the Blue Jackets ice hockey team and the continued self-destruction of the once proud City Center downtown mall, now about to lose its four Limited Brands stores, including Victoria's Secret.[2]

On April 11, an overcast day threatening rain, Christopher Paul walked from his apartment to midday prayers at the Omar mosque. Afterward, he headed back, strolling along the right side of the road, umbrella in hand. He was walking by himself, but he was not alone. A car passed him, then slowed to a stop in front of him. Another car pulled up beside him, a third behind him. A handful of FBI agents materialized, told Paul he was under arrest, handcuffed him, placed him in the back of a car, and drove off. The entire operation couldn't have taken more than a couple of minutes. Frida and Khadija awaited his arrival just a few hundred feet away at 676 Riverview, for a few minutes unaware that their lives had just changed irrevocably.[3]

A federal judge unsealed the indictment against Paul the same day, and Washington released news of his arrest. "The indictment of Christopher Paul paints a disturbing picture of an American who traveled overseas to train as a violent jihadist, joined the ranks of al Qaeda, and provided military assistance and support to radical cohorts both here and abroad," said Kenneth Wainstein, U.S. assistant attorney general. He added: "Our persistence and determination in the pursuit of this case should serve as a strong warning to any American who considers joining forces with our enemy." Tellingly, four years after Faris's conviction, it was no longer the attorney general himself announcing the news of another domestic terror case.

In fact, compared to the arrests of Faris and Abdi, the news about Paul made a relatively small splash in the Muslim community. Perhaps that was because his name had been floating for years as an associate, perhaps because people knew him well enough to think charges might not be far-fetched. But the news sent a shockwave through at least one group: those who remembered the polite, athletic student from high school who, despite his conversion, came across as the same nice kid in chance encounters over the years.

Mark Ellwood, the social studies teacher, recalled being at Chubby's Sports Grill with a group of former Worthington students in 2008, as Paul awaited trial. Among the attendees, the universal consensus was that it just couldn't be right. Glenn Alban, a Worthington lawyer who graduated with Paul in 1983, said repeatedly that the case didn't fit with his memory of his classmate. Sterling Apthorp, the former assistant principal at Paul's high school, commented that Paul never showed any ill will toward the community or country.[4]

Those who knew Paul more recently also professed surprise. His landlord described him as nice, but reserved, with nothing in his apartment that would indicate allegiance to a particular cause or country. Ahmad Al-Akhras, then vice chair of the Columbus CAIR chapter, said the charges were out of character for the man he knew as a loving husband devoted to his family. A friend, Hisham Jenhawi, who attended Paul's initial court appearance, also found the charges hard to believe. "I don't think it's even close to his personality to act upon something like that," he said at the federal courthouse. "He's a very kind person. You would meet him on the street and he would want to hug you with the heart that he has."[5]

There was also a sense among those who had known Paul at the mosque that something was unfair here. Paul had gone to Afghanistan to fight the Soviets: that was something good at the time, wasn't it? And now suddenly, when the tables were turned, he was a terrorist?

Nevertheless, the scale of Paul's alleged wrongdoing was startling, even when compared with the allegations against Faris. The fourteen-page indictment unsealed on April 12 crossed continents, from the United States to Europe to Asia. In particular, it reinforced connections between Paul and the radicalism brewing in Germany over the past two decades. There was the flat-bed scanner, the $1,760 wired to a German conspirator in 1999, the fanny pack filled with ISBNs for incriminating book titles. There was the most serious allegation, that Paul had planned bomb attacks against "European resorts where American citizens are known to vacation" and "governmental facilities, such as U.S. embassies, diplomatic and consular premises, and military bases located in Europe."[6]

Finally, there was the little matter of that postcard addressed to "Brother" Abdulmalek from "Brother" Karim Mehdi, the Moroccan whom Paul had gotten to know in Germany. Mehdi was now a bona fide alleged terrorist, arrested in June 2003 at Charles de Gaulle airport on suspicion of traveling to the Indian Ocean island of Réunion for a possible terrorist attack. Mehdi was also linked to Christian Ganczarski, a German national and Muslim convert who also had been arrested in France. Investigators suspected a link between Ganczarski and an April 2002 suicide attack against a synagogue in Djerba, Tunisia, that killed twenty-one people including fourteen German tourists. There was no evidence Paul was connected with any of those plots, but finding himself tied to people like Mehdi, along with Paul's old acquaintance Mohammedou Ould Salahi, was damning enough. (Salahi's importance to the government was underscored when former defense secretary Donald Rumsfeld revealed in his 2011 autobiography that eight years earlier he had approved interrogation techniques beyond the traditional Army Field Manual for Salahi. Rumsfeld said Salahi was one of only two Guantanamo detainees for whom he approved such harsh techniques. Rumsfeld never mentioned Christopher Paul, but said that Salahi "became one of the most valuable intelligence assets giving information on Al-Qaida.")[7]

Among the information revealed in the wake of Paul's arrest was the visit to the United States the previous year by a top French terrorism investigator interested in talking to Iyman Faris and Nuradin Abdi about Paul and his contacts with Mehdi. It was a mission carried out in vain. Faris and Abdi said they had nothing to say.[8]

FOUR DAYS AFTER Paul's arrest, and a world away, the military tribunal reviewing the status of Guantanamo Bay combatants held the hearing on Majid Khan. Faris was one of several witnesses called by Khan who had provided written comments to the tribunal for the April 15 meeting. Faris was adamant in his three-page statement that he had discussed only religion and business with Khan; the only reason he had visited the Khan family was to talk about investing in the gas station business. He said Khan loved the United States and looked forward to becoming a citizen. "There were never any discussion regarding the fight in Afghanistan—ever," Faris insisted. He also refuted statements he'd made to the FBI years earlier that Khan had called KSM "uncle" and had talked about killing President Pervez Musharraf. Faris repeated the old assertion that he'd been manipulated by the FBI. "If I don't tell them what they wanted to hear," Faris claimed to the tribunal, "they were going to take me to GITMO."[9]

The Ummah Is Angry

JUDGE ALGENON MARBLEY had already shown some sympathy to Nuradin Abdi's arguments. The judge's September 2005 ruling, though eventually batted down by the appeals court, was a robust defense of civil liberties and skeptical jab at what Marbley considered government overreaching. So perhaps it came as no surprise when he ruled in late July 2007 in favor of Abdi's request for a potentially explosive trial witness: one Iyman Faris.[1]

Putting Faris on the stand on Abdi's behalf was a calculated risk. Almost two years earlier, Abdi had argued in court filings that it was Faris and Paul who were the real terrorists, while he was just someone who knew the two and was present when they made incriminating statements. On the one hand, prosecutors likely would have a field day pointing out that Faris was a convicted terrorist with ties to Khalid Sheikh Mohammed, hardly a ringing endorsement of his credibility. On the other hand, Abdi's attorney, Mahir Sherif, said Faris was ready to testify that Abdi had said angry things that day in 2002 at the Caribou Café coffee shop but that he was talked out of any terrorist activity. There was never any conspiracy, Sherif said on July 19, the day after filing the request to put Faris on the stand. "I can't speak for Iyman Faris," Sherif said, "but as far as my client is concerned, it's just a bunch of pissed off people that may have expressed frustration at U.S. foreign policy, and they find themselves in this alleged charge." Abdi, like many in the *ummah,* or community, was angry at the war in Afghanistan and civilian casualties of U.S. bombing raids. "People talk," Sherif said, "and if they're going to charge people with talk, they're going to have to charge the entire Muslim *ummah,* because the entire Muslim *ummah* is angry."[2]

Sherif noted something else that day: the government had offered Abdi generous plea bargains, leading him to believe that prosecutors knew they didn't have a bona fide terrorist on their hands. Sherif told Abdi's family privately, "He's not worth eighty years." Certainly, Abdi's family continued to assert his innocence and to argue that the charges were incompatible with what they knew of him as a person and as a Muslim. Abdi's sister, Kaltun Karani, spoke up outside the federal court building after a hearing on July 5. "A lot of us are American citizens," she said. "We live here because we know that it's a peaceful place. And obviously, if I knew that my brother is capable of doing something to the extent that what they're saying, I wouldn't feel safe living here." Her brother, she went on, was not capable of the actions the government alleged. His faith prohibited it. Moreover, he told her he did not do what he was accused of, and that was good enough for her. "If my brother says, 'No,' he didn't do it, then he didn't do it," she said. It was Abdi's innocence, Karani and other members of the Somali community close to the family would say, that led him to turn down the plea offers over the years.[3]

Karani spoke of justice coming out. Sherif talked of evidence that would emerge at trial. David Smith, Faris's attorney, said his client's testimony could be embarrassing to the government. The mood surrounding Abdi's case in late July 2007 was that perennial favorite, cautious optimism. Yet any celebration over Marbley's one-page order allowing Faris to testify was short-lived. The same day, the judge issued a second ruling, this one sixty-six pages long, that in essence shot down almost every argument Abdi had been making over the past two years regarding his indictment, the use of statements Faris and Paul had made about him, his refugee status, the presence in his house of incriminating photos and jihadist documents from the Internet, the will found in his wallet, and the letter Marbley had received about Abdi from the Franklin County Jail inmate.

In numerous court filings, Sherif had argued several versions of the same point, that there was a line between First Amendment protected speech, which could include advocating violent jihad and amassing material from the Internet and elsewhere about holy war, and participating in or helping others carry out such war. Sherif also argued that any statements Abdi had made about attacking a shopping mall were irrelevant to the actual charges he faced, which were classic counts of violating laws against providing material support to terrorists.

Marbley said Sherif had almost everything reversed. True, Abdi wasn't being charged with advocating jihad, but the allegation was entirely relevant to the government's efforts to prove he was trying to aid terrorists. Case in point: the images on computers at Abdi's business were taken from Web pages about al-Qaida and the dissertation "Pillar of the preparing for Jihad" found in his bedroom. Abdi was free to argue that anyone searching online could have come across these, Marbley said, but added, in essence, not everyone was charged with aiding al-Qaida. In that case, such photos and statements were relevant.[4]

As for the most provocative allegation of the case, that Abdi intended to attack a shopping mall, Marbley said Sherif again had it backward. Rather than having no bearing on the charges that Abdi faced, the threat spoke directly to them. "The fact that he allegedly intended to detonate a bomb in an Ohio mall," Marbley wrote, "makes it more likely that he planned to help terrorist causes in the United States, thus providing material support to them." Marbley concluded the order by saying he would provide further instructions on jury selection in four days, on July 27.[5]

The instruction wouldn't be necessary. Abdi was ready to bring things to an end. Using his brother as an intermediary, Abdi had consulted a scholar in Saudi Arabia about the religious implications of a guilty plea. "I'm not going to lie," Abdi said as he wrestled with his fate. "I'm not going to testify to something I didn't do." Satisfied he'd found a solution he could live with, he made his decision. A week after Marbley's momentous ruling, on July 31, 2007, more than three and a half years after first being taken into custody while leaving his apartment and heading to morning prayers, Abdi announced his intention to plead guilty to one count of conspiring to provide material support to terrorists. In exchange, the government would drop the other three charges and agree to a relatively short ten-year sentence, which would include the years Abdi had already spent in jail. (On paper he faced nearly eighty years in prison if he'd been convicted on all four counts.) The deal also included Abdi's eventual deportation. At a sparsely attended hearing in Marbley's courtroom, Abdi smiled and laughed with Sherif as the hearing unfolded.[6]

Afterward, in a display of verbal gymnastics, a second lawyer assisting Abdi explained that, with the plea, Abdi was acknowledging he'd made certain incriminating statements at the March 2004 immigration hearing in Detroit, but he was not confirming their truthfulness. "He's never said that conversation actually occurred during this plea agreement, he's just saying that he said that in immigration hearings," attorney Aurora Bewicke said. "He's not said that conversation happened or that there was any plans to hurt any Americans." Sherif added that Abdi may have made those statements under the influence of what he called the solitary confinement of his days in the Kentucky jail. Sherif also said Abdi agreed to a plea—against Sherif's advice, the attorney added—to get on with his life and because he was worried how a jury would proceed at this moment in history. "In this climate an American jury, we felt could potentially find him guilty because of all this negative stuff that's coming in, and if they found him guilty he was looking at spending the rest of his life in custody," Sherif said. "The government came back with another offer, so he decided to take it."[7]

Four months later, on November 27, 2007, Abdi returned to Marbley's courtroom for sentencing. Through Sherif, Abdi thanked the judge and thanked his family for supporting him. Sherif said Abdi was grateful to a Pickaway County jailer for seeing he needed mental health treatment after he was taken into custody in 2003 and to a jailer in Columbus for ensuring he received regular visitors at the Franklin County Jail. Abdi followed up with multiple apologies—to the United States, to people in Ohio, to his fellow Muslims. "Islam did not command him, Islam did not teach him to think as he did," Sherif told Marbley. "He wants to make it very, very clear that he does not hate America." Sherif said Abdi came to think the way he did because of Islamic teachings to pay attention to injustice. "Did he really intend to follow through?" Sherif told Marbley. "No, he did not." Abdi opposes suicide bombings and the killing of innocent people and never pledged allegiance to al-Qaida, Sherif added.[8]

In her comments to the judge, Robyn Jones Hahnert, an assistant U.S. attorney who helped prosecute Abdi, pointed out that the case against Abdi went well beyond an angry remark about a shopping mall. Abdi, she said, illegally traveled out of the United States to search for holy war training and provided stolen credit card numbers to buy equipment like laptop computers for use in terrorism. "This is a much bigger scope than one isolated statement in a Caribou Coffee shop," Hahnert said.

"The United States is a country that welcomes people to question—that's what we're all about," she told Marbley. "But that questioning should not lead to criminal activity that can harm people."[9]

Yusuf Abucar, the Somali architect who had emigrated to Columbus in the decade before the great wave of Somali refugees, was serving as the spokesman for Abdi's family. After the sentencing, Abucar said the government exaggerated the facts against Abdi, knowing they would be hard to disprove. "Since this was not a session where everybody has to bring their proof, they could have made any kind of statement," he said. Fred Alverson, a spokesman for the U.S. attorney's office, said in a rebuttal that Abdi had agreed to the lengthy set of facts read into the record at his July plea hearing.[10]

By chance, the following day, in federal court in Chicago, a twenty-three-year-old Rockford, Illinois, man named Derrick Shareef pleaded guilty to one count of attempting to use a weapon of mass destruction. Prosecutors alleged Shareef, a man with ties to other alleged domestic terrorists, planned to detonate several hand grenades in garbage cans at CherryVale Shopping Mall in Rockford. The attack, prosecutors alleged, was to have taken place sometime between November 29 and December 6 of 2006, one of the busiest shopping weeks of the year.[11]

Changing of the Guard

LATE IN 2000, as Iyman Faris and Maqsood Khan returned from their fateful forty-five-minute visit to the training camp where they met Osama bin Laden and Khalid Sheikh Mohammed, they got in a van and sat down in front of two men in camouflage, their faces covered. The strangers' accents gave them away as African Americans. When Faris asked them where they were from, they replied, "All over."[1]

As a black, U.S.-born defendant in a federal terrorism case, Christopher Paul stood out from the majority of alleged conspirators, usually Muslim immigrants or first-generation Arab Americans. But he was not entirely alone. Just as some Muslims had adopted a radical interpretation of the faith they were born to, some black converts took an equally radical step with the faith they adopted.[2]

An al-Qaida defector, L'Hossaine Kherchtou, has testified there were some African Americans with the group when it was based in Sudan in the mid-1990s. Pakistani journalist Hamid Mir was introduced to two African Americans when he visited bin Laden in Afghanistan in 1998. In New York City in the 1990s, former hospital worker Clement Hampton-El, a Brooklyn native who was black, allegedly plotted with blind Egyptian cleric Sheik Omar Abdel-Rahman to bomb the United Nations, FBI offices, two tunnels, and other New York landmarks. Like Paul, Hampton-El was a veteran of the 1980s Afghanistan conflict, from which he'd returned with wounds from a Russian shell and an apparent animosity toward the West common to many foreign mujahedeen.[3]

Jeffery Leon Battle and Patrice Lumumba Ford, both members of the alleged Portland cell, were African Americans; both are now serving time in federal prison. James Ujaama, of Seattle, born James Earnest Thompson, entered a guilty plea in 2003 to a charge of conspiracy to provide goods and services, including computer software and technology, to the Taliban during a trip to Afghanistan. Kevin James, indicted in 2005 for alleged robberies connected to the goals of a terror group he had founded while in state prison in California, was a black convert to Islam, along with two of his fellow conspirators. Kobie Diablo Williams pleaded guilty in 2006 to conspiring to support the Taliban by conducting paramilitary-style training around the Houston area. In total, a 2010 study identified twenty-four African Americans among 139 defendants in domestic terror cases it tracked in the decade after 9/11.[4]

OF THE THREE Columbus suspects, Paul's case proceeded the most quietly and uneventfully. Almost immediately, the government gave notice it would use information gathered during electronic surveillance as part of its prosecution. Paul's attorneys did not respond and in fact did not file a single motion opposing the indictment or challenging any government evidence, other than to ask for a six-month delay to translate documents. Paul's Worthington family refused all interviews, and his lead attorney, Jim Gilbert, was parsimonious with his comments by comparison with the lawyers for Faris and Abdi. After Paul's arrest and indictment in April 2007, the remainder of that year and the first half of 2008 were taken up with housekeeping notices and the setting of status conferences with attorneys. Then, on June 2, 2008, with no formal notice, Paul indicated in a court filing he was going to change his plea to guilty; the government said he would receive a twenty-year sentence in exchange.

Though he would never say so publicly, it was clear that Paul looked at the reality of going to trial as an alleged terrorist in post-9/11 America and, like, Abdi, calculated that the odds were against him. The following day, in the courtroom of U.S. District Court judge Gregory Frost, Paul pleaded guilty to one count of conspiracy to use a weapon of mass destruction—specifically bombs—in terrorist attacks. Prosecutors then agreed to drop charges of providing material support to terrorists and conspiracy to provide support to terrorists. It was a perfunctory hearing. FBI agent LaTisha Hartsough read a statement alleging that Paul plotted with a German terrorist group to bomb Americans at home or abroad, and Paul agreed to the statement's accuracy. Paul's only comments during the hearing were a polite series of, "Yes, sir," and "No, sir," to questions from Frost.[5]

Paul was just as laconic seven months later when he appeared before Frost for sentencing. When Frost asked if he wanted to make a statement, Paul replied, "No, sir."

"Nothing at all?" Frost pressed. Paul shook his head.

So Frost had his own say, lecturing Paul about his crime and telling him that he was an anomaly who had perverted the religion he converted to. "It's hard for me to get my mind around what you were conspiring to do," the judge told him. Afterward, Paul's wife, Frida, left the courtroom without comment, as did Paul's attorneys. The U.S. attorney's office also stayed mum, telling reporters no one was available for comment. "It's over now," Mounir Ayed, president of the Omar mosque, said as Paul was sentenced. "Most of the people that know him very well are gone now."[6]

IF THE FBI had had its way, the allegations against Faris, Abdi, and Paul would have been handled jointly: a package deal. As it was, the case encompassed three prosecutions over six years before slowly winding down. And questions remained. Did the Omar mosque encourage radical thinking or simply serve as an unwitting magnet for such individuals? Were comments tossed out at the Caribou Café in August 2002 conspiratorial statements or just a bunch of hot air? Were there other conspirators?

Faris made multiple choices through his life that likely sealed his fate, from going to Afghanistan with Maqsood Khan in the 1980s to accompanying him to the training camp years later. Even then, had Faris simply come home, put the entire episode behind him, and gone back to driving his rig cross country, it's possible he'd still be a free man today. But always the opportunist, the provocateur seeking some kind of fame or fortune, he was drawn back to the allure of contact with the world's most dangerous men.

Similarly, Abdi had the option early on of pleading guilty to what amounted to a federal slap on the hand and receiving in turn something in the neighborhood of five years in prison. Including time served following his November 2003 arrest, he would easily have been back in society by now. But the deal apparently came with an untenable catch: cooperation in ongoing investigations, which at that time included the case against Christopher Paul. Abdi made it clear he would never testify against another Muslim. The offer he accepted in 2007 was a less rosy arrangement: ten years in prison and deportation to Somalia, a country engulfed in anarchy and violence.

Like Faris, Paul created an extensive wall of allegations over the years, brick by brick, from his decision to go abroad as a wannabe American jihadist to joining al-Qaida and maintaining contacts with terrorists in Germany. Remove one, two, or even several such bricks, and the wall is still standing. That may help explain why Paul chose to plead guilty instead of going to trial. That, and the lingering questions of conspirators. Recall that the training exercises Paul conducted in Burr Oak State Park in 1998 included several other men. There was the unnamed codefendant Abdi drove Paul to meet in Pittsburgh in fall 2002. The U.S. attorney's office in Columbus has always maintained the investigation is ongoing. Paul's decision to plead guilty spared his family the ordeal of a trial and the revelation of even worse facts about his case. But it also may have shielded others he was involved with.

All three defendants made choices that eventually were turned against them. They also had something else in common. As David Smith, the attorney who took over Faris's case, has long maintained, regardless of what the three were charged with or convicted of, none of them actually did anything. They plotted, they conspired, they collected, they visited, they associated with, they spouted off, they whispered, and they journeyed. But they never pulled a trigger.

This is a common criticism of the war on terror, that the government casts too wide a net for wrongdoing. At best, the FBI nipped dangerous conspiracies in the bud before they amounted to anything; at worst they instigated plots through gadfly informants. The FBI operates 106 joint terrorism task forces around the country—up from only thirty five before the 9/11 attacks—and those teams of local, state, and federal officers don't win stripes for not uncovering terrorists. Jonathan Turley, a George Washington University law professor and attorney for accused Virginia Jihad ringleader Ali Al-Timimi, contends the government, aided by the low evidentiary standards of the material support statutes, engaged in fishing expeditions that hampered efforts to root out true terrorists. The focus on investigating and prosecuting terrorism, Turley testified before Congress in June 2008, increased the likelihood of misplaced prosecutions. "If the only tool you have is a hammer, you tend to see every problem as a nail," Turley said, quoting psychologist Abraham Maslow.[7]

The government's response was a variation on the 1 percent doctrine. Namely, 9/11 made it clear there are no second chances available. The FBI was not in the business of needlessly collecting information on American citizens; it was in the business of preventing terrorist acts. In 2009, the U.S. attorney in Georgia, David Nahmias, underscored this argument when he announced the conviction of Syed Haris Ahmed—like Iyman Faris a naturalized U.S. citizen from Pakistan. Ahmed had recorded videoclips of Washington, D.C., landmarks, then provided them to alleged jihadists overseas. "This case has never been about an imminent threat to the United States, because in the post-9/11 world we will not wait to disrupt terrorism-related activity until a bomb is built and ready to explode," Nahmias said. "The fuse that leads to an explosion of violence may be long, but once it is lit—once individuals unlawfully agree to support terrorist acts at home or abroad—we will prosecute them to snuff that fuse out."[8]

Conclusion

ON SEPTEMBER 20, 2009, in New York and Colorado, the FBI announced the arrest of three men on charges of lying to federal agents in the course of an ongoing terror investigation. Four days later, an indictment spelled out a chilling allegation: one of the men, Najibullah Zazi, a permanent U.S. resident originally from Afghanistan, had been plotting to detonate homemade bombs in a plot targeting commuters in New York City. This was unnerving news even for a country desensitized to announcements of terror arrests. Then, on the same day the indictment against Zazi was revealed— September 24—two *more* FBI announcements related to terror. In Dallas, agents arrested a teenager from Jordan, an illegal alien, who allegedly planned to blow up a city skyscraper by dialing a cell phone that would trigger a bomb. In Springfield, Illinois, a man named Michael Finton, AKA "Talib Islam," was arrested and charged with plotting to blow up the city's federal building. As the FBI dryly noted in its news release about Finton: "The arrest of Finton is not in any way related to the ongoing terror investigation in New York and Colorado." In one weekend, three plots aimed at Americans.[1]

Already, 2009 had been a bad year for homegrown terror. In June, Abdulhakim Muhammed, the young African American man who grew up in Memphis as Carlos Bledsoe and lived briefly in Columbus in 2007, allegedly opened fire on a military recruiting office in Little Rock, Arkansas, killing one recruiter and injuring another. In late July, the FBI announced indictments against seven men in North Carolina accused of an al-Qaida plot. Five of the seven were U.S. citizens, the sixth was a naturalized citizen, and the seventh was a permanent resident originally from Kosovo. On November 5, U.S. Army major Nidal Malik Hasan allegedly opened fire at Fort Hood in Texas and killed thirteen fellow soldiers while wounding another thirty.[2] A 2010 report by the Washington, D.C. –based Bipartisan Policy Center aptly summarized the changing threat: "A key shift in the past couple of years is the increasingly prominent role in planning and operations that U.S. citizens and residents have played in the leadership of al-Qaeda and aligned groups, and the higher numbers of Americans attaching themselves to these groups."[3]

On December 7, the Justice Department announced new charges against David Headley, the Chicagoan arrested in October for planning terrorist attacks against a Danish newspaper and two of its employees; the charges alleged he had conducted extensive surveillance of targets in Mumbai, India, preceding the November 2008 terrorist attack that killed approximately 170 people, including six Americans. On December 9, Pakistani authorities announced the arrest of five Americans of Muslim descent on suspicion of carrying out terrorist activities. The five, from suburban Washington, D.C., had disappeared two weeks earlier, telling their families they were taking a trip. And on Christmas Day, twenty-three-year-old Nigerian Umar Farouk Abdulmutallab allegedly tried to combine chemicals sewn into his underwear to detonate an explosive and bring down Northwest Airlines Flight 253 from Amsterdam as it approached Detroit. As so many plots came to light, it was hard not to think things were worse than ever. A Duke University study released in early January 2010 identified 41 domestic terror incidents in 2009, the most since 9/11. A few days later, FBI director Robert Mueller summarized the situation in a January 20 speech to Congress.[4]

> We face threats from homegrown terrorists—those who live in the communities they intend to attack, and who are self-radicalizing, self-training, and self-executing. We face threats from those who may attend training camps overseas—individuals who may live here in the United States and who may be radicalized here or overseas, and those who may live overseas but plan to travel to the United States to perpetrate attacks.[5]

MUCH HAD HAPPENED since Columbus first learned of Iyman Faris in June 2003 and discovered the war on terror was closer than people realized. Census figures showed an increasing number of area residents citing "Arab" for ancestry, growing 11 percent from 2000 to 2008, to as many as 8,343. Those calling themselves Somalis grew more than 100 percent, to as many as 7,059. (The Somali community regularly estimates a central Ohio population three or four times higher.) In suburban Dublin, a huge new mosque, the Noor Cultural Islamic Center, had risen from cornfields in 2006 along with an adjoining subdivision many of whose homes were purchased by Muslims who wanted the convenience of a nearby house of worship. Soaring, airy, built for hundreds of worshippers and with more than ample parking, the Noor Center was light-years from the converted Jehovah's Witness hall on Riverview Drive.

The government's approach to homegrown terror also had changed. Eric Holder, the new U.S. attorney general, signaled in a series of speeches that the time had come to recalibrate resources to crimes besides terrorism. Carter Stewart, the new U.S. attorney in Columbus, echoed this change following his investiture in September 2009. "We don't want to shift all of our resources out of terrorism," he said, "but I think there is probably a balance to be found, between keeping terrorism our number one priority and devoting the resources that are necessary to protect against it but allow for the redistribution of agents and the attention of AUSAs towards other crimes."[6]

One thing hadn't changed since Faris, Abdi, and Paul met for coffee in 2002, a month after the killings in Uruzgan province—civilians continued to die in the crossfire of the U.S. war in Afghanistan. A full seven years after that momentous meeting, the United Nations reported that 2009 was the deadliest year yet for Afghan civilians, with 2,412 casualties reported. The only difference now was that most were being killed by antigovernment forces. But not all. In late February of 2010, again in Uruzgan, NATO jets hit a convoy of vehicles that were suspected of transporting insurgents but turned out to be filled with civilians. The death toll of twenty-seven included four women and a child.[7]

The toll of the war also continued for Ohioans. By early 2010, the state had lost 182 military personnel in Iraq and another 21 in Afghanistan. In January 2010, Lima Company, the Columbus-based Marine Reserve unit that lost a total of twenty-three members in Iraq in 2005, learned it was being redeployed again, this time most likely in Afghanistan.[8]

The stories of Faris, Abdi, and Paul began to fade in Columbus, but they were not entirely forgotten. Faris's name pops up frequently in the news following new terrorist indictments. Some commentators revisit his case as an example of government overreaching with wild allegations—bringing down the Brooklyn Bridge with blowtorches?

Others cite his story as an instance of government success in thwarting a serious threat: Faris was taking his instructions, after all, from Khalid Sheikh Mohammed.

Today, in the nation's most secure federal prison in Florence, Colorado, Faris spends twenty-three hours a day in a segregated cell. He's barred from talking to reporters under administrative restrictions permitted by law and at the request of the U.S. attorney general. In a touch of irony, when Faris is allowed out of his cell to exercise, one of the inmates he chats with is Robert Hanssen, the FBI spy who sold secrets to the Russians. Other fellow Florence residents include shoe bomber Richard Reid, Unabomber Ted Kaczynski, and al-Qaida operative and alleged twentieth 9/11 hijacker Zacarias Moussaoui.

Paul Laws, AKA Abdulmalek Kenyatta, AKA Christopher Paul, has settled into life in federal prison in Terre Haute, Indiana. So far he has refused interview requests. Abdi sees family members who visit him in the federal prison in Marion, Illinois, where he contemplates his forced return to his homeland sometime in 2012. His family doesn't press him on the allegations that put him there. Abdi is assigned to Marion's Communications Management Unit, one of two such units that limit inmates' access to the outside world and other prisoners. Abdi can't have contact visits, and those visits he is allowed are limited to a total of eight hours a month. He's restricted to two fifteen-minute phone calls a week, which must be in English. (A 2010 lawsuit challenged the constitutionality of these units, alleging the Bureau of Prisons was reserving them for Muslims, inmates convicted of terrorism, and inmates with unpopular political views.) Abdi, who is not part of the lawsuit, is resigned to his situation, rarely complaining about the restrictions, while hoping they ease up at some point. He made brief comments for this book in a fleeting electronic correspondence through CorrLinks, an electronic communication system for federal inmates. "I don't know what benefit it will give me 2 give U my permission 2 look 4 my case with the FBI," he wrote on December 4, 2009, at 6:30 a.m. "Also how pious U gonna B or R U going to present the story of the government alone or U want 2 know my side."[9]

Abdi's wife, Safia, still hasn't had the heart to tell her young children where their father is. In response to their frequent questions, she explains he is working and will rejoin them eventually.

Abdi carries on the charade through phone calls and electronic messages from prison, including occasional photographs of himself. He took one of them by a prison wall that didn't reveal where he was. "I don't think he's happy here," his six-year-old son said when he saw the picture.[10]

IN THE FALL of 2009, the Ohio Historical Society and the state Department of Education secured a federal grant to create a program bringing students from a small charter school for Somali children to the historical society's museum for classes in Ohio history and culture. Once a month or so, museum volunteers showed students ancient Indian artifacts, prehistoric Ohio flora and fauna—including the museum's pièce de résistance, a mastodon skeleton—and exhibits on life in the nineteenth century. Except for slight accents, the boys could have been kids at any American school with their jeans and jackets and a variety of shirts, including one boy wearing a sweatshirt with the last name and No. 11 of NBA player Mike Bibby of the Atlanta Hawks. The girls were more distinctive, wearing hijabs and flowing dresses of blue and rose and red and orange and black and aquamarine. The children were inquisitive and mostly attentive and asked the kind of questions any student might have asked, such as why the early Indians were wearing practically nothing. They were briefly stumped when asked to identify the creature represented by one of the state's most famous prehistoric sites, the Serpent Mound in southern Ohio. They kept going for "fish," before finally moving to "lizard," then, with multiple cries: "Snake!"

There was more to this visit than learning about famous Ohio landmarks. In the years since 9/11 and the waging of wars in Iraq and Afghanistan, Somalia had emerged as a new epicenter of terrorism. The country, or what was left of it, was attracting radical Muslims from around the world in a twenty-first-century version of the Afghan Arabs flocking to Afghanistan. The terrorist group al-Shabab set up training camps with a familiar sound to them: ethnic Somalis from Africa, Europe, and the United States received weapons training from Somali, Arab, and Western instructors. At least twenty young men from Minneapolis, all but one a Somali, had traveled to Somalia to fight with al-Shabab. The terrorist group sent dozens of Somali Americans and American Muslims through such training, and at least seven were killed in fighting.[11]

Columbus, with the nation's second-biggest Somali population, had not yet experienced the direct recruiting of young men in the fashion of Minneapolis. But the city was not entirely untouched. Federal investigators questioned Somali women in the city who had raised money in 2008 and 2009 for what they thought were health care charities in Somalia but actually have been a front for al-Shabab. One of these women was identified as an unnamed co-conspirator in a 2009 indictment out of Minnesota charging two women with directly supporting the terrorist group. The number of Somali youth, particularly boys, who started to drift into gangs and crime once they hit high school in the city was a serious concern for community leaders. One explanation was that Somalis have farther to go to integrate, because many families moved directly from rough conditions in Kenyan refugee camps to life in cramped apartments in less-than-desirable Columbus neighborhoods. They also stand out for their dress, their language, and regardless of the increasing diversity of the city, their religion. One of the goals of the historical society grant was to ease the transition for children and make them feel more like residents of Ohio and citizens of the United States and hence less vulnerable to temptation, including online recruiting.

As the children's school bus left the museum after one field trip in December 2009, it turned briefly onto East 17th Street, gateway into one of the city's tougher neighborhoods. For just a moment, a dark chapter in the city brushed up against an effort to prevent another such chapter from being written. As the crow flies, it's less than a mile from the entrance to the Ohio Historical Society to the house on Grasmere Avenue where, once upon a time, Iyman Faris— acquaintance of Nuradin Abdi, best friend to Christopher Paul, and U.S. foot soldier for Khalid Sheikh Mohammed—lived and worked on his truck and played music for hours at a time.

Acknowledgments

Reporting and writing stories for the Associated Press typically requires speaking with a handful or more of sources and the able work of an editor or two. Completing a project like *Hatred at Home* involved the assistance of dozens and dozens of people, all of whom made great contributions to the work and without whom none of it would have been possible. My exploration of the story of the Columbus trio of terrorists began with an assignment from my AP news editor, Deb Martin, to profile Iyman Faris in the summer of 2003. She edited that and many other stories on Faris, Nuradin Abdi, and Christopher Paul, and I am grateful as always for her instruction, guidance, and eagle editing eye. I am also thankful to my AP chief of bureau, Eva Parziale, for her support of my work as an AP newsman as well as for this project. My colleague Liz Sidoti, now national political reporter for the AP, conducted a crucial early interview with Faris's ex-wife, Geneva Bowling, in the summer of 2003 that helped guide much of my future reporting on the case.

Several individuals with close ties to the defendants provided extensive interviews without which the book would not exist. Kaltun Karani, Nuradin Abdi's younger sister, spoke extensively about her brother and responded patiently and graciously to many follow-up questions. Yusuf Abucar, a longtime Columbus resident who acted as the family spokesman in the months before Abdi's plea deal, provided crucial background information on the Somali experience in Columbus as well as Abdi's case. Several other members of the Somali community were generous with their time and information, including Abdulkadir Ali, Jibril Hirsi, and Adam Mohammed, imam of the Masjid Ibn Taymia, who echoed many when he spoke of his gratitude for the United States' acceptance of Somalis fleeing the destruction of their country.

In 2009, Geneva Bowling sat with me for more than an hour to recount the years she spent with Iyman Faris. Virginia Laws McCammon, a cousin to Christopher Paul, was equally generous with her time as she drew a picture of Paul and his family as they grew up in Worthington, Ohio. Mike Brooks, the FBI's chief division counsel for the Southern District of Ohio, and Kevin Cornelius, assistant special agent in charge, provided crucial details and background and context about all three men and the government's pursuit of them; I am especially thankful to Mike and his patience in answering multiple follow-up questions. Faris's former attorneys, Frederick Sinclair and David Smith, both willingly answered questions and guided my reporting. Smith especially was generous with his assistance and answers.

The Muslim community in central Ohio has grown from a demographic footnote to a rich part of the area's cultural tapestry. My recounting of this group's history and growth benefited greatly from the research and writing of Asma Mobin-Uddin and conversations with Jennifer Nimer, Mouhamed Tarazi, and Adnan Mirza. Julia Shearson, of CAIR's Cleveland office, helped put the issues facing Muslims in Ohio in perspective, especially in light of the terror investigations in Columbus and Toledo.

Andrea Murray, an editor at the *Herald-Times* in Bloomington, Indiana, where I came of age as a reporter, was kind enough to read an early draft of the book and make multiple suggestions that lifted the narrative far beyond where it was headed. University of Texas law professor Bobby Chesney, one of the country's leading experts on the prosecution of terrorism, read selected chapters and made pinpoint suggestions that led to important and needed changes. His 2005 article, "The Sleeper Scenario: Terrorism Support Laws and the Demands of Prosecution," was invaluable to my reconstruction of the history of the material support laws. James Benjamin, co-author of *In Pursuit of Justice,* a comprehensive study of terrorism prosecution in the federal courts, also helped improve my understanding of these statutes. Jennie McCormick, the Worthington, Ohio, historian, instructed me on the story of African Americans in Worthington and made sure I distinguished between facts and legend. The city's history is in good hands. I'm appreciative of the support of the Ohio University Press for my work, including Editorial Director Gillian Berchowitz, who guided me toward the narrative that *Hatred at Home* would become, Managing Editor Nancy Basmajian, whose editorial oversight improved the manuscript tenfold, and Rick Huard, whose copyediting skills polished the final product greatly.

There is no creature less deserving of pity and succor than the self-absorbed writer working on his book, and there is no creature more deserving of kudos and comfort than that creature's patient partner. With her usual grace and good cheer, my wife, Pam, happily tolerated all the time at the computer, the after-hours interviews and phone calls, and the blank stares of a man whose mind frequently wandered to realms distant from the conversation at hand. As always she helped me see the forest from the trees, and with a single suggestion—"You know, they have yearbooks at the library"—pointed me in a rich new direction for research. As always, I'm full of loving awe and gratitude toward her.

Notes

Introduction

1. Proof Opening Brief for the United States, December 14, 2005, U.S. v. Abdi (6th Cir.) (No. 05-4199), 8.

2. Indictment, June 10, 2004, U.S. v. Abdi (S.D. Ohio) (No. 2-04-CR-88); Memorandum of Points and Authorities in Support of Motion to Suppress All Statements Allegedly Made by Defendant and All Evidence Seized, May 18, 2005, U.S. v. Abdi (S.D. Ohio) (No. 2-04-CR-88), Exhibit D: Declaration of Nuradin Abdi, 1–5, Kaltun Karani, interview by author, January 26, 2010.

3. Opinion and Order, July 23, 2007, U.S. v. Abdi (S.D. Ohio) (No. 2-04-CR-88), 52; Government's Response to Defendant's Consolidated Motion in Limine to Exclude Statements and Evidence and Preclude Evidence from the Jury Room, June 12, 2007, U.S. v. Abdi (S.D. Ohio) (No. 2-04-CR-88), 3;

4. Declaration of Nuradin Abdi, May 18, 2005, 2.

5. Declaration of Nuradin Abdi, May 18, 2005, 3; Opinion and Order, September 12, 2005, U.S. v. Abdi (S.D. Ohio) (No. 2-04-CR-88), 4.

6. Opinion and Order, September 12, 2005, 4; Defendant's Memorandum of Points and Authorities in Support of Motion to Suppress Statements for Violations of His Fifth Amendment Rights, June 1, 2005, U.S. v. Abdi (S.D. Ohio) (No. 2-04-CR-88), Exhibit A: Declaration of Nuradin Abdi, 3.

7. Declaration of Nuradin Abdi, May 18, 2005, 3–4; Declaration of Nuradin Abdi, June 1, 2005, 4.

8. Memorandum of Points, May 18, 2005, Exhibit L: FBI Report Dated 4/03/2003/Record of Interview with Defendant on 4/03/2003, 2–3.

9. iCasualties, "Iraq Coalition Casualty Count," iCasualties, http://www.icasualties.org.

10. John Ashcroft, "Prepared Remarks of Attorney General John Ashcroft, Plea Agreement Announcement," June 19, 2003, U.S. Department of Justice, http://www.usdoj.gov/ag/speeches/2003/remarks_061903.htm.

11. David Kiley, "Bush Plan Gives Huge Tax Break to Buyers of Big SUVs," *USA Today,* January 21, 2003, http://www.usatoday.com/money/autos/2003-01-20-suvs_x.htm.

12. Testimony of Robert Mueller, House Appropriations Committee, Subcommittee on the Departments of Commerce, Justice, and State, the Judiciary, and Related Agencies, March 17, 2004, http://www.fbi .gov/congress/congress04/mueller031704.htm.

13. David Schanzer, Charles Kurzman, and Ebrahim Moosa, "Anti-Terror Lessons of Muslim Americans," January 6, 2010, National Criminal Justice Reference Service, http://www.ncjrs.gov/pdffiles1/njj/grants/229868.pdf; Richard B. Zabel and James J. Benjamin Jr., "In Pursuit of Justice: Prosecuting Terrorism Cases in the Federal Courts, 2009 Update and Recent Developments," July 2009, Human Rights First, http://www.humanrightsfirst.org/pdf/090723-LS-in-pursuit -justice-09-update.pdf; "Terrorist Trial, Report Card: U.S. Edition," September 11, 2006, Center on Law and Security, New York University School of Law, http://www.landandsecurity.org.

14. Zabel and Benjamin, "In Pursuit of Justice," 13–16; "Terrorist Trial, Report Card: U.S. Edition," 5.

15. Associated Press, "U.S. Deports Ohio Imam for Supporting Terrorist Group," January 5, 2007, AP Electronic Archives.

16. Associated Press, "'Don't Leave a Phone Behind': Cell Phone Makers Fight Resales," September 10, 2006, AP Electronic Archives.

17. Defendant Mohammad Amawi's Request for Reconsideration of Denial of Discovery Relevant to Government Informant, March 31, 2008, U.S. v. Amawi et al. (N.D. Ohio) (No. 3-06-CR-719), 5.

18. Sheik Sherif Sheik Ahmed, October 7, 2009, news conference attended by the author.

19. Associated Press, "Judge Blocks Phone for Suspect in Soldier Shooting," June 11, 2009, AP Electronic Archives; Associated Press, "Suspect in Slaying of Army Recruiter Had Lived in Columbus," *Columbus Dispatch,* July 30, 2009; Melvin Bledsoe, interview by author, September 22, 2009.

20. "Umar Farouk Abdulmutallab Indicted for Attempted Bombing of Flight 253 on Christmas Day," Justice Department news release, January 6, 2010, http://www.justice.gov/opa/pr/2010/January/10-nsd-004.html; Jim Garamone, "Hasan Charged with 13 Counts of Murder," American Forces Press Service, November 13, 2009, http://www.army.mil/-news/2009/11/13/30361-hasan-charged-with -13-counts-of-murder/.

21. Memorandum of Points, May 18, 2005, 7.

22. Indictment, June 10, 2004, U.S. v. Nuradin Abdi, 4–5; Memorandum of Points and Authorities in Support of Defendant's Request for a *James* Hearing, and Motion in Limine to Preclude Inadmissible Hearsay Statements of Alleged Co-conspirators, September 7, 2005, U.S. v. Abdi (S.D. Ohio) (No. 2-04-CR-88), Exhibit A: Nuradin Abdi, FBI-302 interview, transcribed December 1, 2003, 2–5.

23. Proof Opening Brief for the United States, December 14, 2005, 5–6.

Chapter 1: Call to Prayer

1. Asma Mobin-Uddin, "One Faith, Many Hearts," *Islamic Horizons*, September–October 2008, 38.

2. Ibid., 41–42; Felix Hoover, "Islam's Numbers Soar," *Columbus Dispatch*, June 2, 2000.

3. Mobin-Uddin, "One Faith, Many Hearts," 43; Omar Masjid ibn Elkhattab, "Omar Mosque History," Omar Masjid ibn Elkhattab, http://www.masjedomar.org/.

4. Debra Mason, "Moslems [*sic*] Demand Respect They Accord Other Religions," *Columbus Dispatch*, February 25, 1989.

5. Mobin-Uddin, "One Faith, Many Hearts," 43; Mouhamed Tarazi, interview by author, January 21, 2010; Robert Albrecht, "Afghan Guerillas Find U.S. Life Bewildering," *Columbus Dispatch*, May 4, 1990.

6. Mobin-Uddin, "One Faith, Many Hearts," 43; Mouhamed Tarazi, interview by author, October 16, 2009.

7. Tarazi interview, October 16, 2009.

Chapter 2: The Gymnast

1. *The Cardinal*, Worthington High School yearbook, 1983, 104–5 (available at Worthington Public Library).

2. Jennie McCormick, e-mail to author, January 16, 2010.

3. Gladys Beavers Linnabary, "Resources for Teaching the History of Worthington, Ohio, in the Elementary School" (master's thesis, Ohio State University, 1952), 84–85; John Haueisen, *Worthington, Ohio, from before the Civil War and More . . .* (n.p.: self-published, 2007), 202–6; Jennie McCormick, *Worthington Neighborhoods* (Worthington, OH: Worthington Historical Society, 2006), 5; Virginia E. McCormick and Robert W. McCormick, *New Englanders on the Ohio Frontier: Migration and Settlement of Worthington, Ohio* (Kent, OH: Kent State University Press, 1998), 214–16, 269–70.

4. Virginia Laws McCammon, interview by author, September 25, 2009.

5. Ibid.; *The Cardinal*, Worthington High School yearbook, 1964, index of seniors (available at Worthington Public Library); *The Cardinal*, Worthington High School yearbook, 1980, 216 (available at Worthington Public Library); In the Matter of Guardianship of Candace Denise Laws, Probate Court of Franklin County, July 9, 1987 (No. 379678), microfiche.

6. McCammon interview, September 25, 2009; Ohio State University media relations office, e-mail to author, September 17, 2009.

7. Columbus State Community College media relations coordinator, e-mail to author, September 21, 2009.

Chapter 3: Split Personality

1. "What Is Kashmir?" *Washington Post*, http://www.washingtonpost .com/wp-srv/world/kashmir/front.html.

2. Mohammed Rauf and Geneva Mae Bowling, Abstract of Marriage, Franklin County Probate Court (No. 9506917), September 5, 1995; Geneva Bowling, interview by Associated Press newswoman Liz Sidoti, July 2, 2003; Geneva Bowling, interview by author, January 10, 2010.

3. FBI 302, summary of interviews with Iyman Faris between March 20, 2003, and May 1, 2003, contained in pages 162–205 of Joint Appendix, attachment to Brief of Appellant, February 2, 2004, U.S. v. Faris (4th Cir.) (No. 03-4865), 1; Rohan Gunaratna, *Inside Al Qaeda: Global Network of Terror* (New York: Columbia University Press, 2002), 19–21; National Commission on Terrorist Attacks upon the United States, *The 9/11 Commission Report* (New York: Norton, 2004), 55; Daniel Benjamin and Steven Simon, *The Age of Sacred Terror* (New York: Random House, 2002), 209.

4. FBI 302, summary of interviews with Iyman Faris, 1.r.

5. "Sayyid Qutb: The Pole Star of Egyptian Salafism," http://www .pwhce.org/qutb.html, Website copyright 2003–2005, Trevor Stanley.

6. Gunaratna, *Inside Al Qaeda*, 19; Peter Bergen, *Holy War, Inc.: Inside the Secret World of Osama bin Laden* (New York: Free Press, 2001), 51.

7. FBI 302, summary of interviews with Iyman Faris, 1; "Abdullah Azzam," GlobalSecurity.org, http://www.globalsecurity.org/security /profiles/abdullah_azzam.htm; Steve Emerson, "Abdullah Assam: The Man before Osama Bin Laden," *Journal of Counterterrorism and Security International* 4 (Fall 1998), http://www.steveemerson.com/4258

/abdullah-assam-the-man-before-osama-bin-laden; *9/11 Commission Report,* 55–56; Lawrence Wright, *The Looming Tower: Al-Qaeda and the Road to 9/11* (New York: Knopf, 2006), 132.

8. FBI 302, summary of interviews with Iyman Faris, 2.

Chapter 4: Increasing Tensions

1. Kaltun Karani, interview by author, January 26, 2010; U.S. Department of State, "Background Note, Somalia," January 2010, http://www.state.gov/r/pa/ei/bgn/2863.htm; I. M. Lewis, *A Modern History of the Somali: Nation and State in the Horn of Africa* (Athens: Ohio University Press, 2003), 207, 209, 213, 216–17.

2. Karani interview; U.S. Department of State, "Background Note."

3. Motion to Suppress Statements for Violations of Defendant's Fifth Amendment Rights, June 1, 2005, U.S. v. Abdi (S.D. Ohio) (No. 2-04-CR-88), Exhibit A, 1; Memorandum of Points and Authorities in Support of Consolidated Motion in Limine to Exclude Statements and Evidence and Preclude Evidence from the Jury Room, June 7, 2007, U.S. v. Abdi (S.D. Ohio) (No. 2-04-CR-88), 2; Opinion and Order, September 12, 2005, U.S. v. Abdi (S.D. Ohio) (No. 2-04-CR-88), 21; Karani interview, January 25, 2010; Kaltun Karani, text message to author, January 29, 2010; Warwick Ball, *Syria: A Historical and Architectural Guide* (New York: Interlink, 1998), 125; Government's Response to Defendant's Consolidated Motion in Limine to Exclude Statements and Evidence and Preclude Evidence from the Jury Room, June 12, 2007, U.S. v. Abdi (S.D. Ohio) (No. 2-04-CR-88), 5; Memorandum of Points and Authorities in Support of Motion to Suppress All Statements Allegedly Made by Defendant and All Evidence Seized, May 18, 2005, U.S. v. Abdi (S.D. Ohio) (No. 2-04-CR-88), 24.

Chapter 5: On the Move

1. Paul Laws, name change request, approval, March 16, 1989, Franklin County Probate Court (No. 390460), microfiche.

2. Ibid.; Jodi Andes, "Teacher Thought Youth Was Muslim," *Columbus Dispatch,* April 18, 2007; Indictment, April 11, 2007, U.S. v. Paul (S.D. Ohio) (No. 2-07-CR-87), 3.

3. Indictment, April 11, 2007, U.S. v. Paul, 3–4.

4. Ibid., 4–5; Memorandum Order, April 9, 2010, Mohammedou Ould Salahi v. Barack Obama (D.D.C.) (No. 1-05-CV-00569), 12.

5. Memorandum Order, Mohammedou Ould Salahi v. Barack Obama, 2, 14.

6. Indictment, April 11, 2007, U.S. v. Paul, 5–6.

7. Ibid.; Mohammedou Ould Salahi v. Barack Obama, 12.

8. Summary of interviews with Iyman Faris between March 20, 2003, and May 1, 2003, contained in pages 162–205 of Joint Appendix, attachment to Brief of Appellant, February 2, 2004, U.S. v. Faris (4th Cir.) (No. 03-4865); Edgar O'Ballance, Civil War in Bosnia, 1992–94 (New York: St. Martin's, 1995), 94; Rohan Gunaratna, *Inside Al Qaeda: Global Network of Terror* (New York: Columbia University Press, 2002), 132; Dayton Peace Agreement, The General Framework Agreement: Annex 1A, Article III, Withdrawal of Foreign Forces, paragraph 1, http://www.ohr.int/dpa/default.asp?content_id=368; Peter Bergen, *Holy War, Inc.: Inside the Secret World of Osama bin Laden* (New York: Free Press, 2001), 179.

9. FBI 302, summary of interviews with Iyman Faris, 4.

10. Opposition of the United States to Petitioner's Motion to Vacate Judgment of Conviction under 2255, April 10, 2006, Faris v. U.S. 2006 (E.D. Va.) (1:06-CV-132) and (E.D. Va.) (1:03-CR-189) (consolidated actions), 5–6.

Chapter 6: Hardworking Truck Driver

1. Ohio State University Office of Communications, e-mail to author, August 25, 2009.

2. Opposition of the U.S. to Petitioner's Motion to Vacate Judgment of Conviction under 2255, April 10, 2006 (E.D. Va.) (1:06-CV-132) and (E.D. Va.) (1:03-CR-189) (consolidated actions); summary of interviews with Iyman Faris between March 20, 2003, and May 1, 2003 contained in pages 162-205 of Joint Appendix, attachment to Brief of Appellant, February 2, 2004, U.S. v. Faris (4th Cir.) (No. 03-4865), 4; FBI Special Agent Mike Brooks, e-mail to author, March 24, 2010; Transcript, Motions and Sentencing Hearing, October 28, 2003, U.S. v. Faris (E.D. Va.) (No. 03-CR-189), 28.

3. FBI 302, summary of interviews with Iyman Faris, 5; Geneva Bowling, interview by Associated Press newswoman Liz Sidoti, July 2, 2003, in possession of author.

4. Bowling interview, July 2, 2003; Bowling, interview by author, January 10, 2010; "Man's Ex-Wife and Stepson Shocked by Revelation," *Columbus Dispatch,* June 20, 2003.

5. Associated Press, "Pattern of Parallel Lives Forms in Case of Ohioan Who Admitted Aiding Terrorists," September 9, 2004, AP Electronic Archives; Bowling interview, July 2, 2003; Bowling interview, January 10, 2010;

FBI 302, summary of interviews with Iyman Faris, 12; Criminal Information, May 1, 2003, U.S. v. Faris (E.D. Va.) (No. 03-CR-189), 2.

6. Geneva Bowling interviews, July 2, 2003, and January 10, 2010.

7. Michael Bowling, interview by author, October 25, 2010.

8. Evelyn Grannan, interview by author, December 16, 2009; Negla Ross, interview by author, December 16, 2009.

9. Associated Press, "Pattern of Parallel Lives"; Geneva Bowling interview, July 2, 2003.

10. Geneva Bowling interview, July 2, 2003; Ohio secretary of state processing statement, Aymanes Imports, February 11, 1997, searchable document at the Ohio secretary of state's Web site, http://www.sos .state.oh.us/SOS/businessServices.aspx.

11. Transcript, Geneva Bowling interview on *Good Morning America,* June 26, 2003. Mohammad Rauf and Geneva Bowling, Petition for Dissolution of Marriage, February 2, 2000, Franklin County Court of Common Pleas, Division of Domestic Relations (No. DR-02-0448), microfiche 41501, frames J09 and J10.

Chapter 7: Little Mujahideen

1. Indictment, April 11, 2007, U.S. v. Paul (S.D. Ohio) (No. 2-07-CR-87), 9.

2. Abdulmalek Kenyatta, name change request, approval, April 28, 1994, Franklin County Probate Court (No. 427710), microfiche.

3. Steven Emerson, *American Jihad: The Terrorists Living among Us* (New York: Simon and Schuster, 2002), 154–55; Peter L. Bergen, *Holy War, Inc.: Inside the Secret World of Osama bin Laden* (New York: Free Press, 2001), 106, 113; Associated Press, "Inspector: Suspect's Passport Aroused Suspicion," April 2, 2001; "Additional Charges Unsealed Alleging Retired Pakistani Major Conspired in Danish Plot," U.S. Justice Department news release, December 7, 2009, http://www.justice .gov/opa/pr/2009/December/09-nsd-1304.html; Information against David Headley, December 7, 2009, U.S. v. Headley (N.D. Ill.) (No. 1-09-CR-830), 3.

4. Geneva Bowling interview, January 10, 2010.

5. Bergen, *Holy War, Inc.,* 95; National Commission on Terrorist Attacks upon the United States, *The 9/11 Commission Report: Final Report of the National Commission on Terrorist Attacks upon the United States* (New York: Norton, 2004), 47–48, 69.

6. Indictment, April 11, 2007, U.S. v. Paul, 6; Abstract of Marriage, Christopher Paul and Frida Khanum Bashir, February 10, 1997, Franklin

County Probate Court (No. 9700677); Memorandum of Points and Authorities in Support of Motion to Suppress All Statements Allegedly Made by Defendant and All Evidence Seized, May 18, 2005, U.S. v. Abdi (S.D. Ohio) (No. 2-04-CR-88), Exhibit K, 3; FBI Special Agent Mike Brooks, e-mails to author, March 23, 2010, and March 24, 2010; Statement of Facts, July 31, 2007, U.S. v. Abdi (S.D. Ohio) (No. 2-04-CR-88), 1; Memorandum Order, April 9, 2010, Mohammedou Ould Salahi v. Barack Obama (D.D.C.) (No. 1-05-CV-00569), 12.

7. David Wayne, Columbus State Community College Office of Communications, e-mail to author, September 17, 2009; Indictment, April 11, 2007, U.S. v. Paul (No. 2-07-CR-87), 6; Statement of Facts, June 2, 2008, U.S. v. Paul (S.D. Ohio) (No. 2-07-CR-87), 2; Memorandum Order, April 9, 2010, Mohammedou Ould Salahi v. Barack Obama, 12.

8. *9/11 Commission Report*, 70.

Chapter 8: Diaspora

1. U.S. Census Bureau, "PCT18. Ancestry (Total Categories Tallied) for People with One or More Ancestry Categories Reported," American Factfinder, http://factfinder.census.gov.

2. United States' Response to Defendant's Motions to Suppress Statements for Violations of Defendant's Fifth Amendment Rights and to Dismiss for Outrageous Government Misconduct, July 1, 2005, U.S. v. Abdi (S.D. Ohio) (No. 2-04-CV-88), Government Exhibit, 30.

3. Ibid., 31.

4. Kaltun Karani, interview by author, January 26, 2010; Motion to Suppress Statements for Violations of Defendant's Fifth Amendment Rights, June 1, 2005, U.S. v. Abdi (S.D. Ohio) (No. 2-04-CR-88), Exhibit G, 1.

5. Statement of Facts, July 31, 2007, U.S. v. Abdi (S.D. Ohio) (No. 2-04-CR-88), 1; Government's Response to Motion of Defendant to Suppress All Statements Allegedly Made by the Defendant and All Evidence Seized in Violation of the Fourth Amendment, July 1, 2005, U.S. v. Abdi (S.D. Ohio) (No. 2-04-CV-88), 3.

6. Government's Response to Defendant's Consolidated Motion in Limine to Exclude Statements and Evidence and Preclude Evidence from the Jury Room, June 12, 2007, U.S. v. Abdi (S.D. Ohio) (2-04-CR-88), 5.

Chapter 9: Ready at Any Time

1. Lawrence Wright, *The Looming Tower: Al-Qaeda and the Road to 9/11* (New York: Knopf, 2006), 163; Statement of Facts, July 31, 2007, U.S. v. Abdi (S.D. Ohio) (No. 2-04-CR-88), 2; FBI 302 interview with Abdi,

transcribed December 1, 2003, attachment to Memorandum of Points and Authorities in Support of Defendant's Request for a *James* hearing, and Motion in Limine to Preclude Inadmissible Hearsay Statements of Alleged Co-Conspirators, September 7, 2005, U.S. v. Abdi (S.D. Ohio) (No. 2-04-CR-88), 2; Karani interview, January 26, 2010; Abdulkadir Ali, interview by author, January 14, 2010.

2. Statement of Facts, July 31, 2007, U.S. v. Abdi (S.D. Ohio) (No. 2-04-CR-88), 2; Indictment, June 10, 2004, U.S. v. Abdi (S.D. Ohio) (No. 2-04-CR-88), 1–4; Memorandum of Points and Authorities in Support of Motion to Suppress All Statements Allegedly Made by Defendant and All Evidence Seized, May 18, 2005, U.S. v. Abdi (S.D. Ohio) (No. 2-04-CR-88), attachment, 37.

3. Statement of Facts, July 31, 2007, U.S. v. Abdi (S.D. Ohio) (No. 2-04-CR-88), 2–3; U.S. Cavalry Online Store, http://www.uscav.com/.

4. Indictment, April 11, 2007, U.S. v. Paul (S.D. Ohio) (No. 2-07-CR-87), 7–8; Mohammedou Ould Salahi v. Barack Obama, 13.

5. Mohammedou Ould Salahi v. Barack Obama, 18–19.

6. Statement of Facts, July 31, 2007, U.S. v. Abdi (S.D. Ohio) (No. 2-04-CR-88), 3.

7. Ibid.; Government's Response to Defendant's Consolidated Motion in Limine to Exclude Statements and Evidence and Preclude Evidence from the Jury Room, June 12, 2007, U.S. v. Abdi (S.D. Ohio) (No. 2-04-CR-88), 5.

8. Statement of Facts, July 31, 2007, U.S. v. Abdi (S.D. Ohio) (No. 2-04-CR-88), 4.

Chapter 10: Four Hundred Years

1. Mouhamed Tarazi, interview by author, July 25, 2008.

2. Geneva Bowling, interview by Associated Press newswoman Liz Sidoti, July 3, 2003; Tarazi interview, July 25, 2008; Transcript, Motions and Sentencing Hearing, October 28, 2003, U.S. v. Faris (E.D. Va.) (No. 03-CR-189), 6; Motion to Determine Defendant's Mental Competency, July 24, 2003, U.S. v. Faris (E.D. Va.) (No. CR-03-189), 1.

3. Geneva Bowling, interview January 10, 2010.

4. FBI 302, summary of interviews with Iyman Faris between March 20, 2003, and May 1, 2003, contained in pages 162–205 of Joint Appendix, attachment to Brief of Appellant, February 2, 2004, U.S. v. Faris (4th Cir.) (No. 03-4865), 6; Bowling interviews, July 3, 2003, and January 10, 2010; Criminal Information, May 1, 2003, U.S. v. Faris (E.D. Va.) (No. 03-CR-189), 1.

5. FBI 302, summary of interviews with Iyman Faris, 8–10; Criminal Information, May 1, 2003, U.S. v. Faris (E.D. Va.) (No. 03-CR-189), 1.

6. FBI 302, summary of interviews with Iyman Faris, 10; Criminal Information, May 1, 2003, U.S. v. Faris (E.D. Va.) (No. 03-CR-189), 2.

7. FBI 302, summary of interviews with Iyman Faris, 11–12; Criminal Information, May 1, 2003, U.S. v. Faris (E.D. Va.) (No. 03-CR-189), 2.

8. FBI 302, summary of interviews with Iyman Faris, 10–13.

9. Statement of Facts, May 1, 2003, U.S. v. Faris (E.D. Va.) (No. CR 03-189), 2; FBI 302, summary of interviews with Iyman Faris, 18; Brooks e-mail, March 24, 2010.

10. FBI 302, summary of interviews with Iyman Faris, 16.

Chapter 11: Busy Summer

1. "Mukhtar Al-Bakri Pleads Guilty to Providing Material Support to Al Qaeda," Justice Department news release, May 19, 2003, http://www.justice.gov/opa/pr/2003/May/03_crm_307.htm; "Defendant in Buffalo Cell Case Pleads Guilty to Providing Goods and Services to Usama bin Laden and Al Qaeda," Justice Department news release, January 10, 2002, http://www.justice.gov/opa/pr/2003/January/03_crm_014.htm; "Defendant in Buffalo Case Pleads Guilty to Providing Material Support to Al Qaeda," Justice Department news release, April 8, 2003, http://www.justice.gov/opa/pr/2003/April/03_crm_213.htm.

2. Statement of Facts, July 31, 2007, U.S. v. Abdi (S.D. Ohio) (No. 2-04-CR-88), 4; FBI Special Agent Mike Brooks, e-mail to author, March 24, 2010.

3. Government's Proposed Exhibit List, June 7, 2007, U.S. v. Abdi (S.D. Ohio) (No. 2-04-CR-88), 1; Nuradin Mohamoud Abdi and Safia Hussein Muse, Abstract of Marriage, May 2, 2001, Franklin County Probate Court (No. 0102384).

4. "Detainee Biographies," Office of the Director of National Intelligence, September 6, 2006 release, http://www.dni.gov/announcements/content/DetaineeBiographies.pdf; "Summary of Evidence for Combatant Status Review Tribunal—Khan, Majid," Department of Defense, Office for the Administrative Review of the Detention of Enemy Combatants at U.S. Naval Base Guantanamo Bay, Cuba, March 28, 2007, http://www.defense.gov/news/ISN10020.pdf; FBI 302, summary of interview with Iyman Faris, March 21, 2003, 36; Opposition of the United States to Petitioner's Motion to Vacate Judgment of Conviction under 2255, April 10, 2006, Faris v. U.S. 2006 (E.D.

Va.) (1:06-CV-132) and (E.D. Va.) (1:03-CR-189) (consolidated actions), 4; "Detainee Reporting Pivotal for the War against al-Qaida," document obtained by Judicial Watch through Freedom of Information Act lawsuit, released by U.S. Department of Justice, August 24, 2009, http://www.judicialwatch.org/files/documents/2009/cia-ksm-docs08242009.pdf 3.

Chapter 12: We Need People Who Can Vanish

1. Geneva Bowling, interview by author, January 10, 2010; Abdi sentencing hearing, November 27, 2007, attended by author.

2. Geneva Bowling, interview by Associated Press newswoman Liz Sidoti, July 2, 2003; FBI 302, summary of interviews with Iyman Faris between March 20, 2003, and May 1, 2003, contained in pages 162–205 of Joint Appendix, attachment to Brief of Appellant, February 2, 2004, U.S. v. Faris (4th Cir.) (No. 03-4865), 16; Jodi Nirode and Encarnacion Pyle, "Man's Ex-Wife and Stepson Shocked by Revelation," *Columbus Dispatch*, June, 20, 2003; Eric Lichtblau with Monica Davey, "Suspect in Plot on Bridge Drew Interest Earlier," *New York Times*, June 21, 2003.

3. FBI 302, summary of interviews with Iyman Faris, 17; Statement of Facts, May 1, 2003, U.S. v. Faris (E.D. Va.) (No. CR 03-189), 2; Susan Sachs, "A Muslim Missionary Group Draws New Scrutiny in U.S.," *New York Times*, July 14, 2003; Statement of Marc Sageman to the National Commission on Terrorist Attacks upon the United States, July 9, 2003, GlobalSecurity.org, http://www.globalsecurity.org/security/library/congress/9-11_commission/030709-sageman.htm; Dina Temple-Raston, *The Jihad Next Door: The Lackawanna Six and Rough Justice in the Age of Terror* (New York: Public Affairs, 2007), 89.

4. Statement of Facts, May 1, 2003, U.S. v. Faris (E.D. Va.) (No. CR 03-189), 2–3; "Detainee Biographies," Office of the Director of National Intelligence, September 6, 2006, release, http://www.dni.gov/announcements/content/DetaineeBiographies.pdf.

5. Statement of Facts, May 1, 2003, U.S. v. Faris (E.D. Va.) (No. CR 03-189), 2–3.

6. FBI 302, summary of interviews with Iyman Faris, 25; Declaration of Iyman Faris in Support of Motion to Vacate Conviction under 28 U.S.C. 2255, attachment to Motion to Vacate Conviction under 28 U.S.C. 2255, February 3, 2006, U.S. v. Faris 2006 (E.D. Va.) (1:06-CV-132) and (E.D. Va.) (1:03-CR-189) (consolidated actions), 11–12.

7. FBI 302, summary of interviews with Iyman Faris, 19, 31.

Chapter 13: Collateral Damage

1. Associated Press, "Music and Dancing, Then Rockets and Death as Afghans Recall Night of Devastating U.S. Raids," July 3, 2002, AP Electronic Archives; "Afghan Raid Leaves a Trail of Shock, Grief and Anger," *New York Times,* July 5, 2002.

2. Associated Press, "Music and Dancing"; "Afghan Raid."

3. Paul Watson, "As More Bombs Go Astray, More Question U.S.," *Washington Post,* October 29, 2001; Associated Press, "In Bomb-Battered Afghanistan, an Accurate Body Count Nearly Impossible to Come By," October 20, 2001, AP Electronic Archives.

4. "Battlefield Vietnam: A Brief History," PBS online Web resource, http://www.pbs.org/battlefieldvietnam/timeline/index1.html; "Secretary-General Regrets Loss of Life by Conflict in Afghanistan," UN press release, October 15, 2001, http://www.un.org/News/Press/docs/2001/sgsm7997.doc.htm.

5. Human Rights Watch, "U.S. Cluster Bombs Killed Civilians in Afghanistan," Human Rights Watch, December 18, 2002, http://www.hrw.org/press/2002/12/arms1218.htm; Associated Press, "'God Knows' Why U.S. Bombed Hamlet Where Scores of Dead Now Subject of Compensation Claim," March 15, 2002, AP Electronic Archives.

6. Esther Schrader, "Pentagon Defends Strikes as Civilian Toll Rises," *Los Angeles Times,* October 30, 2001.

7. FBI 302 interview with Nuradin Abdi, transcribed December 1, 2003, attachment to Memorandum of Points and Authorities in Support of Defendant's Request for a *James* Hearing, and Motion in Limine to Preclude Inadmissible Hearsay Statements of Alleged Co-conspirators, September 7, 2005, U.S. v. Abdi (S.D. Ohio) (No. 2-04-CR-88), 2–4.

8. Statement of Facts, July 31, 2007, U.S. v. Abdi (S.D. Ohio) (No. 2-04-CR-88), 5; Government's Proposed Exhibit List, June 7, 2007, U.S. v. Abdi (S.D. Ohio) (No. 2-04-CR-88), 4.

9. Statement of Facts, July 31, 2007, U.S. v. Abdi (S.D. Ohio) (No. 2-04-CR-88), 5; Government's Proposed Exhibit List, June 7, 2007, 5.

Chapter 14: Winning the War on Terror

1. Biography, George H. W. Bush, U.S. Senate, http://www.senate.gov/artandhistory/history/common/generic/VP_George_Bush.htm; 2001 event attended by author.

2. Thomas B. Edsall, "Republicans Name 62 Who Raised Big Money," *Washington Post,* July 1, 2004, http://www.washingtonpost.com/wp-dyn/articles/A19026–2004Jun30.html.

3. "Remarks by the President on Iraq," Cincinnati Museum Center–Cincinnati Union Terminal, Cincinnati, Ohio, October 7, 2002, http://georgewbush-whitehouse.archives.gov/news/releases/2002/10/20021007-8.html.

Chapter 15: A Great Chapter

1. FBI 302 interview with Nuradin Abdi, transcribed December 1, 2003, attachment to Memorandum of Points and Authorities in Support of Defendant's Request for a *James* Hearing, and Motion in Limine to Preclude Inadmissible Hearsay Statements of Alleged Co-conspirators, September 7, 2005, U.S. v. Abdi (S.D. Ohio) (No. 2-04-CR-88), 2, 4; Declaration of Iyman Faris in Support of Motion to Vacate Conviction under 28 U.S.C. 2255, attachment to Motion to Vacate Conviction under 28 U.S.C. 2255, February 3, 2006, U.S. v. Faris 2006 (E.D. Va.) (1:06-CV-132) and (E.D. Va.) (1:03-CR-189) (consolidated actions), 8; FBI Special Agent Mike Brooks, e-mail to author, March 23, 2010.

2. "Al Qaeda in America: The Enemy Within," *Newsweek*, June 23, 2003, 43; Statement of Facts, May 1, 2003, U.S. v. Faris (E.D. Va.) (No. CR 03-189), 3; Declaration of Faris, 8–9.

3. Mark Hosenball and Evan Thomas, "The Biggest Catch Yet," *Newsweek*, March 10, 2003, 40; Erick Eckholm, "Pakistanis Arrest Qaeda Figure Seen as Planner of 9/11," *New York Times*, March 2, 2003; Ali Khan, Statement to Combatant Status Review Tribunal, April 15, 2007, Verbatim Transcript of Combatant Status Review Tribunal Hearing for ISN 10020, http://www.defense.gov/news/transcript_ISN10020.pdf; Associated Press, "AP Source: Feds Eye NY Trial for Gitmo Suspect," December 16, 2009, AP Electronic Archives.

4. Geneva Bowling, interview by author, January 10, 2010.

5. Declaration of Jack Vanderstoep, exhibit filed with Opposition of the United States to Petitioner's Motion to Vacate Judgment of Conviction under 2255, April 10, 2006, Iyman Faris v. U.S. 2006 (E.D. Va.) (1:06-CV-132) and (E.D. Va.) (1:03-CR-189) (consolidated actions), 2; Brooks e-mails, March 23, 2010, and March 24, 2010; Mike Brooks and Kevin Cornelius, interview by author, March 9, 2010.

6. Property search, Franklin County Auditor, http://franklincountyoh.metacama.com/do/selectDisplay?parcelid=010109001280&select=SUMMARY&curpage=*.

7. Declaration of Jack Vanderstoep, April 10, 2006, 2–3; Declaration of Iyman Faris, 2–3; Motion to Vacate Judgment of Conviction under 2255 and Memorandum of Law in Support of Motion to Vacate

Judgment of Conviction under 2255, February 3, 2006, U.S. v. Faris (E.D. Va.) (1:06-CV-132) and (E.D. Va.) (1:03-CR-189) (consolidated actions); Faris Interview Log, transcribed April 2, 2003, attachment to Reply to U.S. Opposition to Faris' Motion under 2255, May 24, 2006 (E.D. Va.) (1:06-CV-132) and (E.D. Va.) (1:03-CR-189) (consolidated actions), 1.

8. Declaration of Jack Vanderstoep, April 10, 2006, 3; Faris Interview Log, 1.

9. Declaration of Jack Vanderstoep, April 10, 2006, 3; Declaration of Iyman Faris, 3; Faris Interview Log, 1; Kevin Cornelius, interview by author, March 9, 2010.

10. FBI 302, summary of interviews with Iyman Faris between March 20, 2003, and May 1, 2003, contained in pages 162–205 of Joint Appendix, attachment to Brief of Appellant, February 2, 2004, U.S. v. Faris (4th Cir.) (No. 03-4865), 31; Reply Brief of Appellant, March 26, 2004, U.S. v. Faris (4th Cir.) (No. 03-4865), 11, 15; Faris Interview Log, 2; Brooks e-mail, March 24, 2010.

Chapter 16: I'm Doing This as a Friend

1. Declaration of Iyman Faris, attachment to Motion to Vacate Judgment of Conviction under 2255 and Memorandum of Law in Support of Motion to Vacate Judgment of Conviction under 2255, February 3, 2006, U.S. v. Faris (E.D. Va.) (1:06-CV-132) and (E.D. Va.) (1:03-CR-189) (consolidated actions), 3; Faris Interview Log, transcribed April 2, 2003, attachment to Reply to U.S. Opposition to Faris' Motion under 2255, May 24, 2006 (E.D. Va.) (1:06-CV-132) and (E.D. Va.) (1:03-CR-189) (consolidated actions), 2.

2. Faris Interview Log, 2; Declaration of Jack Vanderstoep, exhibit filed with Opposition of the United States to Petitioner's Motion to Vacate Judgment of Conviction under 2255, April 10, 2006, Iyman Faris v. U.S. 2006 (E.D. Va.) (1:06-CV-132) and (E.D. Va.) (1:03-CR-189) (consolidated actions), 3–4.

3. Faris Interview Log, 3; Declaration of Jack Vanderstoep, 5.

4. Declaration of Jack Vanderstoep, 6.

5. Motion to Suppress All Statements Allegedly Made by the Defendant and All Evidence Seized in Violation of the Fourth Amendment, May 18, 2005, U.S. v. Abdi (S.D. Ohio) (No. 2-04-CR-88), attachment, 41; Government's Response to Motion of Defendant to Suppress All Statements Allegedly Made by the Defendant and All Evidence Seized in Violation of the Fourth Amendment, July 1, 2005, U.S. v. Abdi (S.D. Ohio) (No. 2-04-CV-88), 16.

6. Kevin Mayhood, Jonathan Riskind, and Robert Ruth, "Mall Was Target, U.S. Says," *Columbus Dispatch,* June 15, 2004; Kevin Cornelius, interview by author, March 9, 2010.

7. Declaration of Jack Vanderstoep, April 10, 2006, 7; Declaration of Iyman Faris, 6; Faris Interview Log, 4, attachments, "Advice of Rights," "Consent to Interview with Polygraph"; Declaration of Frederick Sinclair, exhibit filed with Opposition of the United States to Petitioner's Motion to Vacate Judgment of Conviction under 2255, April 7, 2006, Faris v. U.S. 2006 (E.D. Va.) (1:06-CV-132) and (E.D. Va.) (1:03-CR-189) (consolidated actions), 1; Appointment of Counsel for Iyman Faris, memo from Neil Hammerstrom Jr. to clerk of the court, U.S. District Court, Eastern District of Virginia, April 4, 2003, in possession of author.

8. Faris Interview Log, 4.

9. Reply Brief of Appellant, March 26, 2004, U.S. v. Faris (4th Cir.) (No. 03-4865), 4; Hammerstrom online bio, Lawyers.com, http://www.lawyers.com/Virginia/Alexandria/W.-Neil-Hammerstrom-1725780-a.html; Sinclair online bio, Lawyers.com, http://www.lawyers.com/Virginia/Alexandria/J.-Frederick-Sinclair,-P.C.-1726206-f.html; Declaration of Frederick Sinclair, April 7, 2006, 1–2.

10. Declaration of Frederick Sinclair, April 7, 2006, 2–3; Declaration of Jack Vanderstoep, April 10, 2006, 7–8; Faris Interview Log, 5; Transcript, Motions and Sentencing Hearing, October 28, 2003, U.S. v. Faris (E.D. Va.) (No. 03-CR-189), 6, 8.

11. Transcript, Motions and Sentencing Hearing, October 28, 2003, 9; Declaration of Frederick Sinclair, April 7, 2006, 3–4.

12. Jose Padilla, case summary, Human Rights First, http://www.humanrightsfirst.org/us_law/inthecourts/supreme_court_padilla.aspx; "Man Held as 'Enemy Combatant' Now Back in Saudi Arabia," CNN, October 14, 2004, http://www.cnn.com/2004/WORLD/meast/10/14/hamdi; Associated Press, "Former 'Enemy Combatant' Pleads Not Guilty in US," March 23, 2009, AP Electronic Archives; Declaration of Iyman Faris, 7; Declaration of Jack Vanderstoep, April 10, 2006, 6.

13. Declaration of Iyman Faris, 4; Faris Interview Log, 5.

14. Declaration of Frederick Sinclair, April 7, 2006, 5; Memorandum Opinion, November 28, 2006, U.S. v. Faris (E.D. Va.) (No. 03-CR-189), 15; Transcript, Motions and Sentencing Hearing, October 28, 2003, 15.

15. Transcript, Motions and Sentencing Hearing, October 28, 2003, 10.

16. Faris Interview Log, 6–7; Declaration of Frederick Sinclair, April 7, 2006, 7; Declaration of Jack Vanderstoep, April 10, 2006, 8; Transcript, Motions and Sentencing Hearing, October 28, 2003, 15; Mike Brooks and Kevin Cornelius, interview by author, March 9, 2010.

17. Declaration of Jack Vanderstoep, April 10, 2006, 8; Brief for the United States, March 11, 2004, U.S. v. Faris (4th Cir.) (No. 03-4865), 43.

18. Brief of Appellant, February 2, 2004, U.S. v. Faris (4th Cir.) (No. 03-4865), 6; Reply Brief of Appellant, March 26, 2004, U.S. v. Faris (4th Cir.) (No. 03-4865), 18.

Chapter 17: Material Support

1. Memorandum Opinion, July 11, 2002, U.S. v. Lindh (E.D. Va.) (No. 02-37-A), 4–5; U.S. Department of State, Country Reports on Terrorism 2005, http://www.state.gov/documents/organization/65462.pdf, 214.

2. Robert M. Chesney, "The Sleeper Scenario: Terrorism Support Laws and the Demands of Prosecution," *Harvard Journal on Legislation* 42, no. 1 (2005): 4–5, 13; Staff of the National Commission on Terrorist Attacks upon the United States, Monograph on Terrorist Financing, http://www.9-11commission.gov/staff_statements/911_TerrFin_Monograph.pdf, 31–32.

3. Chesney, "Sleeper Scenario," 19; Robert Chesney, e-mail to author, May 23, 2010.

4. John Ashcroft, "Remarks of Attorney General John Ashcroft," Attorney General Guidelines, May 30, 2002, http://www.justice.gov/archive/ag/speeches/2002/53002agpreparedremarks.htm.

5. Testimony of Professor David Cole before the United States Senate Committee on the Judiciary on the USA Patriot Act, May 10, 2005, http://www.fcnl.org/issues/item.php?item_id=1376&issue_id=68; "Overview: The 'Material Support' Statute and its Significance," Center for Constitutional Rights, http://ccrjustice.org/holder-v-humanitarian-law-project.

6. Richard B. Zabel and James J. Benjamin Jr., "In Pursuit of Justice: Prosecuting Terrorism Cases in the Federal Courts," *Human Rights First,* May 2008, 6, http://www.humanrightsfirst.info/pdf/080521-USLS-pursuit-justice.pdf.

7. Memorandum Opinion, July 11, 2002, 42; Chesney, "Sleeper Scenario," 52–57.

8. "Court to Hear Case on Material Support for Terrorists," First Amendment Center, October 1, 2009, http://www.firstamendmentcenter

.org/analysis.aspx?id=22144; Opening Brief for Humanitarian Law Project, et al., November 16, 2009, Humanitarian Law Project v. Holder (U.S. Supreme Court) (Nos. 08-1498 and 09-89, on writs of certiorari), 17; Brief for the Respondents, December 22, 2009, Humanitarian Law Project v. Holder (U.S. Supreme Court) (Nos. 08-1498 and 09-89, on writs of certiorari), 16.

9. "'I Plead Guilty,' Taliban American Says," CNN, July 15, 2002, http://archives.cnn.com/2002/LAW/07/15/walker.lindh.hearing/.

10. Plea agreement, July 15, 2002, U.S. v. Lindh (E.D. Va.) (No. CR 02-37A).

Chapter 18: Guilty

1. "Biography of Judge Leonie M. Brinkema," Federal Judicial Center, http://www.fjc.gov/public/home.nsf/hisj; "Eastern District of Virginia, A Brief History," U.S. Department of Justice, http://www.justice.gov/usao/vae/ourhistory.html; Toni Locy, "Moussaoui Clash Tests Future of Terror Trials," *USA Today,* July 20, 2003, http://www.usatoday.com/news/nation/2003–07–20-moussaoui-usat_x.htm.

2. Transcript, Pre-Indictment Plea Hearing," May 1, 2003, U.S. v. Faris (E.D. Va.) (No. 03-CR-189), 4; Transcript, Motions and Sentencing Hearing, October 28, 2003, U.S. v. Faris (E.D. Va.) (No. 03-CR-189), 32; FBI Special Agent Mike Brooks, e-mail to author, March 24, 2010.

3. Transcript, Pre-Indictment Plea Hearing, May 1, 2003, 16.

4. Ibid., 17.

5. Ibid., 21, 23.

6. Ibid., 40.

Chapter 19: A Secret, Double Life

1. Notice of Motion and Motion for an Order Compelling Discovery Related to Informant Mehmet Aydinbelge, February 21, 2007, U.S. v. Abdi (S.D. Ohio) (No. 2-04-CR-88), 2 i; Opinion and Order, September 12, 2005, U.S. v. Abdi (S.D. Ohio) (No. 2-04-CR-88), 2, 11; FBI 302, summary of interviews with Iyman Faris between March 20, 2003, and May 1, 2003, contained in pages 162–205 of Joint Appendix, attachment to Brief of Appellant, February 2, 2004, U.S. v. Faris (4th Cir.) (No. 03-4865), 25; Declaration of Iyman Faris in Support of Motion to Vacate Conviction under 28 U.S.C. 2255, attachment to Motion to Vacate Conviction under 28 U.S.C. 2255, February 3, 2006, U.S. v. Faris 2006 (E.D. Va.) (1:06-CV-132) and (E.D. Va.) (1:03-CR-189) (consolidated

actions), 11–12; University Relations at Ohio State University, e-mail to author, August 25, 2009.

2. Transcript, Pre-Indictment Plea Hearing, May 1, 2003, U.S. v. Faris (E.D. Va.) (No. 03-CR-189), 43.

3. Opposition of the United States to Petitioner's Motion to Vacate Judgment of Conviction under 2255, April 10, 2006, U.S. v. Faris 2006 (E.D. Va.) (1:06-CV-132) and (E.D. Va.) (1:03-CR-189) (consolidated actions), 10; Transcript of Telephone Conference, June 19, 2003, U.S. v. Abdi (E.D. Va.) (No. 03-CR-189), 2–3; Transcript, Motions and Sentencing Hearing, October 28, 2003, U.S. v. Faris (E.D. Va.) (No. 03-CR-189), 5.

4. Transcript, Telephone Conference, June 19, 2003, 6–7.

5. Ibid., 5.

6. Ibid., 5, 9.

7. John Ashcroft, "Prepared Remarks of Attorney General John Ashcroft, Plea Agreement Announcement," June 19, 2003, U.S. Department of Justice, http://www.usdoj.gov/ag/speeches/2003/remarks_061903.htm.

8. Associated Press, "Ohio Truck Driver Pleads Guilty to Terror Charges," June 20, 2003, AP Electronic Archives; Transcript, Geneva Bowling interview on *Good Morning America*, June 26, 2003; "Man's Ex-Wife and Stepson Shocked by Revelation," *Columbus Dispatch*, June 20, 2003; Negla Ross, interview by author, December 17, 2009; Jonathan Riskind and Jack Torry, "Columbus Truck Driver Admits Helping Terrorists Plot Attacks on American Soil," *Columbus Dispatch*, June 20, 2003.

9. Declaration of Iyman Faris, February 3, 2006, 23; Brief of Appellant, February 2, 2004, U.S. v. Faris (4th Cir.) (No. 03-4865), 8; Declaration of Jack Vanderstoep, exhibit filed with Opposition of the United States to Petitioner's Motion to Vacate Judgment of Conviction under 2255, April 10, 2006, Faris v. U.S. 2006 (E.D. Va.) (1:06-CV-132) and (E.D. Va.) (1:03-CR-189) (consolidated actions), 6–7.

10. Brief of Appellant, February 2, 2004, 20; Reply Brief of Appellant, March 26, 2004, U.S. v. Faris (4th Cir.) (No. 03-4865), 24.

11. Motion to Determine Defendant's Mental Competency, July 24, 2003, U.S. v. Abdi (E.D. Va.) (No. CR-03-189), 1–2.

12. Brief of Appellant, February 2, 2004, 9; Transcript, Motions and Sentencing Hearing, October 28, 2003, 11–13.

13. Statement of Facts, May 1, 2003, U.S. v. Faris (E.D. Va.) (No. CR 03-189), 4.

14. FBI 302, summary of interviews with Iyman Faris, 42.

15. Transcript, Motions and Sentencing Hearing, October 28, 2003, 15.

16. Brief for the United States, March 11, 2004, U.S. v. Faris (4th Cir.) (No. 03-4865), 10–11, 24.

17. Transcript, Motions and Sentencing Hearing, October 28, 2003, 14, 17.

18. Ibid., 6.

19. Ibid., 4, 23.

20. Transcript, Motions and Sentencing Hearing, October 28, 2003, 40.

21. Toni Locy, "Moussaoui Clash Tests Future of Terror Trials," *USA Today*, July 20, 2003, http://www.usatoday.com/news/nation/2003–07–20-moussaoui-usat_x.htm.

22. Transcript, Motions and Sentencing Hearing, October 28, 2003, 4, 35.

23. Ibid., 4, 42.

24. Ibid., 4, 43.

Chapter 20: Get This Done

1. Opinion, September 22, 2006, U.S. v. Abdi (6th Cir.) (No. 05-4199), 3; Government's Response to Motion of Defendant to Suppress All Statements Allegedly Made by the Defendant and All Evidence Seized in Violation of the Fourth Amendment, July 1, 2005, U.S. v. Abdi, 4–5; Kaltun Karani, interview by author, January 26, 2010; Articles of Incorporation, Cell Station LLC, Ohio Secretary of State, http://www.sos.state.oh.us/businessServices.aspx.

2. Mohamed Warsame, interview by author, May 23, 2010.

3. Opinion, September 22, 2006, U.S. v. Abdi (6th Cir.) (No. 05-4199), 3.

4. Opinion and Order, September 12, 2005, United States v. Abdi, 4, 15.

5. Mike Brooks and Kevin Cornelius, interview by author, March 9, 2010; FBI-302 interview with Abdi, transcribed December 1, 2003, attachment to Memorandum of Points and Authorities in Support of Defendant's Request for a *James* Hearing and Motion in Limine to Preclude Inadmissible Hearsay Statements of Alleged Co-Conspirators, September 7, 2005, U.S. v. Abdi (S.D. Ohio) (No. 2-04-CR-88), 4.

6. Opinion and Order, September 12, 2005, U.S. v. Abdi, 3–4; Opinion, September 22, 2006, U.S. v. Abdi (6th Cir.) (No. 05-4199), 7–8, 15;

Brooks and Cornelius, interview by author, March 9, 2010; Brooks e-mail to author, May 27, 2010.

7. Brooks and Cornelius, interview by author, March 9, 2010.

8. Memorandum of Points and Authorities in Support of Defendant's Motions in Limine to Preclude Evidence, September 2, 2005, U.S. v. Abdi (S.D. Ohio) (No. 2-04-CR-88), 2, 7; Notice of Motion and Motion to Compel Discovery as to Nuradin M. Abdi, April 25, 2005, U.S. v. Abdi (S.D. Ohio) (No. 2-04-CR-88), 4–5, 7; Government's Proposed Exhibit List, June 7, 2007, U.S. v. Abdi (S.D. Ohio) (No. 2-04-CR-88), 1–2; Notice of Exhibits D-1 to D-5 in Connection to Second Motion in Limine as to Nuradin M. Abdi, September 7, 2005, U.S. v. Abdi (S.D. Ohio) (No. 2-04-CR-88).

9. Motion to Suppress Statements for Violations of Defendant's Fifth Amendment Rights by Nuradin M. Abdi, June 1, 2005, U.S. v. Abdi (S.D. Ohio) (No. 2-04-CR-88) Exhibit A, 3–4, 6; Brooks and Cornelius, interview by author, March 9, 2010.

10. Memorandum of Points and Authorities in Support of Motion to Suppress All Statements Allegedly Made by Defendant and All Evidence Seized, May 18, 2005, U.S. v. Abdi (S.D. Ohio) (No. 2-04-CR-88), Exhibit H; Opinion, September 22, 2006, U.S. v. Abdi (6th Cir.) (No. 05-4199), 4–5.

Chapter 21: Shopping Mall Plot

1. Douglas Weigle, interview by author, August 20, 2009.

2. Opinion and Order, September 12, 2005, U.S. v. Abdi (S.D. Ohio) (No. 2-04-CV-88), 6–7; United States' Response to Defendant's Motions to Suppress Statements for Violations of Defendant's Fifth Amendment Rights and to Dismiss for Outrageous Government Misconduct, July 1, 2005, U.S. v. Abdi (S.D. Ohio) (No. 2-04-CV-88), 5; Abdulkadir Ali, interview by author, January 14, 2010.

3. Opinion and Order, September 12, 2005, 7.

4. Tamara Audi, "Man's Fate Decided in Secret Hearing; Deportation Is Ordered; His Family Lacks Details," *Detroit Free Press*, March 10, 2004.

5. Government's Response to Defendant's Consolidated Motion in Limine to Exclude Statements and Evidence and Preclude Evidence from the Jury Room, June 12, 2007, U.S. v. Abdi (S.D. Ohio) (No. 2-04-CR-88), 4–5.

6. Opinion and Order, September 12, 2005, 8; United States' Response to Defendant's Motions to Suppress Statements for Violations of Defendant's Fifth Amendment Rights and to Dismiss for

Outrageous Government Misconduct, July 1, 2005, U.S. v. Abdi (No. 2-04-CV-88), 16.

7. Tamara Audi, "Somali Defendant Issues United States a Challenge; He Waives Appeal, to Force Quick Deportation," *Detroit Free Press,* March 11, 2004; Doug Weigle, e-mail to author, December 8, 2009.

8. Kaltun Karani, interview by author, January 26, 2010.

9. Yusuf Abucar, interview by author, November 28, 2007.

10. Ibid.

11. Opinion and Order, September 12, 2005, 8; Weigle interview, August 20, 2009; Associated Press, "Convicted Shopping Mall Terrorist Turned Down Generous Plea Deal," November 27, 2007, AP Electronic Archives; "Sahim Alwan Sentenced For Providing Material Support to Al Qaeda," U.S. Justice Department news release, December 17, 2003, http://www.justice.gov/opa/pr/2003/December/03_crm_699.htm.

12. Opinion and Order, September 12, 2005, 8; "Abuse of Iraqi POWs by GIs Probed," 60 Minutes II, http://www.cbsnews.com/stories/2004/04/27/60II/main614063.shtml; *New Yorker* article: http://www.newyorker.com/archive/2004/05/10/040510fa_fact.

13. Opinion and Order, September 12, 2005, 8–9; Encarnacion Pyle, "Family Says Suspect Loves U.S. but Is Being Mistreated as Part of 'Witch Hunt,'" *Columbus Dispatch,* June 15, 2004.

14. Ashcroft, Mueller news conference, May 26, 2004, http://www.cnn.com/2004/US/05/26/terror.threat.transcript/.

15. Opinion and Order, September 12, 2005, 9.

16. Justice Department news release.

17. Opinion and Order, September 12, 2005, 9; Kevin Mayhood, Jonathan Riskind, and Robert Ruth, "Mall Was Target, U.S. Says," *Columbus Dispatch,* June 15, 2004; June 14, 2004, hearing attended by author; Associated Press, "Magistrate Orders Competency Evaluation for Suspect in Shopping Mall Plot," June 16, 2004, AP Electronic Archives; Cell Station Dissolution, Limited Liability Company, dissolution paper for Cell Station LLC, Ohio Secretary of State, http://www.sos.state.oh.us/businessServices.aspx; Karani interview, January 26, 2010.

18. Opinion and Order, September 12, 2005, 9–10; Kevin Mayhood, "FBI Investigates Whether Jailed Somali Abused," *Columbus Dispatch,* September 4, 2004; Memorandum of Points and Authorities in Support of Consolidated Motion in Limine to Exclude Statements and Evidence and Preclude Evidence from the Jury Room, June 7, 2007, U.S. v. Abdi (S.D. Ohio) (No. 2-04-CR-88), 4; Order as to Nuradin M. Abdi Finding the Defendant Competent to Stand Trial, January 11, 2005, U.S. v. Abdi (S.D. Ohio) (No. 2-04-CR-88), 1–2.

Chapter 22: A Symphony of Unfairness

1. Brief of Appellant, February 2, 2004, U.S. v. Faris (4th Cir.) (No. 03-4865), 16.

2. Ibid., i, ii, 11, 16, 18, 20, 22.

3. Brief for the United States, March 11, 2004, U.S. v. Faris (4th Cir.) (No. 03-4865), 13.

4. Ibid., 36, 50.

5. Brief of Appellant, February 2, 2004, 4.

6. Brief for the United States, March 11, 2004, 21.

7. Judgment, July 19, 2004, U.S. v. Faris (4th Cir.) (No. 03-4865), 6.

8. Ibid, 7–8.

Chapter 23: Life Goes On

1. Mark Ellwood, interview by author, December 1, 2009.

2. Jeff Bringardner, interview by author, February 8, 2010.

3. Noorgul Dada, interview by author, September 3, 2008; Government's Proposed Exhibit List, June 7, 2007, U.S. v. Abdi (S.D. Ohio) (No. 2-04-CR-88), 4–5; Indictment, April 11, 2007, U.S. v. Paul (S.D. Ohio) (No. 2-07-CR-87), 8–10.

Chapter 24: Atypical Psychosis

1. Associated Press, "Kerry Speaks in Forum Where Bush in 2002 Made His Case against Iraq," September 8, 2004, AP Electronic Archives; Associated Press, "President to Visit Republican Stronghold in Southwest Ohio," September 24, 2004, AP Electronic Archives.

2. Opinion and Order, September 12, 2005, United States v. Abdi (S.D. Ohio) (No. 2-04-CV-88), 9–10; Kaltun Karani, interview by author, January 26, 2010.

3. Memorandum of Points and Authorities in Support of Motion to Suppress All Statements Allegedly Made by Defendant and All Evidence Seized, May 18, 2005, U.S. v. Abdi (S.D. Ohio) (No. 2-04-CR-88), Exhibit A, 2–3.

4. James Nelson, Department of Psychology, Valparaiso University, class notes, ttp://faculty.valpo.edu/jnelson/CCWebPage/Notes/CBPPOL.html.

Chapter 25: Radical Role Playing

1. Associated Press, "Informant Says Toledo Terror Suspects Weren't His Initial Targets," April 2, 2008, AP Electronic Archives;

Institute for Preventive Strategies at the Center for Rural Development, "Preventing Jihad in Toledo," case study of Toledo terror case, Somerset, Kentucky, June 22, 2006, https://www.preventivestrategies.net/public/library_file_proxy.cfm?lid=37; Erica Blake, "'The Trainer' Begins Terror Trial Testimony," *Toledo Blade,* April 3, 2008, http://www.toledoblade.com/apps/pbcs.dll/article?AID=/20080403/NEWS02/804030361/-1/NEWS, 10–12.

2. Tarunjit Singh Butalia and Dianne P. Small, eds., *Religion in Ohio: Profile of Faith Communities* (Athens: Ohio University Press, 2004), 289–90.

3. "Three Men Charged with Conspiring to Commit Terrorist Acts Overseas, Providing Material Support to Terrorists," Justice Department news release, February 21, 2006, http://cleveland.fbi.gov/dojpressrel/2006/terrorists022106.htm; Associated Press, "Dad Says Son's Trip to Jordan Was for Business, Not Terror," May 27, 2008, AP Electronic Archives.

4. Superseding Indictment, February 7, 2007, U.S. v. Amawi et al. (N. D. Ohio) (No. 3-06-CR-719), 6–9; Associated Press, "Informant Says"; Associated Press, "Informant: 3 Accused in Plot Had Little Contact," April 23, 2008, AP Electronic Archives; Institute for Preventive Strategies, "Preventing Jihad in Toledo," 3–4; Blake, "'Trainer' Begins Terror Trial Testimony."

5. Superseding Indictment, February 7, 2007, 10–12.

6. Marwin El Hindi's Motion to Compel the Government to Identify Darren Griffin's Handler (AKA "The Boss"), August 15, 2007, U.S. v. El Hindi (N.D. Ohio) (No. 3-06-CR-719), 3; Associated Press, "Man in US Terror Case Says He Was Framed," October 20, 2009, AP Electronic Archives.

7. John Ashcroft, "Remarks of Attorney General John Ashcroft," October 4, 2002, http://www.usdoj.gov/archive/ag/speeches/2002/100402agnewsconferenceportlandcell.htm; Mark Larabee, Bryan Denson, and Maxine Bernstein, "Informant in Terror Case Revealed," *Oregonian,* October 30, 2002; Associated Press, "Two Defendants in Portland Terrorism Case Plead Guilty," October 16, 2003, AP Electronic Archives; Brief of Amici Curiae in Support of Defendants' Motion to Suppress Foreign Intelligence Surveillance Evidence, September 18, 2003, U.S. v. Battle et al. (D. Oregon) (No. 02-CR-399), 15.

8. "Seven Florida Men Charged with Conspiring to Support Al Qaeda, Attack Targets in the United States," Justice Department news release, June 23, 2006, http://miami.fbi.gov/dojpressrel/pressrel06

/mm20060623.htm; Vanessa Blum, "Liberty City 6 Case to Get Third Trial," *South Florida Sun-Sentinel,* April 24, 2008; Carmen Gentile, "Six Suspects Will Be Tried a Third Time in Sears Plot," *New York Times,* April 24, 2008.

9. "Six Individuals Charged with Plotting to Murder U.S. Soldiers at New Jersey Military Base," Justice Department news release, May 8, 2007, http://newark.fbi.gov/dojpressrel/2007/nk050807.htm; Associated Press, "6 Accused of Planning Attack on Fort Dix in New Jersey Plead Not Guilty," June 14, 2007, AP Electronic Archives; Omnibus Pretrial Motions and Brief on Behalf of Defendant Eljvir Duka, June 20, 2008, U.S. v. Duka (D. N.J.) (No. 07-CR-459), 30–31; NPR, "Fort Dix Convictions Seem to Validate FBI Strategy," NPR, December 23, 2008, http://www.npr.org/templates/story/story.php?storyId=98622766; Kevin Whitmer, "Fort Dix Five Guilty of Conspiracy to Kill Soldiers," *New Jersey Star-Ledger,* December 22, 2008, http://www.nj.com/news/index.ssf/2008/12/shell_fort_dix.html.

10. Marwan El Hindi's Motion to Compel the Government to Identify Darren Griffin's Handler (a.k.a. "The Boss"), August 15, 2007, U.S. v. El Hindi (N.D. Ohio) (No. 3-06-CR-719), 3; "Closing Arguments Continue in Terror Trial," FOX Toledo WUPW-TV, June 6, 2008, http://www.foxtoledo.com/dpp/news/Closing_arguments_continue_in_Terror_Trial; Julia Shearson, interview by author, December 17, 2009.

11. Chris Shields, Kelly Damphousse, and Brent Smith, "An Assessment of Defense and Prosecutorial Strategies in Terrorism Trials: Implications for State and Federal Prosecutors," 2008 research report submitted to the U.S. Department of Justice, http://www.ncjrs.gov/pdffiles1/nij/grants/228276.pdf, 134.

12. Associated Press, "Federal Prosecutor Seeks Reports of Mosque Spying," April 30, 2009, AP Electronic Archives.

Chapter 26: American Soil

1. "President Discusses Patriot Act," Ohio State Highway Patrol Academy, Columbus, Ohio, June 9, 2005, http://georgewbush-whitehouse.archives.gov/news/releases/2005/06/20050609–2.html.

2. Ibid.

3. Declaration of Iyman Faris in Support of Motion to Vacate Conviction under 28 U.S.C. 2255, attachment to Motion to Vacate Conviction under 28 U.S.C. 2255, February 3, 2006, U.S. v. Faris 2006 (E.D. Va.) (1:06-CV-132) and (E.D. Va.) (1:03-CR-189) (consolidated actions), 2.

Chapter 27: Bureaucratic Sloth

1. Memorandum of Points and Authorities in Support of Motion to Suppress All Statements Allegedly Made by Defendant and All Evidence Seized, May 18, 2005, U.S. v. Abdi (S.D. Ohio) (No. 2-04-CR-88), 10–14.

2. Memorandum of Points and Authorities in Support of Second Motion to Dismiss Count One, February 21, 2007, U.S. v. Abdi (S.D. Ohio) (No. 2-04-CR-88), 9.

3. Memorandum of Points and Authorities in Support of Second Motion to Dismiss Count One, 15.

4. Government's Response to Motion of Defendant to Suppress All Statements Allegedly Made by the Defendant and All Evidence Seized in Violation of the Fourth Amendment, U.S. v. Abdi, July 1, 2005 (S.D. Ohio) (No. 2-04-CR-88), 2, 33.

5. Ibid., 15–16.

6. Kevin Mayhood, "Judge Questions Lack of Warrant in Terrorism Arrest," *Columbus Dispatch,* August 26, 2005.

7. Government's Response to Defendant's Consolidated Motion in Limine to Exclude Statements and Evidence and Preclude Evidence from the Jury Room, June 12, 2007, U.S. v. Abdi (S.D. Ohio) (No. 2-04-CR-88), 8–9.

8. Opinion and Order, September 12, 2005, United States v. Abdi (S.D. Ohio) (No. 2-04-CV-88), 13–14.

9. Ibid., 15.

10. Ibid., 19.

11. Ibid., 23.

12. United States' Response to Defendant's Motions to Suppress Statements for Violations of Defendant's Fifth Amendment Rights and to Dismiss for Outrageous Government Misconduct, July 1, 2005, U.S. v. Abdi (S.D. Ohio) (No. 2-04-CV-88), 22.

Chapter 28: Dirty Numbers

1. James Risen and Eric Lichtblau, "Bush Lets U.S. Spy on Callers without Courts," *New York Times,* December 16, 2005.

2. Ibid.

3. James Risen and Eric Lichtblau, "Defense Lawyers in Terror Cases Plan Challenges over Spy Efforts," *New York Times,* December 28, 2005; "Lawyers: Did NSA Snoop on Suspects?" CNN, December 28, 2005, http://www.cnn.com/2005/LAW/12/28/lawyers.spying/index.html.

4. "Lawyers: Did NSA Snoop on Suspects?"

5. Declaration of Iyman Faris in Support of Motion to Vacate Conviction under 28 U.S.C. 2255, attachment to Motion to Vacate Conviction under 28 U.S.C. 2255, February 3, 2006, U.S. v. Faris 2006 (E.D. Va.) (1:06-CV-132) and (E.D. Va.) (1:03-CR-189) (consolidated actions), 14.

6. Motion to Vacate Judgment of Conviction under 2255 and Memorandum of Law in Support of Motion to Vacate Judgment of Conviction under 2255, February 3, 2006, U.S. v. Faris (E.D. Va.) (1:06-CV-132) and (E.D. Va.) (1:03-CR-189) (consolidated actions).

7. Declaration of Frederick Sinclair, exhibit filed with Opposition of the United States to Petitioner's Motion to Vacate Judgment of Conviction under 2255, April 7, 2006, Faris v. U.S. (E.D. Va.) (1:06-CV-132) and (E.D. Va.) (1:03-CR-189) (consolidated actions).

8. Opposition of the United States to Petitioner's Motion to Vacate Judgment of Conviction under 2255, April 10, 2006, U.S. v. Faris (E.D. Va.) (1:06-CV-132) and (E.D. Va.) (1:03-CR-189) (consolidated actions), 1–2.

9. Ibid., 35–36.

10. Proof Opening Brief for the United States, December 14, 2005, U.S. v. Abdi (6th Cir.) (No. 05-4199), 17–18, 26–27, 40.

11. Brief of Appellee, March 6, 2006, U.S. v. Abdi (6th Cir.) (No. 05-4199), 11–12.

12. Opinion, September 22, 2006, U.S. v. Abdi (6th Cir.) (No. 05-4199), 9–10.

13. Ibid., 14.

14. Memorandum Order, November 7, 2006, U.S. v. Faris (E.D. Va.) (No. 1-03-CR-189), 10–12.

15. Ibid.

16. Ibid., 18.

Chapter 29: Disturbing Picture

1. Jennifer Nimer, interview by author, January 13, 2010; Mike Brooks and Kevin Cornelius, interview by author, March 9, 2010.

2. "FBI Works Tirelessly to Keep U.S. Safe," FBI press release, April 12, 2007, http://www.fbi.gov/pressrel/pressrel07/seattle_oped041207.htm.

3. Brooks and Cornelius, interview by author, March 9, 2010.

4. Associated Press, "Documents Say Ohio Man to Plead Guilty to Helping Terrorists," June 2, 2008, AP Electronic Archives; Mark Ellwood, interview by author, December 2, 2009.

5. Kevin Mayhood, Jodi Andes, and John Futty, "Local Web of Terror?" *Columbus Dispatch,* April 13, 2007; Associated Press, "Prosecutors Say Ohio Man in Alleged Bomb Plot Was Dedicated to al-Qaida," April 12, 2007.

6. Indictment, April 11, 2007, U.S. v. Paul (S.D. Ohio) (No. 2-07-CR-87), 12.

7. "France Arrests al-Qaeda Suspects," *BBC News,* June 6, 2003, http://news.bbc.co.uk/2/hi/europe/2967202.stm; "French Court Gives Terrorism Suspect 9-Year Sentence," *Voice of America News,* October 26, 2006, http://www.globalsecurity.org/security/library/news/2006/10/sec-061026-voa01.htm; "France Links German Suspect to al-Qaida," *Voice of America News,* June 11, 2003, http://www.globalsecurity.org/security/library/news/2003/06/sec-030611-voa02.htm; Donald Rumsfeld, *Known and Unknown: A Memoir* (New York: Sentinel, 2011), 580 n.

8. Mayhood, Andes, and Futty, "Local Web of Terror?"

9. Iyman Faris, statement to Combatant Status Review Tribunal, April 15, 2007, Verbatim Transcript of Combatant Status Review Tribunal Hearing for ISN 10020, http://www.defense.gov/news/transcript_ISN10020.pdf.

Chapter 30: The Ummah Is Angry

1. Writ of Habeas Corpus ad Testificandum Issued as to Iyman Faris for 8/6/2007 in Case as to Nuradin M. Abdi, July 23, 2007, U.S. v. Abdi (S.D. Ohio) (No. 2-04-CV-88).

2. Mahir Sherif, interview by author, July 19, 2007; Associated Press, "Terror Suspect to Call Convicted Terrorist as Witness," July 19, 2007, AP Electronic Archives.

3. Kaltun Karani, press conference attended by the author, July 5, 2007; Kaltun Karani, interview by author, January 26, 2010.

4. Order, July 23, 2007, U.S. v. Abdi (S.D. Ohio) (No. 2-04-CV-88), 36–38.

5. Ibid., 39.

6. Kaltun Karani, interview by author, January 26, 2010; Judgment in a Criminal Case, December 14, 2007, U.S. v. Abdi (S.D. Ohio) (No. 2-04-CR-88).

7. News conference attended by author, July 31, 2007.

8. Sentencing attended by author, November 27, 2007.

9. Ibid.

10. Ibid.

11. "Illinois Man Pleads Guilty in Foiled Plan to Set Off Grenades in Shopping Mall," U.S. Department of Justice news release, November 28, 2007, http://chicago.fbi.gov/dojpressrel/pressrel07/nov28_07.htm.

Chapter 31: Changing of the Guard

1. FBI 302, summary of interviews with Iyman Faris between March 20, 2003, and May 1, 2003, contained in pages 162–205 of Joint Appendix, attachment to Brief of Appellant, February 2, 2004, U.S. v. Faris (4th Cir.) (No. 03-4865), 13.

2. David Schanzer, Charles Kurzman, Ebrahim Moosa, "Anti-Terror Lessons of Muslim-Americans," January 6, 2010, National Criminal Justice Reference Service, http://www.ncjrs.gov/pdffiles1/nij/grants/229868.pdf.

3. Daniel Benjamin and Steven Simon, *The Age of Sacred Terror* (New York: Random House, 2002), 5, 15; Peter Bergen, *Holy War, Inc.: Inside the Secret World of Osama bin Laden* (New York: Free Press, 2001), 139; Joseph P. Fried, "Sheik Sentenced to Life in Prison in Bombing Plot," *New York Times,* January 18, 1996; Jason Burke, "Mujahideen Trained and Funded by the US Are among Its Deadliest Foes," *Guardian,* January 17, 1999, http://www.guardian.co.uk/world/1999/jan/17/yemen.islam.

4. Candace Heckman, "James Ujaama Speaks Out against Scrutiny," *Seattle Post-Intelligencer,* July 20, 2002, http://www.seattlepi.com/local/79438_statement20.shtml; Ujaama guilty plea, U.S. Justice Department press release, April 14, 2003, http://www.justice.gov/opa/pr/2003/April/03_crm_237.htm; Kevin James sentencing, FBI press release, March 6, 2009, http://losangeles.fbi.gov/dojpressrel/pressrel09/la030609ausa.htm; Williams sentencing, Justice Department news release, August 7, 2009, http://houston.fbi.gov/dojpressrel/pressrel09/ho080709.htm; Schanzer, Kurzman, and Moosa, "Anti-Terror Lessons of Muslim-Americans."

5. Paul plea hearing, June 3, 2008, attended by author.

6. Associated Press, "Alleged Terrorist in Ohio Gets 20 Years in Prison," February 26, 2009, AP Electronic Archives; John Futty, "Worthington Man Gets 20 Years in Terrorist Plot," *Columbus Dispatch,* February 26, 2009; Mounir Ayed, interview by author, February 24, 2009.

7. "Protecting America: National Task Force Wages War on Terror," FBI news release, August 19, 2008, http://www.fbi.gov/page2/august08/njttf_081908.html; Statement for the Record, Jonathan Turley, Hearing on the Executive Office of United States Attorneys,

House Subcommittee on the Commercial and Administrative Law, Committee on the Judiciary, June 25, 2008, http://judiciary.house.gov /hearings/pdf/Turley080625.pdf.

8. "FBI Works Tirelessly to Keep U.S. Safe," FBI news release, April 12, 2007, http://www.fbi.gov/pressrel/pressrel07/seattle_oped041207 .htm; "Defendant Found Guilty of Conspiracy to Support Terrorists," Justice Department news release, June 10, 2009, http://www.justice .gov/opa/pr/2009/June/09-nsd-572.html.

Conclusion

1. "Najibullah Zazi Indicted for Conspiracy to Use Explosives against Persons or Property in the United States," Justice Department news release, September 24, 2009, http://newyork.fbi.gov/dojpressrel /pressrel09/nyfo092409.htm; "Illinois Man Arrested in Plot to Bomb Courthouse and Murder Federal Employees," Justice Department news release, September 24, 2009, http://springfield.fbi.gov/dojpressrel /2009/si092409.htm; "FBI Arrests Jordanian Citizen for Attempting to Bomb Skyscraper in Downtown Dallas," Justice Department news release, September 24, 2009, http://dallas.fbi.gov/dojpressrel/pressrel09 /dl092409.htm.

2. "Seven Charged with Terrorism Violations in North Carolina," FBI news release, July 27, 2009, http://charlotte.fbi.gov/dojpressrel /2009/ce072709.htm.

3. Peter Bergen and Bruce Hoffman, "Assessing the Terrorist Threat," a report of the Bipartisan Policy Center's National Security Preparedness Group, September 10, 2010, http://www.bipartisanpolicy .org/library/report/assessing-terrorist-threat.

4. David Schanzer, Charles Kurzman, and Ebrahim Moosa, "Anti-Terror Lessons of Muslim Americans," January 6, 2010, National Criminal Justice Reference Service, http://www.ncjrs.gov/pdffiles1/njj/grants /229868.pdf, 11.

5. Robert Mueller, Congressional Testimony, Before the Senate Committee on the Judiciary, January 20, 2010, http://www.fbi.gov/congress /congress10/mueller012010.htm.

6. Carter Stewart, interview by author, November 13, 2009.

7. "Last Year Deadliest Yet for Afghan Civilians Caught in Conflict, Finds UN Report," UN News Centre news release, January 13, 2010, http://www.un.org/apps/news/story.asp?NewsID=33473&Cr =afghan&Cr1=; "Iraq Soldier Memorial," online database of Ohioans killed in Iraq and Afghanistan, http://www.cleveland.com/iraq/soldiers/;

"Afghanistan Condemns NATO Strike," *BBC News*, February 22, 2010, http://news.bbc.co.uk/2/hi/8528715.stm6; "Iraq Coalition Casualty Count," icasualties.org; Jeb Phillips, "It's Back to Work for Lima Company," *Columbus Dispatch*, January 29, 2010.

8. iCasualties, "Iraq Coalition Casualty Count," http://www.icasualties.org; Phillips, "It's Back to Work for Lima Company."

9. CorrsLink message from Nuradin Abdi to author, December 4, 2009; Kaltun Karani, e-mail to author, April 1, 2010; Complaint, March 30, 2010, Aref et al. v. Holder (D.D.C.) (No. 1-10-CV-00539).

10. Kaltun Karani, interview by author, January 25, 2010.

11. "Terror Charges Unsealed in Minneapolis against Eight Men, Justice Department Announces," Justice Department news release, November 23, 2009, http://www.justice.gov/opa/pr/2009/November/09-nsd-1267.html; U.S. Senate Foreign Relations Committee, *Al Qaeda in Yemen and Somalia: A Ticking Time Bomb* (Washington, D.C.: GPO, 2010), 9.

Bibliography

Benjamin, Daniel, and Steven Simon. *The Age of Sacred Terror.* New York: Random House, 2002.

Bergen, Peter L. *Holy War, Inc.: Inside the Secret World of Osama bin Laden.* New York: Free Press, 2001.

Burke, Jason. *Al-Qaeda: Casting a Shadow of Terror.* New York: I. B. Tauris, 2003.

Coll, Steve. *The Bin Ladens: An Arabian Family in the American Century.* New York: Penguin, 2008.

Emerson, Steven. *American Jihad: The Terrorists Living among Us.* New York: Free Press, Simon and Schuster, 2002.

Gannon, Kathy. *I Is for Infidel: From Holy War to Holy Terror; Eighteen Years inside Afghanistan.* New York: Public Affairs, 2005.

Gartenstein-Ross, Daveed. *My Year inside Radical Islam: A Memoir.* New York: Jeremy P. Tarcher, 2007.

Gunaratna, Rohan. *Inside Al Qaeda: Global Network of Terror.* New York: Columbia University Press, 2002.

National Commission on Terrorist Attacks upon the United States. *The 9/11 Commission Report: Final Report of the National Commission on Terrorist Attacks upon the United States.* New York: W. W. Norton, 2004.

Temple-Raston, Dina. *The Jihad Next Door: The Lackawanna Six and Rough Justice in an Age of Terror.* New York: Public Affairs, 2007.

Wright, Lawrence. *The Looming Tower: Al-Qaeda and the Road to 9/11.* New York: Alfred A. Knopf, 2006.

Index

Abdel-Rahman, Sheik Omar, 141
Abdi, Nuradin Mahamoud, 1–3, 38, 63, 65, 82
  in Africa, 44–45
  al-Qaida, 95, 98, 138–39
  arrest of, 11, 89
  arrival in Columbus, 40
  childhood in United Arab Emirates, 27
  coffee shop meeting, 59–60, 68, 85
  FBI, 68, 90–93, 95, 143
  ICE and debate over arrest, 90, 91, 93, 94–95
  indictment and prosecution, 98, 111, 120–22, 128–29, 136–38
  Iyman Faris, 96, 98, 101–2, 122–23, 136
  lawyer for, 142
  marriage to Safia Hussein Muse, 50
  mental health, 99, 106–7
  Christopher Paul, 42, 92, 96, 132–35
  plea deal and conviction, 96–97, 138–40, 143
  in prison, 149–50
  September 11, 55
Abdulmutallab, Umar Farouk, 147
Abel, Mark, 98
Abucar, Yusuf, 40, 140
Abu Ghraib, 97
Aden, 50
Afghan Arabs, 24, 30, 150
Afghanistan
  Nuradin Abdi, 2
  civilian deaths, 58–59, 148
  Iyman Faris, 5, 48, 118, 143
  John Walker Lindh, 73
  Christopher Paul, 28, 134
  Portland Cell, 113–14
  Russian invasion of, 24
  Mohammedou Ould Salahi, 29
  Soviet atrocities in, 22
  training camps in, 36, 43-44, 96
  James Ujaama, 142
  U.S. invasion of, 4, 11, 62, 121

African Americans
  history in Worthington, 20
  in terror training camps, 28, 141–42
African Methodist Episcopal Church, 20
Ahmed, Sheik Sherif Sheik, 8
Ahmed, Syed Haris, 76, 145
Akhras, Ahmad Al-, 99, 134
Alban, Glenn, 134
Aleppo, 27
Alexandria, Va., 68, 72, 83
Alexandria City Jail, 85
al-Farooq training camp, 29, 50, 73, 75, 105
Ali, Iyman al-Ibrahim al-, 31
al-Qaida, 58, 64–66, 97, 114, 121, 147
  Nuradin Abdi, 95, 98, 138–39
  creation and growth, 25, 29, 36, 37–38
  Iyman Faris, 69–71, 88–89, 101–2, 122
  government intelligence gathering on, 125, 135
  Saddam Hussein, 61, 64
  Tablighi Jamaat, 56
  Maqsood Khan, 47–48
  L'Hossaine Kherchtou, 141
  John Walker Lindh, 73
  linked to al-Shabab, 8
  North Carolina plot, 146
  Christopher Paul, 105, 133, 144
  training camp, 50
Al Quds Al Arabi, 37
al-Shabab, 8, 150
Alverson, Fred, 140
Alwan, Sahim, 96
Amawi, Mohammad, 112–13, 115
Ames, Aldrich, 79
Annan, Kofi, 59
Antiterrorism and Effective Death Penalty Act, 74
Apthorp, Sterling, 134
Archie, Troy, 115
Ashanti psychosis, 107

Ashcroft, John
  al-Qaida threats, 97–98
  Iyman Faris, 5, 84–85
  government's post–September 11
    strategy, 75, 78, 116
  Portland Cell, 113
Austria, 31
Aydinbelge, Mehmet, 32, 57, 64, 82, 120
Ayed, Mounir, 143
Aymanes Imports, 34
Azzam, Abdullah, 24–25, 28–29

Balkans, 42
Baltimore
  Ali Kahn, 48, 51, 66, 68
  Majid Khan, 57, 63–64, 85, 88
Barre, Mohamed Siad, 26–27
Bary, Rifqa, 8–9
Bashir, Frida Khanum, 36–38, 92, 104,
    133, 143
Batiste, Narsearl, 114
Battle, Jeffrey Leon, 141
Beit al-Ansar, 24, 28
Beit ur Salam, 29
Benson, Matt, 94, 98
Berg, Terrence, 116
Bewicke, Aurora, 139
bin Laden, Osama, 5, 57–58, 60, 62, 64
  al-Qaida, 37, 39
  Iyman Faris, 47–48, 63, 118, 141
  Maktab al-Khidamat, 24, 28
  Lackawanna Six, 50
  John Walker Lindh, 73
Binalshibh, Ramzi, 43–44, 79
Bipartisan Policy Center, 146
Birkhead, James, 20
Black Friday, 11, 89, 91, 107, 122–23
Bledsoe, Carlos. See Muhammed,
    Abdulhakim
Bledsoe, Melvin, 10
Bob Evans Restaurant, 64
Boggs, Danny, 129
Bosnia, 30–31, 38
Bosnian Defense Force, 30
Bowling, Geneva, 32–35, 46-47, 64, 85
Bowling, Michael, 32–34, 85
Bradley University, 70
Brinkema, Leonie, 79–80, 83–86, 88–89,
    100–101, 103
  Iyman Faris appeal, 126–27, 129–31
Brooklyn, 63

Brooklyn Bridge plot
  Iyman Faris, 5, 10, 80, 86–87, 101, 103
  Khalid Sheik Mohammed, 57, 63
  warrantless wiretapping, 125
Burr Oak State Park, 38, 144
Bush, Barbara, 61
Bush, George W., 5, 7
  Patriot Act, 117–19
  speech on Iraq war, 61–62, 64, 70, 98
  2004 presidential campaign, 106–7
  warrantless wiretap program, 125
Bush, Prescott, 61

Canada, 40–41, 43, 44
Capitol, U.S., 63
Caribou Café, 59, 68, 136, 139, 143
Cell Station, 90, 92, 99
Cell-U-Com, 41, 50, 68
Center for Constitutional Rights,
    75–76
Center on Law and Security, New York
    University, 6
Chapman, Seifullah, 125
Chechnya, 43
Cheney, Dick, 61, 106
Chicago, 114
Cincinnati, 61–62, 81, 127; FBI office in,
    3, 91, 93
Cincinnati Museum Center, 106
Circleville, 94–96, 107
Cleveland, 106
Clinton, Bill, 74, 79, 122
Cole, David, 75, 77
Cole, Guy, 129
Coleman, J. D., 119
Coleman, Michael, 119
Columbus, 4, 5, 32, 63, 84
  Nuradin Abdi, 41, 123
  President George W. Bush, 61
  Iyman Faris, 36, 118
  FBI office in, 2, 65
  John Kerry, 98, 106
  Abdulhakim Muhammed, 10, 146
  September 11, 55, 133, 147
  Somali community, 8, 151
Columbus Dispatch, 9, 55
Columbus State Community College,
    22, 38, 104
Congress, 5, 74, 77, 118–19, 144, 147
Corbin, John, 2, 92–93, 98
Cornelius, Kevin, 92

Council on American-Islamic Relations, Columbus chapter, 99, 132, 134
Croatia, 30
Dallas, skyscraper plot, 9, 146
Damas, Mike, 112
Damra, Fawaz, 7
Dar es Salaam, U.S. embassy bombing of, 39, 50
Davis, Jefferson, 79
Days Inn, 71
Dayton, 33, 61
Dayton Peace Accord, 30
Deek, Khalil Said Khalil, 36
Democratic National Convention, 97
Detroit, 32, 41, 95, 98, 138
  2002 terrorism case, 111
  Northwest Airlines Flight 253, 147
Dhahran, 37
Djerba, Tunisia, 135
Don Scott Field, 33
Dowdy, Robert, Sergeant, 4
Drug Enforcement Administration, 112
Dubai, 31
Dublin, Ohio, 65
Duisburg, University of, 29
Duka, Eljvir, 115
Duke University and the University of North Carolina at Chapel Hill, domestic terrorism study by, 6
Dulles International Airport, 40, 44

Eastern District of Virginia, U.S., 72, 76, 79, 127
Edwards, John, 106
Egyptian Islamic Jihad, 50
El-Hindi, Marwan Othman, 112–13, 115
Ellis, T. S., 76–78
Ellwood, Mark, 104, 134
Embassy Suites Hotel, 65–67
England, 37
Essen, 38
Ethiopia, 98
Ethiopian Airlines, 45

Fairfax, Va., 41
Faris, Iyman, 23, 36, 55, 142
  Nuradin Abdi, 3–4, 45, 91, 93, 98, 122–23
  Afghanistan, 25, 29
  al-Qaida, 5, 46–49, 69–71, 88–89, 101–2, 122

appeal, 100–103, 119, 127–31
  Mehmet Aydinbelge, 32, 57, 64, 82, 120
  Balkans, 30–31
  Osama bin Laden, 80, 118
  Brooklyn Bridge plot, 7, 63, 80, 82, 86–88, 148
  coffee shop plot, 11, 59–60, 68, 96
  FBI, 64–68, 70–72, 85–87, 126–28, 135
  Majid Khan, 51, 63–64, 66, 135
  Maqsood Khan, 23, 47–48, 51, 56–57, 85, 141
  mental health problems, 46, 86–88, 101
  Khalid Sheikh Mohammed, 66, 122, 136, 151
  Christopher Paul, 37, 42, 132–35
  plea, conviction, and sentencing, 79–87, 88–90, 121
  potential witness in Nuradin Abdi trial, 136–37
  warrantless wiretap program, 125–27
  written summary of case against, 100–102, 130
Farooq, al-. See al-Farooq training camp
FBI, 6, 9, 44, 55–56, 69, 83
  Nuradin Abdi, 68, 89–93, 95, 121–23
  Academy, 67
  Iyman Faris, 64–68, 70–72, 85–87, 126–28, 135
  Fort Dix plot, 114
  Patriot Act, 118, 133
  Christopher Paul, 132–33
  Portland Cell, 114
  Sears Tower case, 114
  September 11, 6, 75, 116, 144–45
  Toledo terror case, 111–12
  written summary of case against Faris, 100–102, 130
  Najibullah Zazi, 146
Federal Medical Center, 99
Fifth Amendment, 120, 123
Finton, Michael, 146
First Amendment, 74–77, 137
Florence, Colorado, 119, 132, 149
Flowers, Stephen, 2, 90–93
Ford, Patrice Lumumba, 141
Foreign Intelligence Surveillance Court, 125
Fort Dix plot, 7, 114
Fort Hood, 10, 146

Fourth Amendment, 120, 128
Fourth U.S. Circuit Court of Appeals, 102, 126
Franklin County Correction Center, 99, 122, 131, 137, 139
Franklin County Probate Court, 28, 36
Frost, Gregory, 142–43

G-8 Summit, 97
Ganczarski, Christian, 135
Gardez, Afghanistan, 29
Germany, 38, 43–44, 134, 144
    Nuradin Abdi, 98
    Mohammedou Ould Salahi, 29
Gilani, Daood. *See* Headley, David
Gilbert, Jim, 142
Global Mall, 90
Good Morning America, 85
Griffin, Darren, 111–13, 115
Guantanamo Bay, 64, 70–72, 86, 100, 102, 119
    Majid Khan, 132, 135
    Donald Rumsfeld, 135
Gulf War, 61–62

Hacker, Elizabeth, 95–96
Hahnert, Robyn Jones, 139
Hamburg cell, 44
Hamdi, Yaser, 70–71
Hammerstrom, Neil, 68–69, 72, 83, 88, 101–2
Hampton-El, Clement, 141
Hanssen, Robert, 79, 148
Harakat ul-Mujahideen, 73
Hartsough, LaTisha, 64–66, 92, 142
Hasan, Nidal Malik, 10, 146
Hayat, Hamid, 76
Headley, David, 37, 147
Hersh, Seymour, 97
Herzegovina, 30
Hezbollah, 75
Hilliard, 33
Holder, Eric, 148
Hoover Dam, 11, 60
Humanitarian Law Project v. Reno, 76
Human Rights Watch, 6, 59
Hussein, Saddam, 29, 61–62, 64

Ifo refugee camp, 41
Immigration and Customs Enforcement (ICE), 2, 89–94, 97, 121–23, 129

Immigration and Naturalization Service (INS), 41–42
informants, 111, 114–16
Intelligence Reform and Terrorism Prevention Act, 77
International Emergency Economic Powers Act, 73–74
Iran, 30
Iraq
    Abu Ghraib scandal, 97
    President Bush's push for war, 61–62, 64–65, 106
    Lima Company, 119, 148
    Toledo plot, 113
Iraqis, immigrants to Columbus, 17
Islamic Center of Greater Toledo, 112
Islamic Foundation of Central Ohio, 16
Islamic Society of Greater Columbus, 17
Israel, 62
Istanbul, 30
Ittihad al-Islamiya, al-, 44

Jarrah, Ziad, 44
Jenhawi, Hisham, 134
JFK Airport, 82
JFK plot, 7
Joint Terrorism Task Force; in Columbus, 92
Jordan, 36, 113
Justice, Department of, 69, 75, 79, 114, 147

Kabul, 59
Kaczynski, Ted, 149
Kagan, Elena, 77
Kakarak, 58
Kampala, 44
Kandahar, 47–48, 50, 59
Karachi, 47–48, 56, 64
Karani, Kaltun, 137
Karzai, Hamid, 58
Kashmir, 23, 56, 73
Kaster, Joseph, 69, 88, 102
Keller, Jennifer, 65–66, 71
Kenton County Detention Center, 3, 93, 95, 139
Kentucky, 32–33, 92–93, 123
Kenya, 27, 37, 41, 44
Kenyatta, Abdulmalek. *See* Paul, Christopher
Kenyon College, 106

Kerry, John, 7, 98, 106–7
Khan, Ali, 48, 51, 63, 68
Khan, Majid, 51, 57, 63–64, 68, 85, 88
    military tribunal in Guantanamo,
        132, 135
Khan, Maqsood
    Iyman Faris, 23, 29, 56–57, 81, 85, 143
    Ali Khan, 51
    terrorist training camp, 47–48, 141
Kherchtou, L'Hossaine, 141
Khobar Towers, 37
Kilbourn, James, 20
KindHearts, 112
Kismayu, 96
Kosovo, 42–43
KSM. *See* Khalid Sheikh Mohammed.
Kunduz, 73
Kurdistan Workers Party, 76
Kurds, 62
Kuwait, Iraqi invasion of, 29

Lackawanna Six, 50, 56, 96, 125
    government example of alleged
        domestic terrorists, 4, 6, 70
    material support statute, 75, 84
Lane Aviation, 66
Laws, Arnetta, 21
Laws, Ernest, 20–21
Laws, Esther, 20
Laws, Khadija, 38, 104, 133
Laws, Paul Kenyatta. *See* Paul,
    Christopher
Laws, Sandra, 21
Laws, Virdre, 20
Lebanon, 112
Liberation Tigers of Tamil Eelam, 76
Liberty City Seven, 76, 114, 116
Lima Company, 119, 148
Lindh, John Walker, 73, 76, 78
Lindner, Carl, 61
Little Rock, Ark., recruitment center
    attack, 9, 146
London, England, 119
London, Ontario, 40
Los Angeles International Airport, 44

Maktab al-Khidamat, 24
Marbley, Algenon, 106-107, 122-124, 128,
    136-139
Marietta, alleged terrorism cell phone
    plot, 7

Marines, U.S., 119, 148
Marion, Ill., 149
Marri, Ali al-, 70–71
Marriott, 64
Ma'sadat al-Ansar, 24
Masjid Ibn Taymia, 1, 41, 65, 90
Material Support statute, 4, 6–7, 10,
        73–78, 84, 144
    Nuradin Abdi, 98, 137–38
    Iyman Faris, 71, 80–81, 88
    John Walker Lindh, 73, 78
    Christopher Paul, 142
    Portland cell, 114
    Toledo plot, 113
Mauritania, 29
Mazar-e-Sharif, 73
Mazloum, Zand Wassim, 112, 115
McCammon, Virginia Laws, 22
McConnellsville, Ohio, 4
McVeigh, Timothy, 149
Mecca, 43, 46, 98
Medellin, Robert, 2, 3, 11, 93–94
Mehdi, Karim, 29–30, 38, 43, 134–35
Mexico, 4, 41, 68
Minneapolis, 150
Minnesota, 151
Mir, Hamid, 141
Miranda warnings
    Nuradin Abdi, 2, 92–93, 121
    Iyman Faris, 67
Moayad, Mohammed Ali al-, 76
Mogadishu, 96
Mohammed, Khalid Sheikh, 5, 63,
        82, 141
    Iyman Faris, 48, 56–57, 63–66, 121–22,
        136, 151
    Majid Khan, 51, 135
Mostafa, Khalid Ibrahim, 114
Moussaoui, Zacarias, 79, 88, 149
MSNBC Online, 83
Mueller, Robert, 6, 97, 147
Muhammed, Abdulhakim, 9–10, 146
Mumbai, terrorist attack on, 37, 147
Muse, Safia Hussein, 2, 50, 149
Musharraf, Pervez, 51, 135
Muslim Brotherhood, 24
Muslim community, Ohio, 8, 15–16,
        111–12, 133
Muslims, 111
Muslim Student Association, 17

Nahmias, David, 145
Nairobi, U.S. embassy, bombing of, 36, 38–39; 44, 50
Nasser, Gamal, 24
National Commission on Terrorist Attacks upon the United States, 74
National Guard, 4
National Security Agency, 125–27, 130
National Security Service, Somalia, 26
NATO, 148
Newsweek, 64, 83, 127
New York City, 31, 57, 64
   backpack plot, 7, 9, 146
   Brooklyn Bridge plot, 63, 86
New Yorker, 97
New York Times, 125
Nimer, Jennifer, 132
Ninth U.S. Circuit Court of Appeals, 75, 77
No Child Left Behind, 61
Noor Cultural Islamic Center, 148
North Carolina, 75, 146
Northern Alliance, 70, 73
Northwest Airlines Flight 253, 10
Nur, Mohamoud Abdi, 26

Obama, Barack, 77
Odeh, Mohamed, 36
Ogaden, Ethiopia, 43–44
Ohio
   Iraq and Afghanistan wars, 148
   political bellwether, 7, 61
   2004 presidential campaign, 98,106–7
Ohio Historical Society, 150–51
Ohio State University, 15, 21, 32–33
Oklahoma City, 74
Old Williamsburg Candle Company, 63
Omar Ibnelkhttab Mosque, 15–18, 22, 57, 65
   Nuradin Abdi, 41
   Iyman Faris, 33–34
   Christopher Paul, 132–33, 143
"One Percent Doctrine," 117, 145
Operation Rolling Thunder, 59

Padilla, Jose, 70–71, 76, 125, 130
Pakistan, 23, 56
   arrest of suburban Washington residents, 147
   Columbus immigrants from, 15, 32
   Harakat ul-Mujahideen, 73

Iyman Faris, 5, 33, 35, 47–49, 51, 85
Iyman Faris's relatives, 66, 72, 83
Christopher Paul, 28–29
terrorist camps, 6, 76
Park of Roses, Columbus city park, 16, 42
Patriot Act, 7, 77, 117–19, 133
Paul, Christopher
   Nuradin Abdi, 42, 92, 96; 45, 98, 135–137
   Afghanistan, 28, 134
   al-Qaida, 105, 133, 144
   Frida Bashir, 36
   as black convert, 141
   coffee shop meeting, 59-60
   in Columbus, 38, 63, 104
   Iyman Faris, 42, 46, 132, 135
   FBI, 132–33
   gymnast, 19, 21
   name changed to Abdulmalek Kenyatta, 28
   Pakistan, 28–29
   in prison, 149
   prosecution, 134, 142–43
   Mohammedou Ould Salahi, 50, 135
   September 11, 55
   Vienna, 30
Pentagon, 59
Peshawar, 29
Peters, Dana, 66, 72, 99, 121–22, 124
Phillips, Robert T. M., 107
Pickaway County Jail, 94–97, 139
Pittsburgh, 60, 144
Polaris Fashion Place, 1, 68
Port Angeles, Washington, 44
Port Columbus International Airport, 44, 60
Portland Cell, 4, 70, 113, 125, 141

Qaida, al-. *See* al-Qaida
Qatar, 60, 70
Quantico, 67–70, 72, 86, 89, 100
Quetta, 47
Qutb, Sayyid, 24

Ratner, Richard, 85, 87
Rauf, Mohammed. *See* Faris, Iyman
Rawalpindi, 63
Red Cross, International Committee of, 59
Reid, Richard, 129, 149
Republican National Convention, 97

Ressam, Ahmed, 44
Réunion, 135
Riverview Drive, 15–17, 22, 30, 32, 43
    Iyman Faris's apartment on, 47, 63
    mosque on, 38, 148
    Christopher Paul's apartment on,
        37, 104
Roberts, John, 78
Rochester, Minn., 99
Ross, Negla, 84–85
Rumsfeld, Donald, 59, 135

Salafi ideology, 24
Salahi, Mohammedou Ould, 29–30, 38,
        43–44, 50, 135
San Diego, 41, 95
Sarajevo, 31
Saudi Arabia, 29, 37, 43, 62, 71
Scioto Company, 20
Sears Tower, alleged attack on, 7, 76, 114
Seattle Post-Intelligencer, 133
Senate Joint Resolution, 5
Seneca County Jail, 94–95, 97, 99
September 11, 55, 60, 62, 65
Serbia, 42
Shabab, al-. *See* al-Shabab
Shareef, Derrick, 140
Shehhi, Marwan al-, 43
Sherif, Mahir, 99, 107, 120, 128, 136–39
Shine, Daniel, 99
shopping mall plot, 11, 68, 94, 96, 98,
        128
    and other terrorism charges, 137–39
Sidda training camp, 24
Simcox, Andrew
Sinclair, Frederick, 69–72, 79, 83–89,
        100, 102
    Iyman Faris's appeal, 126–27, 130
Sixth U.S. Circuit Court of Appeals, 129
Sixty Minutes II, 97
Sloan, Brandon, 4
Slovenia, 30
Smith, David, 100–102, 119, 126–28,
        137, 144
Sofer, Gregg, 115
Somalia, 8, 26–27, 150
    Nuradin Abdi, 41, 44–45, 91, 95–96, 144
Somalis
    Columbus, 17, 40, 65, 94, 137, 147
    concerns about terror recruitment,
        8, 150–51

South Bend, Ind., 33
South Carolina, 33, 70–71
Springfield, Ill., 9, 146
Sri Lanka, 76
Stewart, Carter, 148
Sudan, 141
Sunrise Academy, 17
Syria, 27, 40, 112–13

Tablighi Jamaat, 56
Taliban, 58–59, 78, 114, 142
Tanzania, 27, 39
Tarazi, Mouhamed, 46, 84
Taymiyya, Taqi al-Din ibn, 41
Terre Haute, 149
Third Battalion, 25th Marines, 119
Thompson, James Earnest. *See*
        Ujaama, James
302s, FBI, 86-88, 100, 127, 130
372nd Military Police Company, 97
Tiffin, 94–95, 107
Timimi, Ali al-, 125, 144
Toledo, 8, 106, 111–12, 115
Toledo/Mettler, 37, 104, 132
Travnik, 30
Turgal, James, 84, 91, 122
Turgal Declaration, 91–92, 123, 129
Turkey, 38, 62, 76, 82
Turley, Jonathan, 144

Uganda, 44
Ujaama, James, 141
Union Terminal, 61,106
United Arab Emirates, 27, 40
Upper Arlington, 59
Uruzgan, 58–59, 148
U.S. Attorney, Columbus, 127, 143–44
U.S. Supreme Court, 75, 77, 126

Vanderstoep, Jack, 64–65, 71, 83, 126
Vienna, 30–31
Vietnam, 59
Violent Crime Control and Criminal
        Enforcement Act, 74
Virginia Jihad, 125, 144

Wainstein, Kenneth, 133
Walker, Arthur, 79
warrantless wiretap program, 125,
        130
Washington, D.C., 57, 63

Weigle, Doug, 94–96, 98–99, 120
White House, 63
Wilkens, Richard, 2, 3, 93, 122
Wilkins, William, 102
Williams, Kobie Diablo, 142
Wiseman, Thomas, Jr., 129
World's Gym, 104
World Trade Centers, 1993 bombing,
   30, 74
Worthington, Ohio, 19–20, 42, 104–5, 132
Worthington, Thomas, 20

Worthington High School, 19–20

Yemen, 10, 56
Yowell Transportation, 34
Yugoslavia, 30
Yusuf, Mohamed Haji, 95–96

Zagreb, 31
Zawahiri, Ayman al-, 37
Zazi, Najibullah, 146
Zenica, 30